RUSTED OFF

RUSTED OFF

WHY COUNTRY AUSTRALIA IS FED UP

GABRIELLE CHAN

VINTAGE

A Vintage Australia book
Published by Penguin Random House Australia Pty Ltd
Level 3, 100 Pacific Highway, North Sydney NSW 2060
penguin.com.au

Penguin
Random House
Australia

First published by Vintage Australia in 2018

Addresses for the Penguin Random House group of companies can be found at global.penguinrandomhouse.com/offices.

A catalogue record for this book is available from the National Library of Australia

ISBN 978 0 14378 928 4

Cover image © iStock
Cover design by Ella Egidy © Penguin Random House Pty Ltd
Typeset in 11.75/16.5 by Midland Typesetters, Australia
Printed in Australia by Griffin Press, an accredited ISO AS/NZS 14001:2004
Environmental Management System printer

MIX
Paper from
responsible sources
FSC® C009448

Contents

Dedicated to Harden-Murrumburrah
and small towns everywhere

Introduction

I don't know if there's a moment when you realise you belong to a place, a landscape or a culture. I do know when I was first offended by an outsider's view of my small town, the town in which my children were born and raised; the place in which I first understood a sense of belonging, of community and the impulse to protect it.

A reporter had appeared on the trail of a missing girl, a sad story of loss. It was a mystery potentially involving foul play, a story that still grips me as a resident and a storyteller. This Sydney-based journalist stayed in the local motel and wrote up a storm. It is something I have done regularly, particularly when I've followed politicians during election campaigns. The headline of the piece was 'From the land of fear, loss and dark secrets'.[1] It portrayed a shire 'masked in shadow'. According to the report, I was living in a deserted, desolate, hopeless town. We had left behind our glory days of the gold rush, the railway era and bumper crops, to become a place in which 'Scarecrows stalk the main street', where 'giant spiders have invaded the town's only motel'. 'Beyond isolation, drought and the desperation of such a combination, there's an unhealthy mix of the unknown, unbe-lievable and uncertain . . .'

Using the true story of the tragic disappearance of a teenage girl, the journalist neatly packaged my home into the quintessen-tial redneck small settlement with a dark past, in the tradition of weirdo country towns featured in horror stories such as *The Cars That Ate Paris*, *Harvest Home* or *Wake in Fright*. Cut to halfwit [in country drawl]: 'You don't come from around here, do ya?'

As someone who has an eye for detail and atmosphere, I couldn't blame the reporter. I had drawn my own fast and loose conclusions of other places, so let she who is without sin cast the first stone. And the scarecrows, made by our local kids, were a gift to a visiting writer. Likewise a hairy huntsman spider. Early on in my country life I hit a high-jump record in the shower when one ran up my thigh to escape the water. Quite the horrifying arachnid if you don't appreciate their fly-catching skills.

Locally, there was a collective gasp of shock at the way we were depicted because towns like ours do not hit the national media often. It felt like guilt by location. My first thought was emotional. Fuck you. As it happened, I had worked at the local one-journalist paper a few years before, run by a major news organisation, for whom I was writing, subbing and cleaning the dunny. I wrote my first thought in an editorial taking the piss out of the city-based journalist and his preconceived notions; frightened of spiders but not of stereotypes. It was not quite Banjo Paterson to his Henry Lawson but it made me and my fellow residents feel better.

For all my fulminating, his intervention was more helpful than I could have guessed, because it gave me a glimpse of what it is to be sneered at for your location or class. To be the butt of swift and uninformed judgements. To live with a pronouncement that cannot usually be met with a reply, save the lottery of sending a letter to the editor of a dying newspaper. 'Dear Sir or Madam, Re your story on my town: get a grip . . .'

I had experienced racism as a kid, but this was the first time I had encountered geographical judgement. And I had the means to fire off an editorial to relieve my frustrations. What of others who noticed those everyday slights, not only of their towns but of their lives, their jobs, their opinions and their choices?

That story was written in 2009. Between 2016 and 2017, the political foundations shifted after a fair swag of the British population voted to leave the European Union, and a chunk (albeit a minority) of Americans voted for Donald Trump as their president. The Australian election in 2016 saw the return of One Nation's Pauline Hanson and an increase in seats for the centrist populist Nick Xenophon, making for a larger Senate crossbench than ever before. People such as Australia's ex-prime minister Tony Abbott were talking about Senate reform: if the barbarians are at the gate, we must change the rules, otherwise governments will get nothing done.

The story of global political disruption first focused on the economic divide in Britain, the US and Australia. The theory went that inequality was causing a breakdown, which was pushing the working class, the under- and unemployed to vote in ways that made no sense to the conservative and progressive establishment. But as journalists and commentators tried to understand the Great Disruption, more and more was, and is, being written on the cultural divide, which might be one of the more significant causes of the electoral upsets we have seen in recent years. I think both elements are at work, and it is messy. Culture more or less divides the city and country, but when it is combined with economic stagnation in particular regions or towns, political outcomes are distorted.

What is undisputed is that there is a divide of some sort, evidenced in the fact that half of Britain, half of the United States and a fair proportion of Australia woke up the day after their respective political disruptions and wondered what the hell had just happened. How had one portion of a country been so unaware what the other half was thinking? Or, in the case of Trump, why would people vote for something or someone who was seemingly inimical to their best interests?

The camps are clear enough. Those on the losing sides of the Brexit vote and the US 2016 election were global citizens, alternatively called liberals, progressives. For this crowd, race, place and cultural origin are less important as identifiers than education and profession. They feel comfortable in most parts of the world, are mobile and are financially sheltered from most economic shocks. These are people who fuss over their kids' every move to ensure their chances are maximised; who are likely to keep their boats lifted by purchasing a 'glass floor' in the form of the best education money can buy. They obsess about the right amount of exercise and nutrients, consume media from around the world but often not from their own backyard. That backyard tends to be the world's larger cities, where the metropolitan landscape changes second by second, a sea of roiling screens. This was my mob.

Across the divide, there is a group of people who are not so cushioned from economic shocks; are often not university educated; have seen the world change and their towns decline and their opinions downgraded. They don't see much diversity apart from economic diversity – with them near the bottom and all these unrecognisable people at the top. In an era of connectivity, they feel disconnected and neglected. Ironically, via social media enabled by smartphones, they can see more people than they ever knew who feel the same way. They are not enamoured with the city; in fact, they care less about career portability than place. They live in the outer edges of cities, regions, larger inland centres and small towns.

I moved to such a town. A small town. One main street. It was about as far from my city-suburban second-generation migrant-kid upbringing as I could get. A Singapore-born Chinese father and an Anglo mother raised me and my siblings in a rented Coogee flat in the eastern suburbs of Sydney, and then the new developments in Sydney's north, with the aid of a large mortgage. When my parents split I lived with my father for a while, then my mother, before leaving home. My father remarried and had two more children. In many ways, my family represents the complex units that are fast becoming the norm – multicultural and many-layered.

While my childhood had its challenges, my family concentrated on education and aspiring to a professional, middle-class life. When I started covering the New South Wales coalition government under John Fahey in the 1990s, I discovered politics is largely played within this professional middle, so the people I saw were either like me – aspirational – or firmly in the 'already made it' establishment camp.

Over that first half of my career, I considered politics a spectator sport. It had impacts, of course, but I guess I was a slow developer. As a young journalist, I loved the game of politics and the factions; to watch how politicians could manipulate the people and the system to achieve their goals. I remember the brilliant political journalist Mike Steketee sighing in the 1990s at the factional war-gaming between the so-called moderates and conservatives within the New South Wales Liberal party. They were wars that included a young Tony Abbott. (In 2018, they have yet to stop.) I cringe, remembering my response. 'Oh, I love the factions, the personalities – it's all so intriguing.' Steketee – always a journalist to concentrate on policy – looked at me blankly. He probably despaired at the future of the trade.

A couple of decades later I rail at the manipulations, and long for politicians who think about the destination rather than the brilliant reverse ferret that will get a party ahead of the other team. And, in defence of my trade, there are wonderful journalists who work this out from the beginning, or at least a lot quicker than I did.

Fortunately, life was about to deliver a few lessons on how the other half lived. In 1996, as John Howard's government came to power and a nervous but defiant Pauline Hanson arrived in Canberra, I married a farmer from a stable conservative Protestant family – something I had never seen before. He lived outside a small town called Harden-Murrumburrah, on the South West Slopes of New South Wales. In my first, wide-eyed visits to the farm in the early 1990s, I had heard Hanson's sentiments bandied around at dinner parties before she'd got anywhere near Parliament. Indigenous people received better treatment than 'the rest of us'. We were being swamped by Asians.

I knew nothing about the town when I married. I knew there were people in the country, but it was Another Country. Rural Australia was a land in a fairy tale, existing only in books and movies. My father had absolutely no experience of it. Neither did my Anglo mother, who, like an increasing number of Australians, had no relatives in the country. We had no wish to go there.

We had done a big road trip once in our white Ford Cortina, when my Chinese grandmother and my aunt came to visit from Singapore – a country that is 50 kilometres long. Dad wanted to show them 'the Country'. We drove across the Hay Plains in western New South Wales. What it must have been for Hay locals to see a Chinese family of seven getting out of a little Cortina in 40 degree heat. I still remember sliding around those vinyl seats, sticking my head out of the open window, nose up like a kelpie as I was blasted with hot air. On the drive down the Hume in 1970, we would have passed the little town that would become my home, just twenty-five minutes off the main route between Sydney and Melbourne.

My home is in Wiradjuri country, which stretches from Hay in the west to Goulburn in the east, up to Condobolin and down to

Albury. The local tribe lived on the creek, which was the best place to find water and food, and therefore the very place that attracted the white settlers. After Hamilton Hume wandered across the Yass Plains in 1821, squatters moved in, even though the area was not one of those the government allowed for settlement, and squatting was illegal, so the squatters were not allowed cheap assigned convict labour or police protection. Still, they stayed, building grass castles and not being overly bothered by any of those rules.[2] Local history notes they were not interested in the development of closer settlements because that would have consumed what they saw as their land. This feeling continues up to this day in some quarters – a number of residents tell me they believe farmers have stopped developments in town proceeding because they don't want competition for labour and land. I have never heard a farmer express fears of labour and land competition.

The squatters were pretty much left alone until the gold rush, when miners took any mode of transport, including shanks' pony, to make their fortunes. Gold was discovered down the reef, along the creeks and over towards Young, then called Lambing Flat. There would have been Chinese gold miners down on our section of creek – an echo that allows me to joke I have come to reclaim it. Once the miners arrived, they demanded housing, infrastructure and services, so the surveyor-general relented and, after drawn-out arguments, in 1857 the site of Murrumburrah, on a creek at the bottom of a hill, was approved as a township.

Twenty years later the railway arrived and engineers worked out that a station at the bottom of a hill made no sense for a steam engine. The solution was to place the train station at the top of the hill – 2 kilometres from the established village – where the train had the downhill run west and a flat run east. Around that North Murrumburrah station developed goods sheds, coal depots and businesses such as hotels servicing the rail. While the advantages of a train station were obvious, the downsides were quickly seized upon by townspeople. It brought in goods that competed with town manufacturing. Whither to for the shoemaker? The dressmaker? They had to compete with goods shipped in from Sydney. The arguments echo current political debates, except now we're talking about the death of national industries.

One of the other byproducts of the railway was a deep split in the new settlement, which still only measures 4 kilometres from end to end. In the great tradition of top bureaucratic decisions, the postmaster-general ensured the split became official and longstanding when he called the receival office Harden and named a street down the middle as a dividing line between Harden and Murrumburrah. No one knows why. All hell broke loose.

Dogged loyalty to one or the other village remained, and there developed two local councils, two clubs and two newspapers, until amalgamation was grudgingly forced and Harden-Murrumburrah was formed. But the anomalies live on. A high school called Murrumburrah in Harden. A sign at the Harden end announcing Harden-Murrumburrah. A sign at the Murrumburrah end announcing Murrumburrah-Harden. There are still arguments over naming rights. According to the Historical Society, individual sporting teams for each town refused to play each other for a time.

One of my first experiences here was walking into a pub to buy a bottle of rum for cooking. There was a barman as thin as a whip, and he was chatting to a couple of drinkers. I might as well have been an alien by the looks on their faces. I asked for the rum. The barman was speechless. I asked again. He shook his head. I walked out.

If he was surprised at this new inhabitant, I was more surprised. The whole place was so far outside my comfort zone, as laid down by a migrant Sydney suburban childhood. There was no diversity to be seen, but there were unexplained cultural divides. I saw a hangover from sectarianism for the first time. I saw class up close for the first time. I saw wider socioeconomic gaps than I had seen in the city. Not because these things do not exist in the city, but because I was cushioned by the suburbs I had lived in as an adult. A country town is like the ant farm, all dirt and ants pressed between two panes of glass. Life is on show.

My children, born in this rural town, pushed me into the school community and its attendant requirements – school councils, cake stalls and incidental chats at afternoon pick-ups. All of these demand involvement and create friendships across class, education and income in a way that rarely happens in a city suburb. I took a job at the local newspaper, and in the process had many conversations with people about their lives, their views, their politics – not only with longstanding residents but also new residents, tree changers who had moved in for a variety of reasons. I discovered people who had a range of opinions, which were so far away from my own as to make me initially recoil – but they were underpinned by their life story. And it struck me that modern political reporting, of the type that is mostly practised by me and fellow journalists, misses in the telling so many ordinary lives and accompanying wider political acts. And I don't know how to fix it, except to write this book.

Since then, I have straddled the dual worlds of country and city, because life changed again when my kids went away to boarding school. I returned to the press gallery in Canberra. It was 2010. Research and production were fully digital, social media was a thing, fellow journalists advised me to get on Twitter. The jump from home back to Canberra was metaphorically further than the ninety-minute drive.

I also noticed distance had stretched between the Parliament and the public. I returned as the Gillard minority government was re-elected in a hung Parliament in 2010. Coincidentally, I had become obsessed with the rural divide and the protest vote.

I had been studying Australian history as it pertained to rural parties such as the National Party and rural independents, past and present. When Tony Windsor, Rob Oakeshott and Bob Katter had to decide the 2010 minority government, commentators thought they had come out of the blue. There was a certain horror that these three country independents were to determine the government. But 'the three amigos' were the modern embodiment of a long strain of discontent with major parties in rural and regional Australia.

Returning to work as a political journalist with fresh eyes and a new focus that took in the rest of Australia, I saw how social media provided a capacity to communicate and find like minds. For the first time I was having conversations with country people around Australia who were dissatisfied with the calibre of rural representation. Social media was also becoming a conduit for anger at governments and politicians. In the political sphere, clever politics were valued over clever policy.

Inhabiting my two worlds, I felt like a woman astride a glacier in a warming climate. Cracks were widening and great chunks were falling off the body politic. Watching the political tribes was like watching groups of penguins floating on those separate icy islands. My fear was, and remains, that there will be no commonality, no community, because there will be no way to speak to people who are not on my bit of ice. And more than that, our Facebook feeds will ensure we don't get to see them anyway.

As a political journalist, I wanted to understand and chart the lives of the people around me, people who live in between the usual stereotypes. Long ago, Anne Summers noted that women were tired of their constant depiction as Damned Whores or God's Police. I got sick of my community – country people – being portrayed as either rednecks or the salt of the earth. I yearned for a more nuanced discussion of country communities and politics. But how to change the debate?

It has been a subject of much media commentary that more often than not political journalists are chained to their desk. We stand, trying to steady ourselves for the tidal waves of incoming information manufactured by political parties, third parties, experts, grifters and spivs. Then we try to make sense of it. Never was this more evident than in my job after the 2016 election writing the Politics Live blog for *Guardian* Australia. I started at 7 am, which required prepping and monitoring political statements in the morning papers, and on radio and TV from 6 am; fired up the production of the blog by 8 am; and wrote up the events of the day until 5 pm, if I was lucky. Later, if a big story was running. During that time I rarely left my desk, save to visit the bathroom or make a quick dash around the gallery corridors to ward off deep vein thrombosis.

But there was a moment during the 2016 election campaign where I went Absent With Out Leave. It involved driving 2000 crazy kilometres away from the parliamentary triangle, down into Victoria then up through New South Wales, following the then deputy prime minister Barnaby Joyce. It was a rare moment of freedom, punctuated by urgent conversations with voters, those rare birds we are always quoting but rarely engaging. It was special for me because in a modern election campaign, unless your media organisation has oodles of money, you don't get on the ground (away from the gallery) very often. If you do, you are stuck on the stage-managed bus tours of the Coalition or Labor. And that means you enter into a dark bargain, in which you hand over your company credit card to cover expenses and you are told to turn up at an appointed time and place. You are not told where you are going because it might leak to the other side. You can ask for hints – umm, warm or cold? – for wardrobe purposes, but that's about all the information you receive. Best (middle-aged) advice is to take a range of clothes, flat shoes, eye drops, plenty of batteries and stay off the grog as much as is humanly possible.

As a result of this structure, we end up with stage-managed affairs; one or maybe two doorstop press conferences a day. Most of the time you don't even know where you are. There are very few voters in plain sight who are not there for a reason (as set up by the parties) and we all file our stories after the press conference, talk about the campaign, joke with the staffers, keep an eye on the latest Twitter outrage and go home.

Barnaby did not do a bus. A former National Party leader, Tim Fischer, made the country election campaign trail, the so-called Wombat Trail, famous. These days a wooden wombat mascot is carried by the Nationals' press secretary, but rarely are there formal wombat trails. So the idea of being in my own car, with the freedom to stray from the trail, was wonderful. I had the drivin' in me, as they say around home about boys who like tractors.

That three-day sojourn confirmed what I had long believed since I'd moved west of the divide. There is another country in Australia. And even though I lived in it, I rarely got to cover it as a political journalist. In the same year as Brexit and Trump, the constituencies that had driven those election results looked a lot like my home town. Older, white and (largely) working class. I became convinced that, by covering politics in Parliament, I was missing the political story of the decade.

So, while sharp political reporting is essential to a functioning democracy, I had two options. I could stay cemented in the press gallery chasing the same stories as a hundred other people, trying to divine workshopped political messages as well as mishaps and mayhem. Or I could return to my small town, where I was part of the community, and work out the political story from the ground up.

I came to the conclusion on that 2000-kilometre road trip that the best way for me to cover politics was to write from outside Parliament. And when I say 'outside Parliament', I'm not talking about the frothing commentators who are sitting in studios or newspaper offices in our big cities but claim outsider status because they are not technically in the press gallery. I'm talking about way outside that insider world. For me, I was talking about going home.

Like a junkie, it was hard to give up the rattle and hum of federal politics. I spent mornings walking, often heading into the jangling easterly around the house paddock, watching the beagle's tail swing in rhythm as she chased down the scent of a fox from the night before. It took months to let go of the need to listen to a wall of interviews, to separate myself from the thought that I would be a lesser human unless I knew what the assistant minister for immigration had said at 11.50 am on cable television. The eventual separation is hard to pinpoint, but months on I was still puzzling how it was that my old workplace, the Parliament of Australia, had travelled so far from my small town, a place only ninety minutes west. I began with little more than a hunch that leaving formal political reporting might yield a better insight into why formerly rusted-on voters were rusting off.

So how can I write about rural Australia when I only know one little bit of it, just a shard of glass in an expansive window that is this big country? Because the first point is that rural Australia is not monolithic. Journalists and shock jocks excel at assuming a demographic is uniform. It is not.

The only way is to write about the people around me. In the past twenty-plus years of covering politics I have written plenty of profiles of politicians. This is a book inspired and informed by the lives of ordinary people and how politics crosses their path.

I wanted to approach political discussions with people from my home town who might think very differently to me. Implicit in my request and their acceptance was an understanding that we both had something at stake. I am no fly-in, fly-out journalist. We share a community. We have to respect each other and we do. And the light-bulb moment for me was that many politicians approach political conversations as if there is nothing at stake and no shared Australian community. They just want a win for their own mob. I can't afford to shout at my town residents if they don't agree with me, like a politician in Question Time or a Twitter keyboard warrior. I live here.

In writing in this vein, I will argue four broad points.

Firstly, metropolitan and non, city and country, are becoming two different nations, and that is dangerous for cohesiveness. The economic and cultural differences between small-town and big-city Australia are vast. These two countries look different, speak differently and make different choices about their lives. Since the 1980s country people have been told our small towns will die out because we represent 'old Australia' – not consistent with the new economic rationalist approach, paying our own way and all that. Yet regional Australia contributes 40 per cent of our economy; Australian society appropriates elements of our lives and symbols – our hats, our landscape and our so-called dying ways. We are given mixed messages about our place in the nation. City narratives of country are confusing and will only increase the divide; country narratives of the city can be equally confusing and divisive.

Secondly, we are faced with the fatal flaws of the people who claim to represent us. On the eastern seaboard there have been a few traditional options. The National Party is considered by most of Australia as the country party, but it associates too closely with a landed class and not closely enough with the working and middle classes that makes up the bulk of towns and regional cities. Country Liberal members have to juggle the interests of the corporate end of big cities, the very rich with the very poor in their own electorates. Then there is the Labor Party, which grew from a traditional country working-class base but in the 1980s walked away from the country to court inner-city voters, who are more numerous, with the effect of damning many regions with cardboard cut-out Labor candidates. As a result, country allegiance to major parties is teetering on the brink, leaving us to look sideways at demagogues and plutocrats and assorted independents, who range from ordinary to excellent.

Thirdly, with the first two factors at play, country communities need to build from within. We need to take responsibility, plan for our own future, then vote for advocates who can take those plans and provide government support in kind, to get the results we have designed for ourselves. We need to take a good, hard look at the old models of rural representation that perpetuate the decline story as if it were happening in a uniform manner. Country towns continue to be very stratified, and if those who care don't want our towns and regional cities to fracture further, we must build this greater cohesion to advocate on behalf of the whole 30 per cent of rural and regional Australia, not just the mobile ones with assets.

Fourthly, and fundamentally, communities are moving ahead of governments. As you will discover, individuals are pushing ahead to find local solutions to issues that governments have abandoned, stalled, mothballed or failed to resolve. Issues such as Indigenous recognition, homelessness, lagging regional education outcomes and small-town economic revitalisation are being tackled by my neighbours with no government support. Frankly, we are tired of waiting.

This has been a political journey for me as much as anyone. I am not a doyenne of the gallery, just an average, often absent, political reporter who has been lucky enough to ride the media wave from a time when the surf was high. I have interviewed and had conversations with many people during the course of writing. My aim was to talk to the people who have no lobby group in Canberra. The people named have generously agreed to take part. Other unidentified conversations are used because hopefully they enlighten the reader on some aspect of small-town politics and culture. As a whole it is partly my story of straddling the divide between city and country; partly my town's story; partly the stories of the particular individuals who kindly agreed to share their lives. These are my lessons from a small town. I hope they shine light on Australian politics from both the back blocks and the front stalls.

PART 1

Shedding my city skin

LESSON 1

WTF? There are people west of the divide

There is a track from the back door to the farm shed, traversed by the farmer every day, first at 7.30 am and then many more times, for morning tea, lunch, to make phone calls, check things on the computer or just hide from an incoming storm. The path is not exactly straight. It curves like the arc of a travelling snake heading across a hot road. In wet times, the track is short grass stamped out of the long grass. In dry times, it is dirt dividing the short, parched pick of the grass on either side. In drought, it hardens to the bald, packed clay next to sand. When I get to the path, coming in from feeding the dogs or the morning constitutional, I follow its curves without thinking. Because that is the way we go. It is literally the path of least resistance. It is habit. And we are nothing if not creatures of habit.

My horses range over their paddock in the same way every day. They start, warming in the morning sun, ranging around the perimeter to pick at the grass, finishing at the water. The sheep do the same thing, following the same tracks, resting in shade or sunbaking in the heat of the day before finishing on the high ground. If I need to make a quick trip to town for provisions in the afternoon, I know I can leave the gate open once the sheep have camped for the night up there, the safest place for them. There is no moving them once settled.

We think we are more than animals. But the longer I see the patterns of politics and animals, the more I think we are fairly close. Every animal, every one of us, has our patterns, which come from our families and our culture. And yet we political class consider ourselves rational creatures, free of ingrained thought, so we ignore the finer details of people's lives and lack the self-awareness to wonder about our own prejudices.

==

My life is split in two. I am in neither one world nor another, and perhaps that is how I was born to be. It was the celadon leaves on black ironbark trunks that lined up for my arrival in 1996, eight months pregnant. I had few possessions to bring into the farm-house, having moved from a three-metre-wide terrace in Surry Hills, Sydney, to a room in the nation's capital to join the *Australian*'s Canberra bureau. By the time I moved to the farm, my possessions had spread thin, between friends and family. It was a shedding of the skin of my previous life – a city life, a media life. I was exposed.

A baby girl was born, a squashy lovely thing who attracted my undivided attention, so the strangeness of my surroundings was muted at first. The days came and went. A big Buddha baby boy followed, and with an older step-daughter, the rhythm of family began. Raucous birds screeched at dawn and dusk. In summer, sheep wandered the perimeter of the garden fence, looking in at the green lawn wistfully. In winter, the troughs froze and frost hung around until midday, forming tiny crystals on the horses' whiskers. I went for my customary morning runs around the paddocks, sticking to the fence lines in an agoraphobic sort of way, unused to the space. The lack of other humans was unsettling, and at night the darkness descended like an absence: an absence of people, an absence of street noise, an absence of light. In Sydney, my inner-city nights were marked by conversations echoing between the terraces, fighting cats, the dump of bottles in the pub bins, the reversing signals of the garbage truck at dawn. In the country, my days began with the cockatoos, the babies' cries, the farmer's alarm, breakfast like a religious ritual, the shed meeting at 7.25 am.

In the early days, I tended to count the absences and not the benefits. My country transition was stretchy, pulled taut on some days when I felt unmoored, before snapping back with a happy twang at this new life. The community health nurse invited me to a new mother's group in Young. There we sat in a circle, young, confused, mostly first-time mothers from a range of backgrounds and demographics, sharing our stories in a community hall. It gave me my first look at this other Australia, a small country town founded on farming. It represented White Australia's original vision of itself. To me it was an Australia so far removed from my own experience as to be a foreign country.

My first lessons were in nature, landscape and animals. On those early-morning runs, I learned to follow the sheep tracks, the path of least resistance; other times I'd wander the paddocks slowly as the galahs announced my arrival. On one of my first runs, I skirted the house paddock and noticed a gate was open. That gate held Mr Nasty, a bull with a face only a mother could love. He looked mean, I knew that from the cartoons. How they stamp and snort. As I rounded the paddock and headed down towards the dam, there he was, rising out of the winter fog, bellowing his two-tone roar. Don't run, the farmer had said. Run I did, but sideways, Bugs-Bunny style, body straight as a board, on tippy toes, all feet and eyes. The bull's regard bordered on nonchalance. I discovered after that day that he was the quietest on the place. A big Charolais shorthorn cross, so quiet that when he had a skin condition he didn't mind having someone stand behind him in the paddock painting his arse in a medicinal wash.

Mr Nasty – my nickname – was a symbol of my fears of the natural world, that nature is dangerous and needs to be tamed. Indeed, I began those first runs wielding a just-in-case stick. I am not even sure what I was expecting, just that it could be bad. The farmer snorted. What do you think is out there?

I hunted through the sheds and outbuildings, looking to understand from whence this farming business came. The sheds were a museum of farm technology, from the scythes used when men cut crops by hand, to air seeders, which deliver the seed directly into the ground. There were yokes for horse and plough, and shelves made from plough disks for myriad odds and sods, the detritus of a century.

I learned the terminology of farming, and the country generally, and puzzled over why the town had a lion-dancing club. My childhood highlight of Chinese New Year were the lion dances, the youths wielding a lion's head, dancing to the beat of drums to snatch lettuces and cash in red envelopes. The farmer was incredulous when I expressed my admiration. Guffaws ensued. 'She didn't say lion dancing, she said *line* dancing. You know, boot scooting.'

I noticed the bone-crushing handshakes. In the country, a strong handshake is a sign of an honest straight-up-and-down person. In my Chinese family, a gentle handshake is polite while a knuckle-cracking handshake is odd, a sign of inappropriate aggression. I have become a squeezer.

I learned about seasons. I realised I'd barely noticed seasons in mild Sydney, apart from the occasional wind tunnel in Macquarie Street. Out here I got to know ground-cracking summers and pipe-breaking winters. My eyes began to see the contours of the landscape and to notice small as well as big variations; the palette changes of drying grass as spring turns to summer.

Now I know that when the cockatoos are chiacking east of the house, it is time to check for fruit. As I write, they are sitting in our apricot trees, heavy with green fruit, which usually ripen a week or two before Christmas. That means fresh apricots, stewed apricots and apricot tarts for a few short weeks. The trees were planted in 1908 by the previous family, who built the rammed-earth house. The trunks are gnarled and there are dead limbs up high because no one has been bothered to get a ladder and a chainsaw to do some judicious pruning. Despite the inattention, the trees still yield in a good year.

The cockatoos land in the top of the trees every dawn from late November, prodding fruit to check. They are much more attentive than me, and when they are bored or just bloody-minded they peck and pick the unripe fruit and drop it on the ground. The bases of the trees are strewn with green fruit marked by one test bite. My office overlooks the orchard and every so often I stomp down to the trees and shake my fist, prompting the birds to rise up squawking. They circle and give me the two-wing salute, knowing I have nothing.

I always hope for a few of those apricots for the family at Christmas. We send the surplus with visiting friends and relatives up and down the Hume Highway, and the message comes back that they taste like apricots used to taste, before the advent of cold storage and long shelf-life. They are old-fashioned fruit in that they last three or four days off the trees, after which they collapse and age like a human face, but the process happens over days rather than years. Their deep orange skin is pitted with imperfections. They would not do for a major supermarket chain – the buyers would not sell them and the customers would not buy them. That is their beauty. These fruit come with no expectations, and they over-deliver.

==

Such is life in a small unremarkable town. I too had few expectations when I arrived, other than spending my days with someone I loved.

I considered the country backwards because I had seen the movies and I knew no one out of the city. In much of metropolitan Australia rural life is seen as old Australia – out of step with modernity – and that was how I thought of it. Political narratives told me that country towns were not built for the transition into the twenty-first century. The way to improve small towns was for farmers to get big or get out, and for those without jobs to move somewhere with jobs: big cities. Economic rationalism told me that from the 1980s onwards.

But life has a way of delivering what you need. A country town has taught me about community. It has taught me acceptance. It has taught me equanimity. It has taught me about diversity of friendships. It has taught me to be less judgemental of people. It has taught me that everyone has a story. Life moves slowly even though country people are as busy as anyone else. Things to do, places to be, bills to pay, but still a certain calm descends. This is good if you are middle-aged. Not so good if you are a teenager, chomping at the bit for freedom and new experiences.

Two disclaimers. Firstly, I do not suggest that community only exists in country towns. In the inner city I knew the Greek family at the corner store and the Chinese family who ran the local laundry. I can see that if I'd stayed in that groove it would have built further, particularly overlaid with children.

My second disclaimer is that marrying someone who was born in this place, from a third-generation farming family, automatically opened up a network of people. The farmer had a social network that enveloped and supported me. In small towns, farmers have had historic influence over communities by dint of their place as land-holders. This fact is as old as Australia's squattocracy, and older in other countries. I realise my privilege because I come from not much.

For this reason, I know that small communities can also shut people out. Small communities can be lonely places without a pathway in. That pathway is usually a family with links into the district. Or it could be a workplace with local colleagues. Social groups tend to be set in aspic. I learned this in those first few years.

For every rule, there is a contradiction. There is a pulling together in disaster. The first markers I saw were human events. The death of a child sent a wave of grief and shock through the small town. Events were untangled and hushed conversations were held on street corners, all of us standing around holding our hands up to shield the unrelenting sun. It exposed the personal connections. Everyone feels more connected because a loss in a small community seems personal. We know him. We knew him. He was one of us. As his family still is.

At first I thought it was odd that pretty much everyone attended funerals, even very distant relationships and connections: a farmer's mother, the agent's brother. It is the coming together that is the thing, a show of confidence and support for the bereaved, as well as a statement of community.

With community comes structure and knowing how people fit in. When considering the glue that holds community together, in our town sport is a constant. Anything involving a ball is a start. I am not usually one for team sports, but when some of my friends formed a netball team sponsored by the local hairdresser, I couldn't resist joining – Reg's Old Grey Roots. Careering around on the netball courts on a Monday night, teaching my kids how to involuntarily barge, was more than therapeutic in the middle of a drought. The competition was fierce and I was perturbed that some people stopped talking to me after I faced them on the netball court. A team member who understood small-town culture better than anyone told me they would talk again when the season was finished.

The touch footy competition is epic – a weekly get-together of thirty-plus teams that form around friendship groups or workplaces. Adults and kids can play together and the competition is stiff: they play for keeps. I sat down with some keen participants, community-minded men and fitness nuts. They train regularly – a bunch of men and late teens. Anyone is invited and it has become like a therapy session. They don't go in for pub culture, though they recognise it's a means of downloading and getting stuff off your chest. These men, in their thirties, forties and fifties, remember a pub culture that taught respect. As teenagers they remember how anyone caught disrespecting older men was pulled into line by the guys in their twenties. These men teach their younger cohorts that respect over weights instead.

There is a value in this sort of physical and mental therapy. At its most basic, again it involves getting together. Indigenous people call them corroborees; more recently, they are called fundraisers, picnic race days, annual shows, community markets, festivals. They fulfil the basic human need to socialise. The country calendar is studded with such events, and many of them have such a long history they have become caricatures of country Australia.

I admit to being quite bewildered at the fuss over the annual race day when I first arrived. It felt cartoonish, like I had wandered into someone's short story. Everyone dressed to the nines, standing in a paddock in heels, swatting away the flies and trying to stay in the shade. The stratification. Who is in whose tent?

Early days were spent standing next to the jumping castle, keeping a lazy eye on the kids. Or negotiating the dunnies with toddlers in pull-ups, while next door a teenager throws up a sausage roll and alcopop. You pick a bookie in the betting ring, perve on the horses and get a tip from the local trainer.

Urbanites may sneer at these events and our dusty fashions, but there is value in large portions of community gathering: in a stratified place, events like race day create cohesion. Yes, there is the separation of social groups in tents, but then everyone unites on the finishing line. And, whether it is fashion in the field, or fancy dress, a dress code helps shed the social classifications that draft us like so many sheep into sorting pens. The races are a micro-cosm, a reminder that society stretches past your own nose, your own social group, your profession and your demographic. I see people I haven't seen for years, and hear expressions of happiness and discontent, joy and anger. In a funny way, we cover most of the ministerial portfolios, traversing health, education, immigra-tion, trade, Treasury, but we do it via the lives of our children, our parents, our businesses, our neighbours and our own lives.

As causes go, education and health remain the top priorities. Nothing inspires both a farmer and a shearer to don a dress more than the thought that a local child might benefit. Our country club has long been the scene of many a fundraiser to help the Harden District Education Foundation, the local chapter of the Country Education Foundation. This highly successful national charity has branches around the country that raise money to pay for children educated in their district to pursue further education and training. It funds everything from apprenticeships and degrees to certificate-level studies. The charity's existence is both a recognition that some kids in small towns need a leg-up and an acceptance that charity begins at home. And these sort of exercises, where communities support their own kids through a formal fundraising program right down to the informal men's support group on the football field, are the best examples of communities helping themselves.

=

My small town is only one of my worlds. I returned to my other world of the national Parliament and the media when my children went off to boarding school for high school. I lived in Canberra like a politician. These were the days of Julia Gillard's prime minister-ship. Home was too far away to commute so I stayed in a little flat, dined on my own, or with contacts or friends in the inner suburbs, and lived out of a suitcase. If I exercised, I swapped my paddock trails for the streets of Canberra's inner-city million-dollar suburbs.

Instead of wheat grass and ironbarks, the streets were lined with clipped box hedges, divided by neat driveways with nary a fallen leaf in sight.

The work day stretched from early morning to evening, watching every move of Australia's politicians, their press-conference doorstops at various parliamentary entrances, ministers' press conferences in the parliamentary 'blue room' and their various interviews on Sky TV and ABC News 24. We recorded any political interview between Radio National's 'Breakfast' presenter Fran Kelly and a minister, and waited for the line of the day designed to set us foxes running. And run we did, knowing full well it was live bait. We monitored 2GB for right-wing commentators Ray Hadley and Alan Jones, with their regular spots for their darlings, including former prime minister Tony Abbott, and conservative figurehead Peter Dutton. Unlike previous jobs in the state and federal press galleries in the 1990s, by 2010 we rarely left the office or the building to report because the truth is we didn't have time, given we had to keep content going for the internet news cycle. All the other bureaus were also producing more stories with less staff.

I did get out on the road once, in 2014. The Abbott government had been in for a year and it was time for the prime minister's promised trip to spend a week in an Indigenous community. Abbott had a regular history of volunteering in Indigenous communities so I was excited at the prospect of him leaving his highly managed media diary behind and watching him engage with Indigenous people. Sit down and chew the fat. Step off the usual dancefloor where journalists and politicians both socialise and spar, and get a bit closer to Indigenous people who are impacted by the long and sorry trajectory of government policy. Here was an opportunity for a politician – the prime minister, no less – to get away from the scripts and for us to report a very human, very important policy story from the ground up. Many of us were hungry to get away from Canberra and understand the front end of policy in order to explain the issues better.

Within a day of travelling to Arnhem Land, it became clear the trip was going to be more like an election campaign exercise. All of us – politicians, staffers, media – turned it into a circus. We were bussed hither and thither to managed events with bewildered or bored participants, many whom had seen it all before. Abbott had short, sharp meetings, prefaced by five minutes of whirring cameras to get the pictures of the day. Journalists were told where to stand, who to talk to and for how long. It was like being taken to a lonely open-air stage where a few actors read out their lines, lit by a single spotlight. All around that stage, there are human lives unfolding, fully realised or fraying badly. They are compelling and complex stories, but you are forced to watch the stage like the protagonist from *A Clockwork Orange*. And every time you look away to the human drama around that stage, a person in a blue shirt says, No, you can't look at those people. You can't talk to those people off the stage. You must only look at those two people on the stage.

This is not limited to one side of politics. A Labor campaign bus trip is equally managed, kept short because of time and logistics. These are regular political campaign exercises, and in order to maintain our access in the Parliament, we media buy into this arrangement. The Arnhem Land trip required press gallery accreditation. Though the *Guardian* was not originally invited, I could not have joined without approval from the prime minister's media team. I was not invited on any of Abbott's subsequent trips, possibly because that team was unhappy with my story, which was critical of its heavy-handed media management. In it, I questioned whether it is possible for politicians to engage in a meaningful way with a full media contingent.[1] That is because competing priorities appeared to outrank the central point of the visit – to inform Indigenous policy. Those competing priorities were getting good positive coverage for the prime minister and feeding journalists so that our news desks received a daily story. It felt like we were part of the problem. As a result, picture opportunities were the order of the day, interspersed with short meetings with Indigenous leaders.

Meaningful conversations between a prime minister and Indigenous communities can only be conducted with more time, and by slowing the pace. That would mean the prospect of the prime minister staying off the news for the day, and modern politics rarely lets that happen. And if it did, cash-strapped media organisations would probably stay home because news editors with limited budgets would find it difficult to justify the trip.

Good journalism also requires time. Longstanding political issues – think Indigenous policy, energy policy in changing climates, school funding – are complex. That is exactly why they hang around the necks of government like an albatross. The modern news cycle chains most political reporters to its wheel, as much as politicians, while the media's impoverished model negates our ability to sit back and look more deeply at issues. To really take hold of an issue, roll it over, shake it, listen to its secrets and think about it deeply is a luxury most journalists don't have.

So even with the frantic line-up of story opportunities in Arnhem Land, the trip told me much more about modern politics than Indigenous policy. It pushed me to want to write about politics beyond the stage.

Don't mistake me. I am not arguing that all my press gallery colleagues should march out tomorrow to west of the divide and leave the politicians to themselves. Good political reporting from the Parliament is more critical than ever for readers who no longer trust government or its processes. But for someone who has a fairly unique view of two very different sides of Australia, I felt I could add more by spinning my reporting on its axis and looking at politics from the reverse. In the world of daily politics, so many aspects of the lives affected by political decisions go unobserved. You can hide in plain sight in the city. There is too much going on. What I have learned from the farmer and the natural world is to hone my skills of observation. An open landscape allows the eye to pick up small changes that would be hidden in a city landscape.

LESSON 2

Place is everything

Farmers refer to a section of land as 'country'. It might be a paddock, or a group of paddocks that have a particular characteristic. For example, 'The country over by the creek has never grown a decent crop of canola.' I suspect it is picked up from Indigenous Australians.

It was not until I moved to the farm that I understood the physical and psychological effect of place because I had so little experience with the natural world and certainly had no connection to a city landscape. No doubt city and suburban landscapes may evoke memories, but I had felt no ties to anywhere I had lived before. Moving to a farm gave me a chance at better understanding the natural world, in contrast to the public world that I had inhabited as a journalist. I saw death and new life play out without sentiment. Lambs born, dead or alive, little noses poking out, waiting for help. In journalism, everything has an angle. In nature, there is no spin. On the farm, as our lives unfurled, the paddocks collected our stories. Those stories were not chosen by place, they just happened, and place wove its way into our shared family history. The pepper tree in the horse paddock still has the kids' treehouse, labelled 'Teraza: X-pirate, Keep Out' in wonky letters. My son broke his arm on the hill towards the shearing shed. I can see the patch in the front paddock where the mare took off on my daughter. I can predict the tree-line where the beagle chases foxes but never succeeds. There is a north-eastern hill down by the creek from which you can see forever. The kangaroos hang out under a stand of birch trees, sitting around like old men in a beer garden, scratching their rumps. There is a clear stretch past the bull-rushes that can be used for swimming practice. The picnic spots, the silage pit, the salt patch. These places have no names. They just sit in my head like an imagined topo-graphical retreat. They will never be displaced, no matter how far I move from this place.

I have a group of women friends who all moved to this area to marry men firmly planted here. We have watched out for each other as we stumbled through the transition from our old lives to our new ones. We've come together over the years for coffee, for school drop-offs, for community meetings and funerals. We have laughed as the kids ran wild at birthday parties; sung best wishes over weirdly shaped cakes. As the kids grew and our lives have stretched thinner to accommodate this pace, we have kept in touch, so when we meet we are right back where we were. When I ask about the importance of place to their lives and particularly to the men who drew us here, the answer is 'everything'. 'He was drawn back to his north star,' says one.

Other friends of mine grew up here, left because dreams or options elsewhere pulled them away, but were drawn back to this small town for one reason or another. Some came back to help out for a while and never left. Some always planned to come back to have kids. Others were expected to come back to take over family businesses, sometimes whether they liked it or not. Whatever the reason, the town that knows them holds them close. They slip back into their place as though it's a comfy pair of pants. Which is not to say everyone loves their town. Those who hate it have already left, but for the ones who stay, place often provides the ballast that tips their decision. So if you can understand that about our communities, if you can understand that place fills a large section in their inhabitants' hearts and minds, then you are more likely to understand these people's other projections. Their stances. Their opinions. Their politics.

Still, as I travelled between the two worlds before I moved to the country for good, it was confusing to observe the fear and rejection of Indigenous land connections during the Mabo debates in the 1990s. In 1992, the High Court recognised native title existed for a group of Torres Strait Island people led by Eddie Mabo. This judgement repudiated the idea of *terra nullius* – that the land belonged to no one. At the time Prime Minister Paul Keating was negotiating to put a workable framework around the judgement, and in typical style he was going to crash or crash through. Many of my new friends were horrified. As owners of very large, productive backyards, farmers were terrified, and voiced white-hot anger towards Keating. I didn't understand how some multi-generational farming families, with a heartfelt emotional connection to place, could not understand more ancient connections. It made no sense to me. Certainly, these farmers were being pushed along by politicians. The Victorian premier, Jeff Kennett, warned at the time that all backyards were under threat. (He has since admitted he was wrong.) John Hewson described the day the Native Title Act passed as a 'day of shame' because it did not extinguish native title on pastoral leases. It was a politically anxious time in rural Australia and the cracks were showing.

One of my favourite jobs every year is working on the release of the government's historic cabinet papers. When I first started looking at the papers in the 1990s, the National Archives held the documents for thirty years, though that's transitioning to twenty. In December each year journalists were briefed and given access for the release of stories on 1 January. My family long suffered during the festive season as I simultaneously celebrated Christmas, did the Santa thing and worried about whether I had wrongly interpreted the 1967 cabinet file on the Indigenous referendum or missed something in the file containing the contents of Harold Holt's briefcase.

The real value of scrutinising these files was the bracing historical slap across the face it gave us journalists, too often mired in the irrelevant detail of the daily outrages. The cabinet release reminds us to focus on substance, the issues that will be talked about decades on. If you stick around long enough, the cabinet papers start to give you a perspective on the years you reported decades before.

In 2016 I was reminded of the anger over Mabo I had experienced at those first country dinners when I found a transcript of Keating's conversation with a talkback caller. It gives you a whiff of why John Howard, in the lead-up to his 1996 election, began reframing Indigenous law reform debates (and later race and gender debates) as political correctness.

On 17 June 1993 Paul Keating was interviewed by 2UE's talkback king, John Laws, one of the prime minister's favourite commentators via which to talk to the average punter. A caller rang in and asked Keating why his government saw Aboriginal people as 'much more equal people than the average white Australian'. Keating challenged the caller, suggesting he wanted discrimination in favour of non-Aboriginal people, and an argument spiralled, with the caller protesting, 'I'm not racist.'[1]

'That's what they all say, don't they? They put these questions, they always say, "I am not racist, but, you know, I don't believe that Aboriginal Australians ought to have a basis in equality with non-Aboriginal Australians." Well, of course that is part of the problem.'

The caller took issue with Keating's statement that Aboriginals had been dispossessed of their land. While he admitted knowing nothing of the High Court decision in favour of Mabo and those Mabo represented, the caller asked, 'Why does the average white Australian feel that he is prejudiced against?' He blamed Keating's government for that feeling.

'Well, why don't you sign off?' said Keating. 'If you don't know anything about it and you're not interested – goodbye. You can't challenge these things and then say "I don't know about them."'

Once the caller had hung up, Laws said the man was typical of 'the feeling that exists' and he wanted to know what Keating would do to placate those people who felt they were being 'disadvantaged by what is being given to the Aboriginal people'. Keating explained that all that was being granted were limited land opportunities, income support and Commonwealth programs for education, health and social justice.

I remember hearing those Keating-esque conversations at the time and cheering that he did not take a backward step in arguing the case. I was not alone in the press gallery. Resolving the first stages of the native title issue by facing down critics and detractors, and steering the act through the Parliament, remains one of Keating's great achievements – quite apart from the Hawke–Keating government's economic reforms. But in 2002, on the tenth anniversary of the Mabo judgement, Keating admitted that a lot of people in the Labor Party had got pretty nervous at the effect of his comments on voters. Keating told *Four Corners* journalist Liz Jackson twenty years after the Mabo decision that 'a lot of my colleagues did not want a bar of it.'[2] He admitted that the issue had caused huge political damage to his government (even if his 1996 election loss was hard to uncouple from the age of the thirteen-year-old Labor government). Keating reflected on talkback callers like the one above: 'You can deal with it. It doesn't say that you send everyone away as satisfied customers. I mean, I think the Native Title Act was material in the decline in the standing of the government, you know, from 1993 onwards – particularly in Western Australia and Queensland.'[3]

I commonly heard sentiments like the one expressed by the talkback caller when I first moved west of the Canberra press gallery, and it was shocking to hear such comments from people I knew and liked. They personally knew Indigenous people in town – not that there were many who made their presence felt – but there was a separation of the accepted Indigenous individual and the rejected Indigenous group. I have found this quite common on issues of race more generally. One person is okay, but en masse? Not acceptable. I heard the old myth about Indigenous people in bush communities being given brand new LandCruisers and leaving them on the side of the road when the vehicles had run out of petrol. I heard scathing criticism of Aboriginal drug and alcohol problems without consideration of history. The Mabo judgement provided my first stark reminder that I was in a very different world with different conventional wisdoms than inner-city Sydney.

After floating around in liberal media circles, it was shocking to hear some opinions, but don't misunderstand me. The business of journalism is to call out factual errors. Opinions you consider to be wrong but that are based on facts – people should be free to be express them. It was also ironic to come from a supposedly diverse city group, where people around me had similar views, to a more homogenous community that had diverse and, to me, sometimes jarring views. There were farmers, for example, who'd supported the Mabo decision. Opposition to the High Court ruling in rural areas was not hard and fast.

The farmer was characteristically calm in the face of a certain level of hysteria as I argued my point, ranting and railing long after guests had gone home. Immaturity made me insist back then that everyone else should think like me. That was isolating until a like-minded friend said to me, 'Find common ground. If the only thing you share is a cake recipe, that's okay.'

As I have evolved, the whole political debate has reverted to my old mindset. That is, if you don't agree with me, I have nothing to say to you. If you say one thing I disagree with, everything you ever say from henceforth is devalued. That is how the political debate runs these days. Every day, on social media and in comments threads, people make personal attacks on journalists who have reported facts they don't want to hear and opinions they don't like. Journalists operating in these times are working in a more polarised environment than ever before. Certainly, spending our days in colosseums like Twitter compounds that feeling. Most days on social media you get covered in verbal shit simply for reporting politicians' utterances. But those 1990s debates also felt pretty polarised. And farmers complaining about Aboriginals back then were not operating in a vacuum. Here is what Tim Fischer, National Party leader at the time and later deputy prime minister, told a New South Wales party conference in 1993:

> Rightly or wrongly, dispossession of Aboriginal civilisation was always going to happen. Those in the guilt industry have to consider that developing cultures and peoples will always overtake relatively stationary cultures. We have to be honest and acknowledge that Aboriginal sense of nationhood or even infrastructure was not highly developed. At no stage did Aboriginal civilisation develop substantial buildings, roadways, a wheeled cart as part of their different priorities or approach ... Mabo has the capacity to put a brake on Australian investment, break the economy and break up Australia – a brake, a break and a break-up we can well do without.[4]

Fischer went on to say that it was important to remember there was 'a very fragile set of circumstances applying, as people began to realise that that which they thought was a fair dinkum title to lands that they were operating on may not have any legality whatsoever'.

Comments like that, along with Kennett's backyard scare and Keating's fiery lectures to voters, provided fertile ground in the next three years for a young Liberal candidate called Pauline Hanson. She wrote to the *Queensland Times* in 1996: 'How can we expect this race to help themselves when governments shower them with money, facilities and opportunities that only these people can obtain no matter how minute the Indigenous blood is that flows through their veins, and that is what is causing racism.'[5]

The letter got her disendorsed, and that was when her career really took off. Once Hanson was let off the political leash of a major party, her persona flipped. In a parallel universe, she might have been just another disgruntled Liberal backbencher. Instead she became the ultimate anti-politician, one who was, therefore, bound to be a popular candidate in the bush. The outsider with all the benefits of the insider.

The native title debates were explosive because they threatened place. It is the ultimate irony that the Mabo judgement, centring around ancient Indigenous connection to land and place, threatened more recent white connection to land and place. Both a physical place – land – and place in terms of social standing. And by threatening place, it threatened identity and, potentially, livelihoods. This was not a reason to fail to resolve it for Indigenous Australians, but it was a reality that sat under the surface of political debates that I saw play out at the time. Hanson and her views had a fair swag of support in the 1990s around here, and Hanson 2.0 still does in certain circles, as you will see.

In my urban life, people moved houses and cities regularly. They established a home in a new place and set about building their identity. With the advent of social media trails it is now harder for the global wanderer to remake their identity, but it is still entirely possible. Yet those who have lived in the same place all their lives cannot erase their identity, their family background or their histories. Individual histories travel out and down like a root system. This can be limiting if there is something you'd rather people forget, but it can also create pride for those individuals and families who have earned the respect of their community through their work ethic or reputation, no matter on which rung of the ladder they sit in that community.

If I think of place, I think of many families I have been able to get to know by moving to the country. Tim* was 'born and bred' in a housing commission house, in a large family. His mother cleaned houses. His father was a tradesman and a worker but an alcoholic. It was a tough start. The family didn't have anything, but they had work. All the kids are now middle-aged, having carved out good working lives, mostly close to home. They are trusted and respected in the community. Tim has never been unemployed, and he instilled the same work ethic in his kids. You never ask for anything and you don't expect anyone else to ask for anything. When his kids got teased at school for having a nice house, Tim calculated that those doing the teasing probably had more 'welfare money' than he earned in a week. 'Don't let anyone tell you that it has been easy for us,' he said. 'It hasn't. But don't whinge about being picked on, either. It only happens a couple of hours a day. Wait till you get to work. Then you'll cop shit all day. And don't come home whingeing, or I'll get stuck into you.' He told the kids, 'Just say hello every day and don't say nothing else.' It soon stopped. 'But I've learned,' he tells me. 'I tell my kids, if someone offers you something, say thank you and accept it.' It took him a long time to learn that.

Tim's family is well respected for their self-reliance and their work ethic, and this personal history is well known because the family has

---

* Some names have been changed.

been of this place for generations. If Tim chose to move elsewhere, his family history starts from scratch. My identity is built largely around my job; no one knows much about my family. I didn't really give a rats about my physical location until more recent years. Similarly, people around me in the media, in politics, constructed their identities based on their professions. I don't know their families' identities, or their back stories, unless they are very close friends. My colleagues move seamlessly between cities, parliaments and other countries. Their jobs take precedence over most other things. I held on to that work identity like grim death. It was one of the reasons I struggled when I took time out for the kids. To me, having meaningful work was more important than place because it went to my identity.

My skill base meant I could still move and work and carve out a life. When we were faced with a family farm restructure, we looked at other farms, other towns, other places. I concluded that the decision to leave was not mine to make because place was less important to my identity than my work. I felt like a weed that would grow anywhere. The penny finally dropped about the importance of place to identity.

===

'I never lost this place. It was a really important memory. I used to say to people in Sydney my soul is here. I left at eleven but I never lost touch. I always knew I would come back. But I could never see any reason to get back.'

Lorraine Brown is descended from fifth-generation families in our town. Her father, George Bruce, came from a family of shop-keepers, originally from Tumut. Lorraine's mother, Edith, was from a large local clan. Lorraine was born in 1945. Her father was older and quite Victorian in his attitudes: children were to be seen and not heard; there was to be no speaking at the dinner table from the kids.

When Lorraine was seven her father died of a stroke. Edith had had just four years of education at the local one-teacher school, and George's death forced her into a job in a clothing factory on the town's main street, which used to employ dozens of women making garments for the Koala brand. When the factory closed the family had no option but to move to Sydney, where Lorraine's older brother was living with his new wife and young kids. There was not a lot of cheap accommodation in Sydney even then, so there was no choice but for mother and daughter to split up. In her first year of high school Lorraine lived with her brother's family, and her mother lived with her sister in Manly. They could only see each other on Sundays. Life for Lorraine with her brother's new family was hard. She held her feelings close. Self-expression was not encouraged: 'It was not uncommon in that era.' As an adult, she can see that it was not easy for her brother's family either, having been 'dumped' with a teenager while their own children were so young.

'I hated it. I found it really hard to adjust, and on top of that the emotional things of being separated. Mum had been my only parent for years. My whole life changed and I found it emotionally difficult as a child and I became quite withdrawn and shy, as I was anyway; as many country children are. It had a fairly traumatic effect at that stage. It wasn't until later in my life I came to terms with lots of those things. As an adult you can see why things happen, but as a child you don't, and in those days people didn't explain much to you.'

Lorraine had a letter of recommendation for the selective Sydney Girls High School, but she was rejected because Edith didn't have a job at the time and would not be able to pay for extras. Lorraine was sent to Crown Street Girls, the overflow for families who could not afford to go to Sydney Girls. She went to school with a lot of children from the first wave of migrants who came after the Second World War. She was befriended by two Jewish girls, and one of their families lived in a flat in the beachside suburb of Coogee. It was her first close experience with another culture. 'It didn't matter to me as a child, as it often doesn't.

'They were so good to me, I can remember being accepted in their homes, taken to different places to see their friends. They treated me as their own daughter.

'It really had an impact on me. And, you know, I never kept in touch with the family, and I wish I had but they disappeared from that point in my life.'

Lorraine would have loved to have been a school teacher, but there was no money for that so she left and took a job as an office girl in a tannery in Botany. She did a secretarial course at night to learn typing and shorthand. She delivered letters, messages and did some typing, traversing the streets of Sydney in the late 1950s with shipping bills for the wharves. The tannery sent her for further training in office skills, and she progressed up the ladder – such as it was for women then. Typing, telex, adding machines.

She met Englishman Mick when, confused about the Australian male tradition of standing with other men to drink, he came over for a chat. Mick is a specialist in scientific instruments. He came to Australia as a skilled migrant with one of the instruments he built when it was installed in the University of New South Wales. He and Lorraine were engaged after three dates. She was just eighteen.

She had always kept in contact with friends in her small town, and missed her birthplace. She told me that she knew in her bones she would come back one day. But there seemed to be no way back because Mick's business was thriving and their son was at school. After he left school, though, they had an opportunity to buy a place here and decided to have a go at relocating Mick's very specialised business to our little town. He had more clients than ever, retaining his old ones and building a new base. Lorraine threw herself into community work and set up a drapery shop, selling craft supplies and gifts.

'Because I'm third, fourth and fifth generation of local families, that in itself provides a security blanket for you. It is some sort of security of being part of community. Is that the security I had that drew me back? Sydney to me was very frightening, where I was totally anonymous, and for a child who had grown up in a small community where I knew so many people and had a lot of relatives, that security blanket is gone, so you are isolated. When you come back you feel that security again, and I'm sure that's part of the reason.'

It has been different, though, for Mick, who Lorraine says is the 'alien'. Like I was. We have to build connections from scratch, and in all honesty I would not have looked twice at a country town unless I'd had a very good reason to move from the city. There has to be a push or pull. We agree that a personal connection is every-thing. Even many older people who have retired from the city have a reason for coming– a distant relative, an old friend. Some thread that pulls them here.

'These days I understand how the Aborigines feel about their land because that same feeling was within me all my life about this place.'

=====

Two central themes emerge from my conversations on the main street when we talk about place. There is no confidence that government understands place, and as a result there is inadequate consideration by governments and politicians of the effect of policy templates on rural areas. When I talk about a consideration for rural areas, I do not mean the endless lofty rhetoric from some country MPs about the importance of farmers. (Barnaby Joyce used to take at least one question every Question Time on how the government is singlehandedly increasing commodity prices subject to global forces.) I am talking about the absence of policy thought given to the concept of place and its importance in small communities. I mean any flicker of recognition of the fundamental importance of place to small town and rural residents.

In rural communities, education policy, welfare policy, aged care policy, so many policy concepts, take on a new meaning. Solutions that work in the city need anything from tweaking or major surgery to transplant to rural areas, and if there is one thing that keeps coming up in my conversations with locals about government it is the one-size-fits-all policy. In other words, a disregard of place.

A glaring example is the welfare changes the Abbott government attempted in 2014, one of which was to remove unemployment benefits for anyone under twenty-five. This proposal assumed every unemployed person had access to the kinds of transport networks a metropolitan centre has; and that there is a large pool of jobs for every dole recipient. It assumed the main problem with unemployed young people is laziness. In fact, in small towns, getting to a Centrelink fortnightly interview is problematic without a car. The nearest Centrelink office to our town is forty minutes by car, and there is no public transport system. We are an inner regional area; it would be harder in outer regional and remote areas. I know of a local man who has walked the 35 kilometres for his dole interviews. Other times, he has been driven by a good Samaritan.

When this policy was revealed, I rang a federal government MP to ask how kids just out of school in small towns would survive without local work or support payments. The MP told me they'd have to move to a centre with jobs – a larger regional town or a city. Yet some kids know no other place and don't want to leave the home they know so well. We are fewer than four hours from Sydney and at a pinch I can do the return drive in a day. The transition between city and country is second nature for me, and to any country person who has boarded in a city school or has work experience there. Yet there is a whole other demographic in country towns. Every year, when our primary school does an excursion to the city, there are twelve-year-olds who have never been to Sydney. It is not within their experience. The idea of moving to a larger centre is like moving to another country. The policy was never implemented – it did not pass the Senate.

Consider a young teenager, struggling with drugs of addiction, thrown out of his family home in a small town. In that community where he was raised he may have other significant adults who will keep an eye on him. If there is no crisis accommodation in that place, the kid has to move to a larger centre. In this community that might mean Wagga or Canberra, where he can really get into trouble without a watchful eye. This has happened in our town – young people who are homeless have had to move away to access underage crisis accommodation. We hope to find a way to address the issue and this is where an acknowledgement of place and a little targeted government funding could help a community help its own.

Or consider the other end of life's trajectory – aged care. People who have lived their lives in a small community usually want to stay in place. So often those communities are told that certain services are uneconomic. Small nursing homes are just not viable. Governments and businesses like to consolidate and rationalise, but this disregards the social dislocation caused by removing people from the support of their local community. The dislocated nursing home resident is removed from the former neighbour who drops in with a cake, or the adult child of an old friend stopping by for a cup of tea. In Bundarra in northern New South Wales, a town of 400 people and about 600 in the outlying district, an aged care facility was deemed uneconomic by the service provider because it had ten beds. The community mounted a fierce fight to save it, with the help of the then local MP Tony Windsor, and the facility remains, making a profit and keeping aged people in place.

=

When I think about place, I think of two political elements: granular policy arguments like the ones mentioned above (and I'll go into more detailed discussions about policy in Part 2); and broader threats to place, which take on a more emotional aspect.

On policy arguments, I see continual disregard for the people and places that do not fit into a metropolitan or regional city model. Nearly everyone I have spoken to for this book has remarked on this. Policy solutions that satisfy rural areas and their voters should be more bespoke and involve real consultation with local communities. A tweak here or there to take into account place may be all that is required to satisfy a small town.

The second element – broader threats to place – are more difficult to solve. More than twenty years after the Mabo debates of the early 1990s that shocked me, those same farmers acknowledge that the threats were overdramatised in the heat of the political moment. Nevertheless, the fears came from a strong sense of their place in their world. It was only time and hindsight that healed that particular sore.

In recent times, farmers' livelihoods have been more secure, with strong agricultural land prices, rising global demand for agricultural products and reasonably buoyant commodity prices. Instead, the threats now relate not to physical place but cultural place in the world, and are felt not so much among farmers but among those in rural and regional towns with less economic, cultural and political clout.

The solutions to both the finer policy arguments and the broader threats to cultural place seem contradictory. Metropolitan and rural are like two different countries with different priorities. Yet if governments were to take account of those differences and respond to them in conjunction with the community, the rift between country and city could improve.

Of course, governments have every right to continue business as usual. And perhaps, after so many cost–benefit analyses, they will continue to disregard place by cutting services to small communities. Every government has the right to change policy as it sees fit, but they also need to wear the consequences.

LESSON 3

Diversity is waiting to be found

The night sky in rural Australia remains one of my favourite views, clean and crisp with definition. So it was enlightening to discover there are Aboriginal stories that reverse the view of the sky at night by interpreting the spaces between the stars rather than the stars themselves. They consider the dark sky like a photographic negative, with the stars as holes in an inky blanket. As a concept, it appealed because it forces an abrupt reversal of focus, and so much of political reporting involves straining to see the bits that are out of sight. Political reporting teaches you to take what is presented and then try to figure out what is missing.

Country towns differ enormously. Inner regional areas like ours, closer to larger towns and cities, do not have the same make-up as those further inland. My first impressions of moving into the country was the obvious absence of an Indigenous presence. And yet, as you will see, Aboriginal Australians have a larger presence than was first apparent and have emerged in plain sight as a result of an unlikely alliance in our little town.

Still, in many towns you have to seek out Indigenous stories because they are not evident. These stories do not stand in the road, forcing you to face them. They are traces, like a groove in the stones I have passed every year for the past twenty on the way to one of our favourite Christmas holiday beaches. There is a single flat rock at this south coast beach that the kids used to jump on to – an island in the spiky grass at the edge of the sand. It wasn't until an archaeologist showed us the axe-grinding groove on the rock that we realised what we had been missing for all these years. Previous lives, untold stories.

I remembered those apparent Indigenous absences after watching one of the most memorable speeches I've seen in Parliament. In sitting weeks, Thursday mornings in the Senate are usually pretty ordinary because there are readings of private bills: bills not sponsored by ministers or the government of the day and ones, therefore, that don't usually get up. Private members' business gives senators a chance to raise matters important to them, but journalists don't often watch these debates because they don't materially affect the outcome of government – unless a bill sparks an interest. In November 2016, though, it was all about Section 18C of the Racial Discrimination Act.

Labor senator Pat Dodson has a rare presence in the upper house. He speaks with a certainty that comes from hard-fought experience; not many of his lines come from work-shopped political talking points.

He began. 'It is interesting that bigotry is back in favour.' He talked about the filters through which we see the world, and how our family and cultural upbringing create a frame of reference through which the world is interpreted. It was a speech urging Australians to find a way to 'accept and appropriate' the most positive elements of the diverse cultures that make up the nation rather than continuously dividing and denigrating fellow Australians.

'There is nothing wrong with freedom, particularly if you are from the ruling class. There is a hell of a lot wrong with freedom if you have to battle to experience it – if you have to fight for it. I was born before the 1967 referendum, when we as Aboriginal people were not even counted in the census of this country; when this government did not have any power to make laws for Aboriginal people because it was excluded by the crafters of our Constitution in 1901. The whole battle for recognition – for freedom to enjoy the basics of being a citizen – in this nation had to be fought for by black and white Australians: Jessie Street, Faith Bandler and many others.

'What I see today is the ideological creep back to bigotry and to racism. It is fine if you sit in some leafy suburb and never rub shoulders with people who are battling to interpret and navigate their way through modernity in this land of Australia, with its highly-sophisticated culture and its complexities of protocols and procedures and social ethos. We have to understand that today is not the day to be changing this section of the Racial Discrimination Act.'[1]

He was followed up by a number of other senators, and finally by Pauline Hanson. Over her life, she said, she had been involved with many people of different cultures. A Laotian refugee had managed her fish and chip shop and they had worked well together. She had rented a property to an Aboriginal woman and her child. Her children had grown up with Aboriginals in the same street. 'Respect is earned by the person, not purely based on who they are or their race,' she said. When the Greeks and Italians came, she continued, they were called wogs and they got on with it. 'Because when the Aussies had a go at them, in that Aussie way, they became part of the community – they assimilated.

'We are told constantly, time and time again, that we must be tolerant. Well, I have had it up to here with my tolerance.'[2]

It's easy to be into tolerance if there is nothing to challenge it.

Likewise it is easy to do tolerance on your own terms when you have power.

===

I have never chased up local Indigenous history, partly because I have not had the time and partly because I've had no insistent reason to. Roy 'Jacko' Levett is a local Wiradjuri man. His dad was also named Roy Levett. Roy Senior was from the little town of Wombat (population 180), about fifteen minutes from Harden-Murrumburrah. Like so many around here, he was a fettler on the railway. Jacko's mum, Maisy Bush, was from Boorowa. She worked at Young Hospital. Jacko was one of twelve kids, one of whom died at birth. He reckons he was always a bit different, even from his siblings.

He was born in Mittagong and his father chased work up and down the railway line. He took Jacko out into the bush every weekend. Jacko remembers natural features, a rock chair to rest on, and trees on which his father carved their initials. 'I could still take you there now.' Roy Senior did not talk much about Indigenous culture, but from a young age Jacko was keen to learn. Now some of his own kids and grandkids are interested, but what do you teach them, he asks. 'You can only teach them what you know yourself. I find a lot in old books and old things.'

Jacko was born in 1951; left school at twelve when his mum and dad split. Jacko and his dad headed to Bundaberg and lived on the beach at Burnett Heads. He worked for the Fairymead Sugar Mill in his early teenage years, picking up rocks over thousands of acres. They had a tractor with a cart on the back and he would throw the rocks on, fill it up, take it back and tip it, then bring it out, fill it up – clearing paddocks to plant sugar cane. Rock picking is one of the staples of farm work. 'It's a different life,' he says.

Eventually he settled down, had four kids and moved back into our town. He has been in work all his life, mostly on farms and orchards. Jacko put together casual work across a number of farms, one day a week on each to make up a five-day week. He had plenty of work to get by.

Over the years, he split with his wife and settled on the divorce. 'You can't do more than that – that's the world.' These days, Jacko spends his time helping out the local Land Council, talking to schools, painting and doing woodwork. His hobby is collecting Coca-Cola memorabilia. He was keen to find a poster of Taylor Swift advertising Coke, finally tracking one down in a nearby town. 'They're worth $200 now. Some of the old Coke bottles are worth $100.'

Jacko is one of a number of local keepers of Indigenous knowledge in a town where the Aboriginal heritage is largely unseen. He talks to schools about the history of the area, shows the kids tools, artefacts, paintings and Indigenous culture. He surveys local sites and traces Indigenous routes travelled. At the annual show he organises an annual Indigenous display, which also features his paintings and those of his family.

His Indigenous role is not how I know him. His granddaughter was my daughter's best friend at school. They were thick as thieves. We meet in one of the many coffee houses that have grown up on the highway at the western end of town, servicing the locals, the grey nomads and the Sunday motor bikers who have increased the traffic on the main highway over the past two decades. Jacko says there was a local tribe living two doors down on a site beside the Murrumboola Creek, a Wiradjuri word for 'two canoes'. Murrumboola was his people's summer camp. Their winter camp was on a nearby hill, which must have been as cold as charity.

Everything has a meaning, Jacko says. He has found hammer stones and culturally modified trees that mark travelling routes. These tell you where you are. He looks after them for the local Land Council and answers any queries that come through local government. He doesn't want anything for it. It's interesting just tracing it. Jacko makes it his business to get things right, get evidence and 'cover your own tail so it doesn't come back and bite you'.

So much of modern bush culture must have seeped from Indigenous culture. Jacko knows where the Ngunnawal (Canberra) tribe used to come into Wiradjuri country. He knows the natural features of the landscape that act as boundary markers for the edge of Wiradjuri country. When I first moved here, I was regularly flummoxed by the directions given, not in house numbers or roads but in natural terms. Turn left at the big gum tree, travel for twenty-five minutes, turn right at the silo and follow the dogleg after the bridge. I think, Just give me the address! It still confuses my Singaporean-born father to navigate on the farm – he can't easily find his way around the paddocks. He once asked me where the house was when we were still in the house paddock. Dad grew up in a fully urbanised world, as did I. Nature confounded me for years. The daughter of my best friend, born in the city, asked on a visit, 'Who knocked all the houses down?'

In the latest census, 8.4 per cent of the local area identifies as Aboriginal or Torres Strait Islander, compared with 3.3 per cent nationally. Jacko says the number equates to a couple of hundred people registered.

'I don't know what house they hide under because they are part-Aboriginal and the children are still identifying, but they don't get involved in anything. I talk at the school and try to tell them what I am doing. They all see me up the street and say, "Hi, Jacko," and I try to get them involved doing some painting or something, but nuh.'

It is me who steers Jacko's conversation to the frontier wars and how the Wiradjuri people were pushed off their land.[3] He doesn't think there was much violence. But do we know what happened to these particular families living on the creek here? Probably like everywhere else, says Jacko, they moved on. 'They stayed here and stayed here and stayed here, and eventually most of them moved on.' Looking for somewhere better, he says. The Murrumburrah post office was built on their camp on the creek.

I want to know what it was like growing up Indigenous in a rural area. 'I didn't take any notice. It doesn't matter to me whether you are green, yellow or white. I used to cop a lot of stick, but I was a good fighter and that's what it was. If you could look after yourself, you would look after yourself and that's the way it was in those years. If you were a scrawny little kid – well, every bugger picked on them, didn't they?'

Jacko's manner is low energy and relaxed. He reminds me of people who are good with stock. He wouldn't spook a horse. He's chilled, as the kids would say. I suggest he is pretty laidback.

'Yeah, I have made a lot of friends over the years. I can get on with anyone. If I don't get on with someone I usually tell them. You've got to be like that in the world.'

He was born at a time when the notorious Cootamundra Training Home for Aboriginal Girls was still operating. Cootamundra is forty minutes from our place and while the home is infamous, I don't think I have ever heard any locals, Aboriginal or non-Aboriginal, talk about it. It's as if it never existed. Full erasure. The home was run, with sad irony, by the Aboriginal Protection Board. It took Indigenous girls away from their families to be trained as domestic help for farms and businesses. It has a firm and ugly place in the stories of the Stolen Generation history and the 'Bringing Them Home' report of 1997.[4]

Jacko knew no one out of the 'Coota' Girls' Home, but he says his parents would have known people. He tells me the story of one girl out of the home: she was working at a nearby pub and was repeatedly raped and belted around the legs with barbed wire by the owner.

'Things like that – you don't really want to hear them, do you? It must have been a terrible thing. They let them out into these home-steads, you may as well say as slaves. People don't realise – there is supposed to be that many children in the wells, a well at the front and a well at the back. Dead babies and that. It's a place that you don't feel like going to very often.'

Our conversation is interrupted by a phone call. It is the Indigenous optometrist, who's coming to a nearby town to do an eye check for Jacko and anyone else who wants to see her. We talk about government services and the role of government in ordinary people's lives. He addresses the unspoken suggestion that Aboriginals get more than other people. It is a direct repudiation of Pauline Hanson's complaint that Indigenous people are 'showered' with benefits.

'This is the part I can't work out. Your glasses and things – anyone can get that if they are on a pension. People say, "Oh, because they are Aboriginal they get this and they get that." You don't get no more benefits. I don't think, anyhow. Well, I don't. You probably put more back in than what you get out, sorta thing.'

Jacko references his work in schools and the Aboriginal Education Council. He helps out if schools want Indigenous dancers, or if they apply for funding. He encourages schools to identify their own Indigenous kids and to teach them Indigenous culture if they don't already have an understanding. It needs to come from within, he says, but he doesn't see it as community-minded.

He worries that some in the community always have their hand out. It's the way of the world, he says. 'You can give one person $100 and they have it tomorrow; and another person won't have it ten minutes later.' You can't help some people – 'I'll guarantee that.'

So as far as government goes, best to treat it like hospital: something to avoid if possible. Jacko thinks life is pretty much up to the individual – to chase down work or services – because government is a monster. It is a theme I have heard again and again.

'It's up to yourself. That's how I've earned a living all my life. I have found my job and worked my job, and it's up to everyone else to think the same way. There's a job out there for you if you want it.

You just have to go and find it. It's no use going into Centrelink and saying "I need a job, I need a job." They are not going to get you a job, are they? You're just a number to them and I think if they went out looking, Harry down the road will probably get you a job before Bill up in the Centrelink office. I've never been short of work in my life, there's always been something there. There is still work around today if you want to go and find it. Just potter around and do this and that.'

Again, here is the importance of place in small towns. 'Harry down the road' will know Jacko is honest, and that is what makes place so powerful for rural residents. Avoiding government is a theme. That's why Jacko tries to steer clear of government grants – because the accounting process is a pain.

'It's better to do it off your own bat because you feel more comfortable. I do anyway. I don't have to answer to anyone. You've got to tell some bloke how much you spent on this or that. The paper was $2 – you gotta account for that.'

Not that he doesn't have time for unemployment benefits. They are needed in places that are worse off. Jacko feels other places are worse off, out further west. (This is another recurring theme. Every town on the eastern seaboard thinks towns further west are doing it tougher.)

'If you get out in the bush country and the west and that, they have a bad year and can't afford to put anyone on. They are the people who need the help, I reckon. You don't need it at Wollongong or down around the coast because there is plenty of work around. If you can't do one you can do something else, can't you? But remote areas still need it. I think everyone needs some help at some time through their life, it don't matter who you are. That's my opinion and I think that's the way to live by.'

Like many I talk to, Jacko is not one for politics. What's the point? 'You hear them arguing about a ten cent piece or something. I can't see the sense of that.' The way he sees it, there doesn't seem to be much difference between the parties. 'You vote Labor because you work, and you vote Liberal because you've got a business, and that's the way it's worked from day one.

'I look down the middle and I sorta decide who I like each time. I don't just pick a person. I'm not going to vote for someone who is "I'm going to do this, I'm going to do that." I'm not a person who is gunna do something. I do it straight away. I think you have to have a good think with your own mind before you say something, and look at what they think they are going to do.'

If government does have a role, says Jacko, it should be to bring families out of the city and into the country. To help people see that there is a life beyond big cities. If they would only try it for six months, they would never look back. He also wants the government to protect parks and Crown land for future generations because in Indigenous life everything is connected. He pulls out a hand-drawn diagram of the Indigenous understanding of moiety. In the middle is a circle – your family – and everything branches off from there: your elders, your country, your stories, your art, your occupation, your habits.

Jacko is right. All these things are connected, if only people would look for the links. Pat Dodson is right. Our families and cultures create our frames of reference, the filters through which we see the world. And with observation comes the lesson that no one fits neatly into a little box. The culture warriors who dominate, weaponise and monetise the political debate tell us you can never escape that little box. If you support one idea then you stand over in that corner, and if you believe another idea then it's over there. And once you are pigeon-holed, everything else you say will be referenced through that original assessment.

What I have learned, though, is that as the political conversation polarises and governments become captive to cultural warriors, communities are moving beyond them to find their own solutions.

One of my farm neighbours, Judy McFadyen, drives me out to the other side of town at 5.30 one morning in the dry autumn of 2018. We have not connected for years, since she taught my kids at the local primary school. We yammer all the way into the dark dawn, slipping through farm gates to an outcrop, fenced off because of its rocky ridge and established trees. The sun is just rising and it is the only pointer to where our farm lies, somewhere in the shadows of the largest mound, which marks the way to Canberra.

Like sheep, we make our way through the rocks to the highest point of the rocky knob. The boulders here are in random patterns, occasionally clearing to circular spaces about 10 metres wide. We walk mostly in silence, through pockets of icy air. There are snatches of painterly views across the landscape to horizons stretching in all directions. Judy remarks, and it's true, that it all has the feel of a scene in Peter Weir's *Picnic at Hanging Rock*. There is something prehistoric about the place.

Soon two other women join us; landholder Julia Atkin and Jacko's daughter, Amanda Levett. Hers is just one Indigenous story, but in it I see the wrestle of recent political history. While politicians are fiddling, Jacko, Amanda and this little group have moved beyond the national debate.

Their story started with a development challenge to land usage in the valley. The nature of the perceived threat is not important, the point is the challenge brought people together and forced a reassessment of the value of their place. What does this land mean to us? The group included Judy and her farmer husband, Don, and Julia and her husband, John Taylor – who with his family served the area as vets for many decades – as well as a number of others.

It is rare for farmers to visit other farms, apart from the house for a social occasion, a field trip, or the shed to pick up an errant dog or a piece of machinery. It is even rarer for them to visit outer paddocks – there's just no reason. But in the process of working out what their place meant to them, the landholders began walking the land, following the waterways and discovering the landscape with fresh eyes.

Amanda and Jacko had never visited these particular farms but Judy had mentored Amanda at our local primary school when Amanda was a teachers' aide. Amanda subsequently completed a teaching degree and is working in a larger town nearby. Like Jacko, Amanda has a stillness to her. She is the mother of my daughter's best friend at school so I've known her for nearly twenty years, but she and I have not caught up much since my daughter left for high school. We have certainly never talked about Indigenous issues or the history of the area, but I know from the bush telegraph that she and Jacko have learned how to read landscapes and over the years have been discovering their heritage. Neither of them grew up with culture, they sought it out; began mapping the Indigenous history in the area. Judy and Amanda had always stayed in touch, bonded by their friendship and mutual interest in education. As the land-holders discovered their land more closely, Judy consulted Amanda and Jacko on the Aboriginal heritage in the area. From little things big things grew.

So Amanda and Jacko were welcomed into the group and everyone made their contributions to build a more complex picture of their place. For some, it was childhood memories of the landscape as it was. For others it was more specialised skills. Having retired from his vet practice, John – an environmentalist from an early age – channelled his energies into comprehensively researching the biodiversity of the valley and the interlinked Aboriginal cultural heritage. He worked closely with Jacko to combine the science and the Indigenous cultural heritage of the landscape and they have developed a strong friendship. In the end, the group agreed on a simple statement that enunciated their position as landhold-ers, custodians and community members. It acknowledged their valley was 'of cultural significance including natural, Indigenous and historic places with cultural values'. It recognised the historic land use in the area by traditional Aboriginal custodians, European pastoralists, Chinese gold miners and family farms amongst some 'complex biodiversity'. It said in part:

> Places of cultural significance reflect the diversity of our communities. They tell us about who we are and the past that has formed us and the Australian landscape. We embrace the important role of education to cultivate an increased awareness of Aboriginal culture and history as integral to this landscape. A respect for the principles of inter-generational equity will ensure that the future of this valley is not lost or spoiled.

This connection between farmers, landholders and the Indigenous residents would have seemed inconceivable for some in the group in the 1990s when I encountered those early Mabo conversations. The key in 2017–18 was the bond formed between people, which brought together various cultural strands – Indigenous and non – in a way that did not threaten anyone's sense of place. John's careful crafting of their valuing of place cemented the bonds between the group. And it was as if the landscape played its own role. Landholders were aware of one or two 'scar trees', Indigenous culturally modified trees from which bark was taken to make coolamons or shields, but none were aware of 'ring trees', a much rarer phenomenon. A 'ring tree' has been modified early in its growth, either by placing a stone or another object in a partial split of a sapling's trunk, or by binding a branch to another section of the tree, using kangaroo tendon, perhaps. Some of the finest examples have distinctive loops that can be seen from a distance. 'Ring trees' are thought to act as a marker for ancient walking tracks, or songlines, or to indicate a place of abundance. One of the landholders whose property contains a significant number of culturally modified trees says it is like having a natural wonder of the world that no one else can see.

'Everything here points towards something pretty impressive,' says Amanda. 'They lead you towards something. If you think of it not as a single thing, but connected to each other, it really helps. I thought this is bigger than me. I have felt that way for a long time.'

Reflecting on it with us on that rocky outcrop, she says she was worried by any immediate threat to the land, the water and the people. 'This turned into a greater concern for the cultural landscape as a whole. This is a whole landscape at stake. Not a single culturally modified tree or artefact: without one, the others lose their context, their meaning and their significance. And there are many, many features of significance in this landscape.

'We discovered we had many in our community who have similar values to us. Many of them have an appreciation of, and respect for, Aboriginal cultural values. This has strengthened our determination to preserve our history and increased our desire to learn more.'

Jacko and Amanda had discovered their connection to country, and the connection to its people, including to the white landholders, who were previously largely disconnected from her and her dad.

I assumed that everyone who lives on this land has an emotional story map of their place, on which they remember the events that have taken place on this land. I ask Amanda about her thoughts on the Mabo debate that hit me when I arrived. What was it like for her? 'It's fear. Everything has a knock-on effect.'

While the smaller group had welcomed Jacko and Amanda, Julia and Judy felt the powerful change in the farming audience came at a meeting over land developments. 'When we got up to meet with the farmers, we said, "Look, we are not here to steal your land," Amanda says. Judy and Julia, who were both present at that meeting, underlined the importance of that moment. 'Pivotal,' says Judy. 'A real moment,' says Julia.

'From that, more farmers [were] aware and interested in the history of their property, which is fantastic,' Amanda says. She and Roy have since been invited to see places they have never accessed before.

Sitting on an ancient fallen log, we pour coffee from a thermos and the sun rises, sending shafts of light into the eucalypts above us. My own lack of knowledge gives licence for my companions to ask things they've wanted to but never had the opportunity. I want to know whether Amanda feels it's convenient for farmers to use the concept of Indigenous heritage when land they see as theirs is threatened.

'I can't get my head around what it would feel like to have been almost ignored or dismissed, and then find kids and some adults in an awakening about it all,' Julia says.

'Initially, but it has moved way past that – way past that,' says Amanda. 'Gosh, yes, I would not have stayed such a part of it if I felt otherwise.'

Julia and John have a longstanding interest in Indigenous issues and history, but the impetus for them to come together with the Levetts was the exploration of land and their introduction through Judy.

Julia describes their first meeting. 'I suddenly thought, How would this feel – for everyone to be keen to meet you; to seek your help? Roy engaged with us straight away, talking away as he does, jokes, stories; but at that first meeting Amanda is holding her distance, and I thought, Oh, sheesh, I think we might have done the wrong thing here . . .'

Amanda smiles. 'That's quite normal for me.' She explains to us only half-jokingly that when she is thinking it takes quite an effort, and I understand it. I am not a fast thinker; I would prefer to order my thoughts while writing.

'I did not grow up with culture,' Amanda tells us. 'Everything is like a learning experience for me. It is not like coming home, but it's just reaffirming some stuff.'

Judy reminds her of Jacko's comments at the first public meeting over the development, that the whole thing has come to him in a very strange way. He told the meeting he felt that through this process he had 'come home'. It was the acceptance.

'Dad has found his identity because since then he has been asked to do "Welcome to Country" twice in town. He had never been asked before. No one has ever done it before. It is 2018,' said Amanda.

Amanda's story strikes me for her generosity of spirit, given that she would have every right to resist becoming involved in a fight which benefits some local farmers. I say that in her shoes I would be crankier. Julia agrees.

'I understand what you are saying, but this is the only life that I know, where culture was hidden for sixteen years,' Amanda told us. 'I knew nothing. No connections with family, no connections with country. So to be able to continue finding it, and having support to do so, is winning.'

It dawns on me that three of us four women have grown up with expectations of having a place and a connection to wider culture. We expect to be treated respectfully; we expect a job and a career and a family. We are proprietorial about that place in the world and our landscape and through all of that, we create our identity. So when we put ourselves in Amanda and Jacko's shoes, we imagine we would be angry at our treatment. Amanda was raised with no such expectations. If you grow up with no expectations, everything might be a bonus.

'I am removed from this area. It's not my daily life to come out here. I have empathy for you guys. I think, Oh wow, what if that was me?'

This bridge between the Indigenous residents and the farmers has led to regular expeditions to discover heritage on farms. Out of the connections and with Judy's support, Amanda has developed the Yalbinyagirri program to advance an understanding of Indigenous culture for primary school students. She has brought children out here to show them the culturally modified trees and the land. She has run professional learning sessions for staff, and four local schools have worked with her to develop the units to engage students in learning about the foundations of Indigenous culture. Amanda says the idea was to get kids out on country, connected, and then for them to take it back and teach other children, even their own parents. She is confident that it will change the way Indigenous kids think about themselves. 'By the end of the year it will change things for them because they will have more self-awareness and self-pride, and I find that a really difficult thing to judge because I find those things shift when I am at a school, anyway.'

Before retiring from full-time teaching in 2017, Judy invited Jacko to help her two-teacher school in Jugiong create a traditional Wiradjuri garden and landscape. The kids are learning about totems, local culture and practices, and Dreamtime stories. They are also growing a bush tucker garden with a state government grant.

We talk about the cultural fear of 'doing the wrong thing' in an era of identity politics. Teachers, like a lot of us, find it hard to tackle information from other cultures, so if they can't get access to knowledge or help they avoid it. Amanda has been often approached by teachers who want to know how to incorporate Indigenous painting or history into their classroom in the 'right' way, worrying otherwise it will be culturally inappropriate.

'It's a two-pronged effect, in that you have teachers saying, "I didn't want to do dot art or a stencil or whatever,"' Amanda says. 'I also spoke to a young Aboriginal man who is very passionate and wants to get into schools and I gave him an idea of the project and what's going on and he just went, "Yeah, but that's my culture. Why should they be teaching it?"

'I said, "Because they have to. Can you be in every classroom in every day? Can I be in every classroom? No. They have to – so isn't it up to us to make sure it is done right?"'

Amanda describes the clear tensions within her community over whether to share culture and heritage; whether to tell stories and show sites that will signify the complexity and breadth of Indigenous culture. She is adamant that sharing culture will change attitudes towards Indigenous people. 'My values and ideas aren't the norm. I learn that more often than not.'

Amanda believes that reconciliation 'must be a two-way street'. 'Reconciliation as a buzzword rubs me up the wrong way because a lot of Aboriginal people don't show the values themselves and don't put in the effort themselves. [They] believe it's all for them but don't give it back.' She understands constitutional recognition is 'important to some people' because of past policies, but she has yet to read the Uluru Statement from the Heart, which urged a 'First Nations Voice enshrined in the Constitution'.[5] She is too busy with her approach, which, along with that of her father, Jacko, has led to reconciliation on their own patch.

Her 'goosebump moment' was when a farmer's child whom she had taught explained an Indigenous painting to her parents in a major gallery two years after this girl had learned about the symbols. Her mother proudly reported her daughter's story back to Amanda, who says, 'I'm amazed that she kept that.'

Amanda is convinced that although a greater understanding between black and white may take a generation, it will happen – and because of local actions across the country. Not through Parliament. She notes the sweep of history and its changes even in her own lifetime. 'There was the Stolen Generation, the Hidden Generation because of the Stolen Generation, and then the Forgotten Generation. My kids want to know [more]. They don't know who to ask but they want to know.'

Julia says it is the small acts of kindness that have affected her most. 'It is that generosity that I have experienced multiple times from Aboriginal people that for me is – even though I wasn't involved in the atrocities – it's the forgiveness. That's where the real human connection is and, I'd say, [where] reconciliation really occurs, as opposed to the token stuff.'

There was a moment at the height of the local land usage debates when Judy felt on the outer in her own community. She tells Amanda, 'When we were so isolated from our community, it was a tiny, tiny taste of what you might have experienced.' Amanda shrugs. She had been fully involved in the debates but says she never cares what people think of her.

On that rocky hilltop, I learn two things: one personal and one national. Firstly, that although I've known the Levett family for twenty years, I have not known them. We often get to know people on a superficial level, without asking about their deep stories. Sometimes they don't want to share them. Sometimes they are more than willing to open up. For that to happen requires us to reach out, and this has become my personal project.

Secondly, I learn that our political leaders are falling behind communities. At a time when communities are looking for more active government, politicians are being dragged to decisions. There was majority voter support for a banking Royal Commission two years before Labor and four years before the Coalition agreed it was needed. There was majority voter support for same-sex marriage several years prior to it being finally passed by the Parliament in 2017. Malcolm Turnbull has dismissed the idea of the Indigenous voice requested in the Uluru Statement from the Heart, describing it as a 'third chamber' incapable of winning the constitutional change required, even though the manner of the voice has yet to be fully enunciated by Indigenous Australians. We don't know what level of public support is out there yet, but, given what I see on this rocky hilltop, I would not dismiss it. My hope is that Indigenous recognition will again prove that community is ahead of government. Reconciliation may yet build from the ground up.

LESSON 4

Social divisions are highly visible in small towns

In big cities, hierarchies have postcodes. In small towns, hierarchies are in full view. In a small town, individuals and their families are on show. Friendships and interactions are evident. Influence is palpable. The social ladder is in plain sight. Just as there is a division between city and country, there are divisions within the country, too. There can be a division between living on a farm or in town. There can still be elements of sectarian division between Protestants and Catholics. There can be a division between new money and old money; between locals or blow-ins. I've heard a lot of talk along the following lines: 'He was a so-and-so from Yass'; or, 'She was a so-and-so from Goulburn.' To which I would say, 'I am one of the Singapore Chans, not far removed from the Chinese Chans.' Cop that! Biggest family network in the world! Then, when the divisions between public and private schools widened as my own children grew up, city acquaintances from posh schools asked my country kids more and more, 'Which school did you go to?' In the country, I have seen snobbery: 'Why would you invite them?'

And reverse snobbery: 'She's thinks she's too good because she lives on a farm.' None of this is hard and fast. It is tangled and fluid.

Growing up in the city, I never noticed the concept of class. We lived in a suburb with a similar aspirational demographic, and kids at the local high school seemed to come from similar backgrounds as I did in all but race. As I reached adulthood and moved into the media, the financial divisions were clear, but distant from my life in the inner city, even though talk of silvertails and bogans was ever present.

Still, many city-based, middle-class professionals such as us in the media rarely encounter other classes. Historically, Australia has tended to disavow class, at the same time as much of our culture makes fun of one class or another. Think of Kath and Kim: 'Oi wanna be effluent, Mum.'

'You are effluent, Kim.'

Or Chris Lilley's Ja'mie: private school girl to the public high school kids on exchange: 'Some of you come from povo families, but that's not your fault.' Chris Lilley also bells the rural–city divide when Ja'mie introduces her posh private school. She says she is nice to pretty much everyone except the boarders (my kids). Lilley identifies differences of class and geography, which combine to create an oddity. 'I don't even know why I don't like them,' Ja'mie says in her mockumentary. 'They are just really annoying. You know what I mean? They are sort of fat and weird and they have stupid haircuts.'

Every single person in my hundreds of conversations for this book thinks class is a very real thing in Australia, though it is barely mentioned in political commentary, because we don't know how to talk about it. The people in my main street have no qualms discussing class. With the 2016 Brexit and Trump votes, however, class is becoming less of a dirty concept in public debate.

J. D. Vance's *Hillbilly Elegy* documented Vance's childhood in a poor white family in Middletown, Ohio, and became an explainer of the 2016 Trump voters. Vance's story of the complexities around poverty, unemployment, substance abuse and trauma reflected both the systemic hurdles and self-sabotage experienced by aspirants to the American dream. It was a story that shocked a fair portion of the United States. It represented a culture and people they found foreign.

The post-war years in Western countries have been marked by people striving for a middle-class life in the entirely understandable effort to achieve a comfortable existence. My parents worked their arses off in the 1970s to get out of a rented flat in Sydney's beachside Coogee, before it was fashionable, and into a three-bedder brick veneer project home on a quarter-acre block in the suburbs. We eventually climbed into a middle-class existence and stayed there, courtesy of education. It was something to strive for. To join the so-called elite meant not having to struggle.

In 2016 the worm turned, and we have now entered a climate in which it's not done to brag about having a comfortable existence, let alone to desire entry into the elite or upper classes. When chasing down an essay by Professor of Law at UCLA Joan C. Williams, 'What So Many People Don't Get About the U.S. Working Class', I had to laugh when an advertisement popped up for Harvard University courses: 'Arrive an elite executive. Emerge a visionary leader.'[1] This nod to the horror of being elite, and from one of the most elite institutions in the world, is becoming more common. It seems as if every woman and her dog is fighting to prove their working-class cred, or, at the very least, their self-awareness of being elite. Guilty as charged.

In her essay and subsequent book *White Working Class: Overcoming Class Cluelessness in America*, Williams argues that Trump's election hung a lantern over the cultural divide between the largely white working class (WWC) and the professional managerial elites (PMEs) – a class she places herself squarely within.[2] She married a working-class man. When she talks about the working class, she is talking about the middle – or median – income. She uses cultural touchstones like television shows to identify the contempt held for the white working class. Williams names *All in the Family*, a 1970s American sitcom I grew up watching. My father and I used to laugh at Archie Bunker, the dumb, white working-class dad in the series. We identified with the views of his son-in-law, who was pro-gun control, pro-civil rights and myriad other progressive causes. We considered Archie a loser because we knew he was so last century. Even in the seventies, the world was leaving him behind. Now Archie is back and he is pissed off.

In his 2017 book *The Road to Somewhere*, British journalist David Goodhart splits the Brexit divide into 'Somewheres' and 'Anywheres'. According to his theory, Somewheres voted for Brexit. Somewheres have deep roots in location and place. They are often less educated, more likely to live in regional areas and to be socially more conservative. Anywheres voted to stay in the European Union. They are marked by their global mobility.

Williams and Goodhart are just two of the many commentators who have had a crack at explaining the 2016 political disruption in terms of class and cultural revolt. While more recent academic research suggests that Trump's support stemmed from a more classical working Republican base than a straight working-class revolt, I am thankful that it spawned interest in constituencies outside of the big cities.[3] In moving between the Canberra press gallery and a small country town, I have seen first-hand the two worlds, which may be termed the Somewheres and the Anywheres, or the WWC and the PMEs. There is definitely a division, and with the rise of minor-party voting in Australia (discussed in Part 2), it behoves the political class to understand that division better. Regional voters are rusting off the main parties at a greater rate than city voters. That is a bald fact.

To understand how small communities like mine function, we need to talk about class. This has been one of the biggest lessons I've taken from my little town. Class demarcations are a window into how country towns work. Those demarcations in turn drive influence and therefore political representation. It begins with class.

Attempting definitions of Australia's class alone would be enough to throw the focus of this book into a bog of income brackets, education levels and status symbols. Suffice to say that in considering small towns like my own, it is clear that as you travel up the class ladder, so too do your opportunities increase. Or, to put it another way, as you head towards the bottom rungs, your opportunities shrink. There is a role for personal agency, but the climb to success is longer the lower down the rungs you stand. That might make you cranky.

The thing about class is that it's nebulous. Class is about money, but it is also about other things. It's status and a place in the economy. It's education but not all the time. It is often intergenerational. Or sometimes not. As you climb the class ladder, networks become invaluable. When it comes to stratification in the country, advantageous connections count for a lot, both in terms of acceptance and when you are trying to strive for something outside the community. Connections help knock down a few of the hurdles between a small town and whatever dream you hold. That is partly why some country people send their children to the city for their schooling. Understanding the city and its tribes can provide a head start from a small town. The seamless transition between the two worlds makes jobs and social interactions easier. Lack of connections or any kind of network pile further weight in the saddles of children trying to get ahead in small towns.

Global research would tell you that Australia is generally seen as doing not too badly in terms of income mobility. A study published by the Stanford Center on Poverty and Inequality in 2017 found that for Australians the income of our parents mattered less than in most other countries, though we were beaten by Denmark, Norway, Finland, Canada and South Korea.[4] But often that is not how it feels on the ground in a small town.

Ken Pearsall's parents had a soldier–settler block, the small farms given to soldiers returned from the First and Second World Wars. It was a tough gig, given many of the soldiers had no experience in farming. Ken worked on the place until his parents sold the farm. He was determined to do anything but fruit picking or the abattoirs, so he found a job in an asphalt company, then he carted bread for a decade and did a variety of other jobs over his working life. But as the work dried up, and with a family to raise, he did find himself looking to the abattoirs. And when the abattoir closed and the workforce was turned out, the orchards were his only option. 'Can you imagine? The two places I swore I would never work!'

From there, he went on to the Newstart unemployment benefits and later got credits for his volunteer work in the Harden-Murrumburrah Historical Society under mutual-obligation requirements. These rules require all participants to do something in return for the dole or youth allowance. It might be looking for work; it might be work for the dole; or, if you're over fifty-five, you might do at least fifteen hours per fortnight of approved voluntary work, or a bit of paid work, or a combination of the two. Since that time, Ken has moved to a disability pension but is still voluntarily involved in the Historical Society and the State Emergency Services (SES).

As a result, he spends a lot of time ferreting through files for requests, sorting pictures and manning the local museum. For a donation, you can see the local history collection on most weekends and one day in the week. He can give you all sorts of details about it, and has spent a great deal of time scanning in old films, collecting information and ensuring records and local newspapers are kept up to date. I see him once a week with his mates at the gym and in our conversations, he regularly underestimates his brain.

'When I went to school in the 1970s, you could really see your classmates, you could pick out who was going to work where,' Ken says. 'We had the abattoirs there, so anyone in the lower end of the year went to the Cootamundra abattoirs. The middle group did apprenticeships and other jobs.' The one up top? 'One guy in our form, well, he's the judge at Wagga now.

'A lot of that was the attitude in town. My son went to work [in the abbatoir] after Year 12 and one fella there said, "What? A Year 12 working in the abattoir?"'

Ken's understanding of class underlies his politics – a common element for the Brexiteers and the Trump voters. Trump's ironic exhortation to drain the swamp appealed to main-street perceptions of politicians, media and their privilege as a class or club. Ken makes the distinction between the late Alby Schultz – an abattoir worker, and a former local MP – and most politicians in more recent times. 'They go to big schools, and costly schools, and do all law and university and all that. We are just the scum of the human chain for them. "I'm it" – you know? They are not with the common people. Alby was an abattoir worker.'

Ken voted for the Liberal party when Alby Schultz was in Parliament because Schultz was one of those 'common people'. But when Pauline Hanson returned to Parliament in the Senate one parliamentary term after Schultz retired, Ken stopped voting for the Liberals. He says he can no longer identify with major party politicians: he feels they have abandoned ordinary people. He considers himself working class, separate from the political class, and studies show people are pretty good at self-identifying.

A 2015 survey by Jill Sheppard and Nicholas Biddle of the Australian National University found that most Australians (52 per cent) considered themselves middle class. A lesser proportion (40 per cent) viewed themselves as working class; only two per cent identified as upper class in Australian society.[5] Six per cent did not answer the question.

Sheppard and Biddle then went beyond self-identification to try to build a more objective picture of social class in Australia, which was based on what we do, who we know and what we have. That represented economic capital (income and property), social capital (who your contacts are and what they do) and cultural capital (how you spend your free time: sport, opera, choice of music, ballet or video games). The authors found that when they asked people to describe their social class and then assessed it based on their economic, social and cultural capital, their self-assessments came pretty close to those based on the measures. The authors found that the self-described working class were more dissatisfied with the way the country was heading than the self-described middle and upper classes. The affluent classes were the most satisfied with the direction in which the country was heading, which is not surprising. If you are more comfortable financially, it tends to take the economic hard edges off life.

Trust in governance is falling across the board, but if the less affluent classes tend to be crankier with the political system, it might explain a definite split I found between the established farmers and the town. While almost every person I speak to in my town is distrustful of politicians and the media, it is those sandwiched between the established upper and middle-class asset holders and the poor who are most angry about politics. If you want to know where the middle (as opposed to the middle class) is, the median taxable income in Australia, according to 2014–15 taxation statistics, was $54,543.[6] That is, if you earned more than that, you earned more than at least half of all Australians. This group is hard to label as straight working class or middle class because it blurs at the edges. You need to understand the contours of their lives, though even if you do, the most common factors are anger at the system and the feeling of being neglected by politics.

=

I am sitting in Trish and Adrian Stadtmiller's living room in their house in town. Our interview is scheduled for 2 pm on the day the

High Court decisions on the eligibility, or otherwise, of the (then) deputy prime minister Barnaby Joyce and six other members and senators are about to drop. The television is on ABC News 24 and it is clear from the conversation that the Stadtmillers are avid news watchers. They watch Fox and Sky News a lot and enjoy broadcasters Paul Murray and Rita Panahi. It has been a shift, as they used to watch the ABC more than they do now, but they say the national broadcaster has swung too far to the left.

'It's embarrassing,' says Adrian. 'We've watched ABC current affairs programs for years, but as soon as someone is a bit right-wing, one particular host closes them down. He tends to let people who are quite possibly black or lesbian or transgender, or whatever marginalised group, rabbit, rabbit, rabbit on; but if they are a bit more right-wing he will shut them down. I can imagine his job must be difficult, but a lot of the left on the ABC do not perceive the difference between conservative and what they call hate speech, which is the right. They think the far left is normal, but I'm thinking the left is here, the right is there, hopefully I am somewhere in here.' Adrian points to the centre.

You consider yourself centre? 'Well, yeah. The older I get I'm probably more to the right. I'm not saying that's a good thing.'

In 1975, when Gough Whitlam was sacked by Governor-General John Kerr, Adrian was working for the parliamentary bills office. He collected his wife Trish from the Department of Social Services, where she was working in the public relations department. The two of them rushed to the front steps to see Gough, surrounded by fellow Labor MPs and chanting Labor supporters. The comedian Garry McDonald, whose best-known character at the time was Norman Gunston, climbed the steps.

'We're on the front steps and there is Norman shoving the microphone in Gough's face,' says Adrian. 'It was such a charged atmosphere. You had Labor supporters down the bottom screaming,

"Sack Fraser" or "Kill Kerr", and Gough at the top saying, "Men and women of Australia." I just felt, boy, this is a momentous time in history . . . politically I wasn't one way or another, but I thought it's a momentous incident. I was just watching it unfold.'

Trish had voted for Gough before the events that took place on those steps that day in 1975. She and Adrian have been married for forty-four years and these days she classifies herself as a swinging voter but rarely votes Labor. The last time was for Kevin Rudd and she considers that a mistake. 'I just thought Gough tried to achieve far too much in too short a time. Labor do that every time when they get into government. They go like bulls at gates and then they get pulled up and people think they are wasting all this money.'

Adrian doesn't have much time for Labor's policies. 'They get chucked out of office, so their attitude is they have to get in and go hell for leather and try to achieve as much as possible, but then the general populace gets a bit nervous. In the public service, which is more a Labor voting body, I think there was an awareness that, boy, things are happening fast here. But you just have to admire Gough's style.'

Trish's father migrated from England to the Harden district in 1926. He was the second son of a wool merchant from Manchester. He married a local girl whose father was a share farmer. Trish was one of five kids, and her mum was a Labor woman. It didn't matter what that party did, Trish says, her mum always voted Labor. Trish thinks her dad probably leaned towards Labor, given he was 'a working man, even though he came from a middle-class background'. He was a bulldozing contractor, building dams for farmers around town. He converted from the Anglican Church to Catholicism for the sake of his wife, and quickly became a more committed Catholic than many born to it. It was a big thing to convert in those days, when there was still a strong sectarian feeling around here – a division that has since calmed down as churches have combined in ecumenical services to try to increase attendance. If proof was ever needed of her father's commitment to the faith, it came when Trish's brother married an Anglican woman. The family had planned to go to the wedding but their parish priest forbade their attendance. Her father acquiesced. 'It was the only day I saw my father cry. It was dreadful.'

Adrian was also raised Catholic. He and his four siblings, his parents and his grandparents lived in the old Binalong convent west of Yass. His father had a falling-out with the priest, prompting an argument at the presbytery door, after which he left the Church and declaring he was an atheist. The Stadtmiller family was denounced from the pulpit, according to Adrian. His father never returned and would not let a priest see him on his deathbed. Adrian wouldn't know how his parents voted. He feels they had little influence on his vote.

When Adrian thinks of the mechanics of class, he thinks of his maternal grandmother. She and her daughter, Adrian's mother, came from a 5000-acre property. Adrian's parents met when his father was working for his mother's family. It was the late 1940s and they fell in love. 'Grandma made it quite clear my mother was marrying beneath herself. She was an old snob.'

Adrian was sent away to a Sydney-based Catholic boarding school. It was a violent time to be boarding – 'I'm still recovering.' It seems like only half a joke. He tells stories about being hit for failing to understand mathematics, and will never forget the day another Year 11 boy, pushed to the brink, punched the principal in front of the whole class. 'It was a lot different school in the late sixties than it is now.'

Trish finished Year 10 as dux at the little Catholic school in town but couldn't face the idea of two more years of schooling. She took a job teaching first grade because, well, 'It didn't take Einstein to teach seven-year-olds.' After five years teaching she went to Canberra and started working in the department of social services, delivering files. She briefly considered joining the police force but eventually moved to the male-dominated public relations department.

From a small, socially conservative town, she registered that her workmates were all on their second and third marriages. They were all big Labor supporters and she thinks that also influenced her at the time. People like Bill Hayden were often visitors to her workplace.

Adrian and Trish had their first two children in Canberra and then moved back to Harden. The decision was based on lifestyle, says Adrian. That and he could see he was not progressing in the public service. 'After ten years I couldn't stand it anymore. Excuse the French but one thing I am not is an arselicker. I didn't go and play squash and drink with the powers that be. And coming from the country I felt too hemmed in in Canberra. I didn't want to hear the neighbour and his wife fighting every night. Trish liked Canberra a bit more.'

They started a clothing business in town, with no experience in clothing or business. Adrian did the buying and the shop survived for seven years and paid their way as two more children arrived. Eventually Adrian added a diploma of education to his arts degree and taught locally. Though Trish had four young kids, and an ageing mother, she decided to do a BA in social welfare and then worked in adult education and the welfare area.

'I always felt I lacked the education that I really wanted. When I went to Canberra in the public service, I started in the lower division because I only had Year 10. I thought, I am going to fix that, and did the Higher School Certificate. Later on . . . I am not belittling motherhood and bringing up kids, but I needed something more than that.'

Adrian and Trish Stadtmiller are very aware of the stratification of small towns. When I ask Adrian what class he identifies with, he says, 'It is not so much which class we identify with, it is which class identifies with us.' He thinks class is certainly about money – at least to some extent. And here he apologises to me for what he is about to say, given I am married to a farmer.

'There's a stratifying of classes. If you want to try and cement it down, I'm not saying all but some of the landowners only stick with [other] landowners, and they operate with that social clique. They all tend to drive a certain kind of car that comes from money. You know – BMWs, Mercs – and that's great.'

My VW is parked in the driveway. Trish points out that Adrian has a Bentley. 'Yeah, but it's 1960.'

Adrian sees class as defined, too, by the physical manifestations of standard of housing, though it is not a hard and fast rule. He says you can also see how it plays out in friendship groups, including your friends on Facebook. Who you accept and who you don't says a lot.

'Due to my parents' example – especially that of my father – I believe I have no problem associating with whoever; for example, the bloke in the pub with more schooners in him than teeth through to the bloke who owns 20,000 acres. From experience, the bloke with few teeth is probably more likely to be happy to associate with you than the 20,000-acre bloke, but you can't lump everybody in the same basket.

'Then you have the middle, the business people, tradies and whatever; and then in a town this size, down the bottom you've got people who probably don't have a lot of money, maybe a dysfunctional family background. People who've had problems in life – drugs and whatever. It's not a situation that is yelled out, but it's implicit and I think it's insidious.

'There are boundaries. I don't think [class] is a good thing. Some big landowners around here would be fine, they would talk to anybody. But if people overstep the mark they are told to get in their box. It goes right across Australian society.'

Trish says their approach when raising their four children was to tell their kids they were no better than anyone else, but no one was better than them. After the clothing business, she worked in welfare in a larger regional centre. 'You could see a definite class [there] – two or three different classes, if you like.'

She thinks 'new money' can be as problematic as 'old money' in Australia. 'There is also a thing with the nouveau riche,' says Trish. 'I know people who are really well-off who are down-to-earth, nice people; and then people who have come into money and made a lot of money and moved up in society – they can be more snobbish than other people.'

Adrian believes people who marry up can lose their grounding quite easily. 'One couple we know came from a poor background. They became quite well-off. Trouble is, she didn't have the sophistication of attitude that would have gone with the acquisition of money. It was very much, Oh well I'm not dealing with you anymore. I've seen it here: they marry up and suddenly the nose goes up in the air. If I walk past somebody in the street and say hello and they walk past me without speaking, that's the last time I say hello to them. Bugger you.'

=====

So, yes, stratification in small communities is clearly visible. And there's a certain resentment if 'self-appointed' landowners are perceived to be 'running the town'. There are regular complaints that farmers and agricultural businesses dominate local councils or other leadership groups. Leadership can be executed quietly or with condescension, and done badly it breeds discontent. Conversely, in other groups there can be a lack of will or confidence to step up and contribute, though there are many examples of those who do. Some with no tertiary education or business skills think they have little to contribute, but I would argue it is vitally important to get community perspectives across the board for issues that affect the town. People have told me that in regard to town development committees they can't be involved because they don't know about business, or the way council works, even though they have definite views on the direction of the town. Often community contribution is firmly rooted in family cultures inside and out of town, and you can see the same families stepping up year after year, generation after generation. A number of those people consider it their responsibility to put their money and time into contributing to improve the town and its children's prospects in whichever way they see fit. I know of country families who are taught this from the start. They learn that the luck of their birth into a comfortable existence requires their contribution. No doubt some people see it as wealthier residents throwing their weight around. Sometimes, though, it is just a quiet vocation. Here, again, is the class divide within the town, as old as humanity, as present as in any city but just more visible in small towns. I worry that it is these divides that have the potential to widen as we see political disruption take hold around the world, because class has been at the heart of the great political disruptions in the West in recent years.

The term 'landed gentry' has made a comeback in the post-Brexit/Trump era. The Australian National Party is considered the party of farming as well as of a section of the rural business class, and as such is most often labelled the landed gentry of rural Australia. When Barnaby Joyce had to recontest his seat of New England because he had been found to hold New Zealand dual citizenship, Labor's Joel Fitzgibbon used the term in launching Labor's campaign against Joyce. Fitzgibbon was critical that while the Nationals represented some very poor electorates in the Parliament, they were not 'of' the people. 'Their modus operandi is to keep them poor and to throw them a few crumbs from time to time,' he said. The agriculture shadow minister claimed that the by-election had come about because 'Barnaby Joyce thought he was above the law'.

'Forget about the plea of ignorance, Joyce's crime is that of arrogance. He presents as a man of the people, but he is typical landed gentry. He recently said the people in the weatherboard and tin needed him here. It was his way of making reference to the battlers. But the truth is, they are struggling because he is here!'

Rural society does not operate in a vacuum. Class warfare has never really left the parliamentary political debate, even if terms such as landed gentry have come in and out of favour. Tony Abbott accused Julia Gillard and her treasurer, Wayne Swan, of class warfare in their 2012 budget. Gillard suggested Abbott did not understand working families because he was cosseted on Sydney's north shore. Mining billionaire Andrew Forrest described Labor's planned mining tax as a class war. Malcolm Turnbull is often drawn by cartoonists in a top hat to convey his wealth. Abbott's former chief of staff turned Sky News commentator Peta Credlin famously nicknamed Turnbull 'Mr Harbourside Mansion' in the 2016 election campaign. Turnbull made fun of Bill Shorten as a class traitor – 'a social-climbing sycophant if ever there was one'. In Question Time in early 2017 Turnbull said of Bill Shorten, 'There was never a union leader in Melbourne that tucked his knees under more billionaires' tables than the Leader of the Opposition . . . There has never been a more sycophantic leader of the Labor Party, than this one and he comes here and poses as a tribune of the people.'

This is where main street and politics converge. In Parliament, attacks on the wealthy are often criticised by the Coalition as class envy. Or Labor has used class to depict the rich as out of touch. On the main street, class is used to get at those with perceived privileges not accessible to the majority. I have also heard it used to dismiss families that are racked by domestic violence, petty criminality and poverty. A particular family was dismissed: 'Always have been feral, always will be.'

There has long been a myth in Australia that the nation is a class-less society, and it is not uncommon to hear about our egalitarian attitudes in public debate. A well-used example is sitting in the front of taxis with the driver. Farmer, country woman and Labor aspirant for the federal Parliament Vivien Thomson lives down the Hume in New South Wales. She attempts to explain the myth of the classless society via her entry into the district some years back with her partner Robert. '[Class] is still there, but it's not talked about and it's not acknowledged. I would probably have to assume it's because we like to think of ourselves as a fair society, and as soon as you put class structures in, it's not seen as fair. Robert was told when he moved [here]: You will never move in the right circles because you didn't go to the right boarding school and you didn't play in the right football team. He was told that quite bluntly by a friend who would be considered in that class.'

Most people who have lived in regional Australia have a story of the visibility of its stratification. Jack Archer's grandfather was the mayor of Goodradigbee Shire Council and he had a fine wool property which was part of the original selection in the Mullion, north-east of Canberra. Jack's father was raised on the farm but moved to the Hunter Valley where his parents were both teaching. That is where Jack was raised. As chief executive of the not-for-profit Regional Australia Institute, he speaks to many different rural communities to better understand their issues.

Jack's first insight into class hit him when he arrived in the city, straight from high school. He was moving into Wesley College at Sydney University when an enthusiastic young fresher bounced up and asked him which school he went to. Jack told him Maitland High. 'He never talked to me again. Not in a completely rude way. It was just, "I'm not sure what to do now so I'm just going to leave." That gave me a real insight into class in Australia. I think that it certainly exists. If you're not a significant asset owner in the regions, if you're people who don't own business, don't own a significant house, don't have a government job, there is definitely a divide there, in terms of wealth and culture, but it's messy.'

He does not claim to know any communities deeply enough to know whether the bones of stratification in rural areas has changed, though he knows where it came from historically: 'Class is there from squatters. They were the original upper class in Australia, even if they weren't particularly upper class when they started. The landed gentry are definitely part of it.'

The disturbing thing for someone interested in politics and policy is that the visibility of small-town stratification means you can see children you know following family patterns, or at least finding it difficult to stray from those family paths. This might be fine if your parents are professionally well connected and have the resources to improve your life opportunities by ensuring a good education or an unpaid internship, or introducing you to contacts who can open the door to your dreams. It's not fine if you come from a family without those same social and financial resources: that's likely to lead to a failure or at least a stunted opportunity at pursuing your goals.

Of course, this dual carriageway of opportunity happens in cities, too, but in small towns the visibility of family pasts makes it harder for those down the ladder to remake their identity if that is what they want. Longstanding residents of small rural communities rarely need an investigation by the SBS-TV show *Who Do You Think You Are?* to discover their family tree. Their antecedents tend to be well remembered, for better or worse. In short, what becomes clear in a small town when you watch those family patterns repeat is that the very simplistic language employed by politicians that divides Australia into 'lifters and leaners' cannot adequately explain this complex terrain. From a small town, it is often possible to imagine where kids at preschool may end up. I am married to a third-generation farmer. We both have university degrees. We have a good income. We have handy connections. Do my kids get a head start over other kids who have not had the same income, parental education levels, social networks and opportunities to adequately pave over the geographic and cultural divides that exist between city and country? The answer is yes. Of course.

==

Even in the ant farm environment of a small town, it's still possible to disappear. As the kids went through primary school, I, and any parent taking part in the reading program or helping at the canteen, could see children who were vulnerable, who came to school without lunch. Those little faces were like open books, as curious as the next child, but their parents stood away from the main social gatherings at pick-up time. Sometimes they were not there at all, and if they were there it was hard to break through to them. We did not come across these families on school councils or P&Cs. The regular Education Department exercises collecting socioeconomic data on the school community for funding rounds was like extracting teeth. We organised morning teas to help parents fill in the surveys, but it was still hard to get the families doing it tough to share information. It was so easy for them to slip under the radar. There was also a certain transience, so that the next time you notice, the children have moved on, a result of the insecurity of work, dysfunction at home or the vagaries of changing economic and relationship circumstances.

While these people are accessing and interacting with government services continually, and Centrelink is a constant presence in their lives, the underclass or the working poor don't express their political anger in the usual channels of the street-corner conversation or a letter to the local paper. They are too busy surviving. I have learned this through the work of Glenn and Ros Stewart at our Harden community gym. Ros is a social worker and Glenn an electrician, with a history of ministering through the God's Squad Christian bikie group. A family working sabbatical to the UK-based Zac's Place, an outreach service for those on the fringes of society, gave Ros and Glenn the model. After deciding there was a need in rural areas for crisis accommodation, they set up Zac's Place in Yass, in an old building with a disused tennis court. It's a drop-in centre from where employment programs for marginalised people are run. Through that process, Ros and Glenn were given the use of a house in Harden-Murrumburrah for crisis accommodation, which is part-funded by the gym.

Glenn has since begged, borrowed or used online auctions to gather an extraordinary array of equipment for a community gym in an old Harden supermarket building, leased at a peppercorn rent. Ros's social-work skills have come in handy to deal with the increasing number who stop by to get help. So now those of us who use the gym to keep fit are getting to know another side of town, a side we used to see far less often. It has made it a comfortable place for anyone to come, regardless of the label on your active-wear. Musclemen and gym junkies lift and sweat as aged residents and disabled folk stretch, and a marginalised youth eats toast at the breakfast bar in the middle. As far as Glenn and Ros know, theirs is a unique model: a community gym, and private donations funding the maintenance of the crisis accommodation.

The first family was welcomed into the crisis accommodation. Mark* is a father with three children who needed short-term accommodation after a separation. He tells me that the dearth of men's crisis accommodation makes it difficult for fathers with children. Glenn and Ros's not-for-profit enterprise ensured Mark didn't have to move to a larger centre to try to find public housing. It allowed him to take a breath, gather his forces, find a steady job and save to move into his own accommodation. The crisis accommodation has cemented his loyalty to the town. 'I'm always telling people to move here,' he says.

Unless you work in services like Zac's Place, or in health or education, it is hard to see the marginalised, and to understand their challenges. Many are dealing with domestic violence and abuse, or have drug and alcohol issues, and mental health issues. Government will not offer services to address these problems without certain numbers, because it has to justify its programs. Ros worries that small towns miss out because they cannot tick those boxes. 'You can't pick up a model from the city and put it in a country town. There is just not enough people. It's not that the issues are different. Drug addiction is drug addiction and kids' behaviour is kids' behaviour. But in a city you might run a parenting course that you can guarantee you will get twenty people to. You would never get twenty people here, and they won't fund something that doesn't get the numbers. But still, isn't it just as important to get four people and change the lives of those families so that we have improved outcomes for everybody?'

Ros and Glenn's model has not just connected social groups who would not usually come across each other. Their advocacy has increased understanding and cohesion in the community by high-lighting the needs of our own people who are going without. For every lesson, there is an exception. For all the clarity of the small community, people still fall through the cracks.

=

Since I moved from the city, the political dynamics have been changing in my region. The rise of the professional political class has taken the occupation further from the average voter in my main street. That means that only the most connected individuals have the capacity to relate to politicians, or have relationships with them. This has occurred while there has been a shrinkage of major-party options, as Labor has walked away from rural areas to court more populous metropolitan and coastal audiences – thus reducing the pool of viable candidates.

At the same time, at two levels there has been the continued decou-pling of rural populations from metropolitan. The decoupling can be seen at a broad cultural level, in that rural and regional populations tend to be more Anglo and cities more multicultural. The decou-pling has also occurred at a family level: metropolitan people are less likely to know someone in a small town. So the gap between rural and metropolitan attitudes has been exacerbated, feeding a feeling of geographical divide. All of this has happened at a time when there has been a rise of higher-profile, branded independents who are able to get their messages across much more effectively via social media than they could have in the past. Minor-party brands run by the likes of Pauline Hanson, Nick Xenophon and Derryn Hinch have become lightning rods for discontent with major party politics.

As a result of these dynamics, I have witnessed a cleaving between the Parliament and ordinary voters around me. While class has been relevant since European Australian settlement began, it is the interaction of class and political sentiments that has surprised me in the past two decades of country life. Connected, influential classes in country towns remain as frustrated as most Australians with the past decade of politics, but they remain more rusted on to their political party of choice. In rural areas, this is most likely to be the Coalition. However, those further down the ladder of assets and opportunity are angry. In the past, those voters might have been likely to follow the country party voting tradition because their lives were more intimately linked with agriculture. But as agriculture has got more efficient, requiring less employees, the links between the two groups are more distant. Those voters are rusting off their traditional choices. If we are really looking down the barrel of an extended period of political disruption, as reflected by global patterns, there is value in understanding the role of class in any cleavages between metropolitan and rural and regional Australia, because class is not just about education, income and cultural capital. It also about opportunity. Opportunity is about finding a good, steady job and having the capacity to address most hurdles life can throw at you, including personal health. If certain swathes of regional people continue to feel locked out of opportunity, political disruption in Australia is more likely.

LESSON 5

There is an education divide

If you are a kid from a small town, negotiating a city landscape and city institutions is like landing in an alien world. Yet country kids have a range of experiences that are unquantifiable. Navigating a wild landscape or even a domesticated farm landscape were skills that confounded me when I first arrived here; to a country kid none of that is rocket science. Understanding the life cycles of animals, seeing the patterns of seasons, identifying the hard edges of social strata in small communities can teach a kid a lot about people and the way we interact. I am reminded of a student, not academically inclined, who became the go-to guy on the bush campus of his city school. Turns out he knew stuff that was invaluable when learning to survive. Suddenly everyone wanted to be on his team.

Unless you are dropped into an episode of *Celebrity Survivor*, those skills can't be measured. And in our education system, if skills can't be measured they are not valued, and therefore they don't help you make the leap from school to tertiary education. Year 12 subjects are carefully weighted and ranked, and the 'harder' subjects are pushed by elite schools to ensure their students get the top rankings, to ensure the schools get the top rankings, to ensure the schools get the top-ranked students, to ensure the schools get the top ranks. You get the picture.

I told Labor MP and economics professor Andrew Leigh how rare it was for our local high school to offer three-unit maths. There is simply not the demand. Leigh went to the selective public Sydney school James Ruse Agricultural High – the holy grail of school education for migrant families like mine. James Ruse tops the state every year. I would not have got within a bull's roar of qualifying for entry. Leigh said at James Ruse, he could only do three-unit maths, or four unit. He did not get a choice.

If you have a small school with limited enrolments, it goes without saying that the subject choices will be limited – there are not the students to fill the classes. That limits the outcomes for students, unless they can double back and re-sit subjects, or take the long road of picking up extra subjects in the form of bridging courses. It requires drive. And where does drive come from? It can be innate, it can be learned and it can happen through a significant mentor, or a combination of all three.

Dr Martin Parkinson credits his grandmother with instilling his drive and encouraging him to 'think big thoughts'. In the airy conference room at the top of the Department of Prime Minister and Cabinet (PMC), one block from Parliament House, Martin looks like the ultimate insider, but the road he's travelled is longer than most. A former Treasury secretary and secretary of PMC, Martin came to economics by accident. He was born in Stawell, a town of about 6000 in western Victoria. His parents divorced and left town when Martin was a baby and until he was five he was raised by his grandmother. His father died, and his mum, a nurses' aid, worked elsewhere. She eventually returned to Stawell and remarried. She and her new husband took Martin to Sydney for a year, then returned to Stawell again. The family followed work through two other regional towns before landing in Adelaide. By then Martin was in his senior high school years.

His grandmother was smart. When Martin's grandfather was killed in Libya in the Second World War, she was left to care single-handedly for six children under the age of six. Having raised them, years later she suddenly had a grandson to bring up, and she focused all her energy on Martin. He has an early memory of sitting on the front porch with her quizzing him. 'You can see all the stars. What's out there? You need to know – you need to have intellectual curiosity.'

In country Victoria, Martin noticed that the 'bright kids' who were aiming at white-collar jobs and university went to high schools that had a Year 12. His school only reached Year 11. The boys learned woodwork, carpentry or sheet metal and the girls learned typing. 'The thing that was striking to me in this period . . . we talk about being a classless society: it is just garbage,' he says. 'I went to the state schools in Stawell and Mansfield and Ballarat. I went to a primary school; there was a technical school over the road, which went to Year 11, or a high school that went to Year 12.

'The smart kids, or the kids that were going to get the white-collar jobs or go to university, they went to the high school; and the rest of us went to the tech school. I was the first person in my family to finish high school.'

It is exactly this sort of split from early childhood that is harder to see in the city, where similar demographics are housed in whole suburbs, sometimes whole regions. When your classmates move into different school or job realms you mostly never see them again. In small towns, kids who have played together in their preschool and primary years move to local, regional and city schools from Year 6 onwards, and often don't speak much again. But if they choose to return to their town, they'll almost always run into their classmates. They live alongside them.

These children know that life is not uniform and the world doesn't revolve around their own experiences and attitudes: they share classes with people who have nothing and people who have everything, and it can have nothing to do with their parents' choices. Or it can be completely as a result of their parents' choices. It reminds me of the famous *Seven Up* documentary by UK director Michael Apted, which took as its subject children from different socio-economic backgrounds and returned to interview them every seven years. Apted traces their journey, their loves, their jobs and their life outcomes. If you live in a small town, you can see these journeys playing out before you. Martin watched those patterns in his younger years, and when his family moved to Adelaide, he came up against the reality that school limitations can affect opportunities.

'I hadn't done English grammar – that is all self-taught,' he says. 'I hadn't done English literature at that point. Frankly, social studies was a teacher picking up cheque book application forms and [teaching] kids the fundamentals of that. English was listening to Cat Stevens records and trying to work out what the hell he was on about. There was no structured teaching of grammar, no exposure to English literature. I read widely – again that was a function of my grandmother pushing books on me; and my mother's an avid reader, too, so there were always books around the house.'

In fact, when the family eventually decided to move to Adelaide, Martin considered staying behind. By then he was in Ballarat, at Sebastapol Technical School. The option he was given was to stay with his aunt in Snake Valley, just outside Ballarat. He decided to give the move to Adelaide a chance.

'I had ambition, but I didn't know what the world was. I didn't know about the study of economics. I thought if I made it some way through, it would be doing something like industrial chemistry, something that was technically based but was a step up on the ladder from where I had come from.'

He landed in Adelaide's Salisbury East High School. It was a contrast with his previous school in that a lot of the parents' careers were in either technical or professional roles: there was a weapons research facility nearby, a teachers' college next door, an institute of technology not far away. Four or five kids from the school went to Adelaide University every year.

Essentially, there was a presumption that students would go on to some form of tertiary education. Because Martin had been at a technical school, he did not have the prerequisites to do a lot of the subjects offered at Salisbury East, but economics was one that stood out for him. By the end of his first term of Year 11 he was hooked on the subject, even though he didn't quite understand it. He sensed a glimpse of how the world might work. His spare time was spent trying to grapple with Samuelson's *Economics: An Introductory Analysis*, Keynes' *General Theory* and Karl Marx.

It was 1975. Gough Whitlam was prime minister and would be dismissed in fewer than twelve months. It was a period of massive social change but not, in Parkinson's words, of economic success. He watched as university education was made free, but stayed out of reach of most working-class kids. 'The abolition of university fees was a massive financial windfall for the middle class. It did absolutely nothing to help the working class break through. You really have to see subsequent waves of [earlier childhood intervention] reform before you begin to see changes in opportunities flowing through for kids from different backgrounds. I think it's really important that you don't wait until then. You realise the barriers to successful education occur a lot earlier, a lot younger in people's lives.'

It made him reflect on why it was that the poor remained poor, no matter what. 'I had grown up with this question mark: why is it that our people always seem to be at the bottom of the income distributional ladder? Where was social mobility – the thing that broke people through? What was it that stopped people being totally stratified? I didn't know and I couldn't work it out.

'It was really economics that taught me about the value of human capital and property rights, and the ability to marry [those two factors] to then be able to access financial capital to create pathways up and out for people. So that's always given me a really strong sort of emphasis, which is echoing my parents and grandmother, [as to] the importance of education and the importance of the quality of education.'

Martin got into an economics degree at the University of Adelaide. For students from less advantaged socioeconomic backgrounds and/or small towns, it is at this point that their families lose their capacity for granular guidance because of the unfamiliarity of this world. You don't know what you don't know. For Martin's family, they were supportive of him 'in an abstract sense'. This is not a criticism. They had no lived experience of what he would be facing, or the opportunities that may present, so while they were proud, they didn't know what to do with it. 'It's very hard to have aspirations for your child if you yourself don't know that part of the world.'

Even for Martin, thinking his big thoughts, his ambition was modest. Towards the end of his undergraduate degree, he saw that the Commonwealth Treasury were offering cadetships. He did not think Treasury would be interested 'in a kid like me' but his university friends and his lecturers encouraged him to apply. He paints a picture of 1977 Adelaide and it echoes Jack Archer's experience at Sydney University. 'Adelaide is pretty class-conscious. I go to Adelaide Uni and you knew who the kids that had come from the private schools were, and you always knew that, well, there were probably more of us [public school kids], but we were a bit discomfited and kept our heads down a bit more, but you had a sense that you were in a different place and I suppose I just projected on to Treasury that sort of experience.'

He had married his high school sweetheart in university (they have since split) and in those years they joked that their ambition was to get a job. 'She would be a teacher, I would get a job in a bank and we would get a house in the Adelaide Hills; and that was the bit where you could push your imagination out. It was really uni that pushed my imagination on beyond that, but I just assumed that something like Treasury – that looms up there and you are a lowly student down here – would be looking for the sorts of things that somebody like me would not be able to bring. Then I got there and found that it was actually full of a lot of people like me.'

Martin got in to Treasury, and a chance for postgraduate study at the Australian National University, before doing a PhD at Princeton University. It was during a conversation with a friend at Princeton that he understood the value of his life experience. His friend's father had a similar socioeconomic background to Martin. He was a poor farmer from the plains of Canada.

'My friend said, "You and my dad are very similar in the sense that you are the ones who have crossed that socioeconomic divide. It's not an intergenerational divide, it's a cultural and social divide, and you are comfortable talking on either side of that."'

That insight gave Martin an understanding of cultural and social divides that might be valuable for policy-making. By coincidence, he is one of four Treasury heads, including Bernie Fraser, Ted Evans and Ken Henry, who hail from working-class families. Henry was born near Taree and spent his early years on a leased dairy farm before his father returned to timber cutting to make a living when the dairy farm was crushed by drought. Henry's interest in tax policy was sparked by his childhood, watching his father work hard for not very much. He learned about the state tax royalty system when he asked his dad who got the money for a massive tree his father had felled.

Martin regards his and Ken Henry's upbringing as 'critical' to understanding the role of government. 'That's one of the things that struck me,' he says. 'When you look at Treasury, Treasury has been a consistent place for smart kids to be able to come up and have opportunity to thrive, because it had a definition of merit that is entirely about analytic capability. You didn't get caught up in the sort of thing you see elsewhere, where it is important where you have gone to school.'

So there are two things here. The first thing involves the lost opportunity for the child, because limited subject choice can handicap kids from small or under-funded schools. Martin says that one of the things that saved him was a strong maths and science bent at his technical school, and the ability to do the equivalent of three- and four-unit maths at his Adelaide school. He wonders aloud how many state high schools in the Adelaide suburbs are still teaching higher-level maths in 2018. He worries that once schools lose the capacity to teach serious maths, physics, chemistry and English, 'You really start to hamstring kids.'

The second thing involves a lost opportunity for the nation resulting from unfulfilled potential. Breadth of life experience is of immeasurable value and surely is worth something to public policy. It accrues when you travel a longer road. What if we lock the current young Martin Parkinsons out of the future leadership? It is hard to imagine Australian economic reform without the Treasury leadership of Martin Parkinson, Ken Henry, Bernie Fraser and Ted Evans. If governments and large employers come, increasingly, from the same backgrounds – middle-class, urban people taught in private schools – what diversity of experience will overlay policy formulation for the whole of Australia?

'If we end up with this situation where we create this big divide based on the opportunities kids have had and not based on their aptitude and interest, then I think we are worse off as a society.'

=

Bernie Minogue was born in 1938 in Warren, in northern New South Wales, where his father was a stationmaster on the railway.

The family moved south to Quandialla and he went to school there. All he wanted to do was muck around and break in horses, so boarding school in Goulburn came hard. He dreamed about home and cleared out pretty quickly. The local agent pleaded with him to join Elders, the stock and station agent, but he refused. He worked as a drover, often taking Queensland bullocks off the trains to Sydney for a spell and a feed.

He muses over how things might have been different if he'd taken up the offer. 'That's just the way it went.'

Bernie married Maureen and had four kids, while spending every spare moment buck-jumping, riding bulls and bareback in local rodeos. He worked on farms, share farming at one stage, until quotas to control the production of wheat were introduced in the 1970s. The quota was designed to control the amount of wheat going to the Australian Wheat Board because of global stockpiles.[1] Bernie had invested in $43,000 worth of machinery, but ended up with 'not an acre to plough'. He managed a few places, then bought his house and acres on the edge of our town in 1981, just as eastern Australia was sliding into the 1980s drought. Farmers were paid to destroy their sheep during that drought because the price of transport would never cover their sale at market. He shrugs. He got by carting wheat and stock, working on farms; and then became the stockman at the local abattoir. When it closed, Bernie decided it was time to retire, though he was confident he could have got other work. He was in his sixties. His retirement did not last, though, and he went back to carting stock until he was diagnosed with emphysema in his late seventies.

'I have never been out of work all my life, but that's in the bush. I wouldn't like to lob myself in the cities. There's always a bit of work here.'

His daughter, Cate Minogue, is his youngest, born in 1968 in Gunnedah Hospital when the family were living in a little town called Manilla in northern New South Wales. They spent some time in Canberra but soon came home to be near their extended family. 'They were doing it tough. Mum and Dad were battlers, all the way through,' Cate says.

Woodwork was the only thing that lightened Cate's school days, and eight weeks into Year 11 she left. She drifted towards the caring professions because you can always get a job, even if they are some of the lowest paid around. She nannied for a year for a local farming family, then headed to Canberra for a childcare course, which she did not complete. She found a live-in job at a disability centre, looking after kids when their parents went out.

She applied for a job in a disability service in Wagga, but after moving there and taking up a six-month lease on a flat, her employer informed her she did not have the job. She took a job in an abattoir. There was a lot of lifting and carrying, time in the slaughter room, the offal room and the chillers, but she didn't mind it. There were other women working there and she was not the squeamish type. To supplement her income, she drove taxis. Bernie, or Gramps, was a constant presence in the family's life.

Cate had been seeing a bloke who was living down in Albury. She was pregnant with her first child when the couple decided to get married. The church was booked, as was the local caterer, but six weeks before the date Cate got cold feet. She decided to have the child by herself.

Even though Cate's waters broke that hot November, little Maggie-Kate was not born until the following January. The girl grew up with her three older cousins, Amy, Sarah and Claire. She still talks of them as sisters. Her extended family was her world. 'We have always been a pretty close family, the lot of us,' Bernie says. Losing Maureen when she was only fifty-five was difficult, but with her gone the kids kept Bernie going.

Seven years, one month, seven days. Maggie-Kate can recite her age to the day when her little sister Deanna was born. Cate had injured her back while doing some nurses' aid work and had been in a lot of pain for most of the pregnancy. She was also suffering placental insufficiency. After two false starts having been induced, she had an emergency caesarian. Afterwards, a nurse told her that her baby was fine but one look told Cate that her little girl was blue. Deanna was tiny, five pounds, like a 'skun rabbit'. Her friend had rushed to the hospital with a camera, and was told she better take a lot of photos because photos might be all that Cate would have in the end. No one told Cate.

When Deanna was two weeks old, the black ugly umbilical stump was hard to get the nappies around and Cate's mates told her how close she had come to losing her baby. They organised an appointment with a paediatrician in Wagga and bundled up Deanna and Maggie-Kate in the car for the ninety-minute drive.

The paediatrician took off the top of the umbilical, which was a bit like a tiny appendage, with a little scalpel. There is a duct that, in utero, joins the baby's bowel to the umbilical cord. It is supposed to close over before a baby is born, but Deanna's had not. So when the cone came out, so did some of her bowel. Cate was told to drive straight to Canberra – a three-hour journey. Maggie-Kate took directions straight from the specialist. He bandaged Deanna up and told the seven-year-old to sit in the back next to her little sister. 'If there is any colour on this bandage here, you tell Mum.' So they left Wagga in a terrible hurry, rang ahead so Cate's mates could pack some bags. In the back, Deanna was getting antsy, starting to grizzle and cry like the newborn she was, but Maggie-Kate stayed calm.

Doctors operated on Deanna when she was sixteen days old and Maggie-Kate came home and declared she wanted to be a doctor. Cate didn't really take it seriously at first. After all, at that age little kids want to be astronauts, high divers and pop stars when they grow up. But as the years passed Maggie-Kate's dream did not abate, so Cate told her that if she put her mind to it she would achieve it. She was in our little high school, and there were 163 kids in the whole joint when Maggie-Kate was in Year 10. As far as Cate knows, no one had qualified for medicine straight from school before, but only one teacher raised an eyebrow at her ambition.

There was talk of Maggie-Kate going to a private boarding school, where she might be pushed in a larger, more competitive group. The HSC marking system can improve student results for individuals in schools that do well as a whole. But Maggie-Kate made the decision to stay in town. 'A lot of the private school kids are spoon-fed to pass exams. We thought about it in Year 10. There was the option of going away for Years 11 and 12, and I made the choice to stay at Murrumburrah High, and I stand by that choice and fully encourage it.

'The choice was actually emotional. My mum and my three older cousins all did school there and I wanted to finish where they went. In the end I had such strong support from the school that I got all of my preferences I wanted so I had a teacher for each subject.'

There are moments in all lives that can be turning points. Baby Deanna's medical condition was one moment. Another was a visit Maggie-Kate made to the careers day at the University of New South Wales (UNSW). She met an anatomy lecturer who had come to Australia as a refugee. He told her that he never compared himself to anyone else. Only compare yourself to what you did yesterday. It is wise advice whether you come from a school with very little competition or a lot of competition. She learned motivation comes from within.

Maggie-Kate looks back at those times as pivotal, particularly as she moved through her degree and on to the UNSW Wagga campus, where she felt a little intimidated by the calibre of the medical students. 'There is always the [subconscious] pressure to live up to them. And if you start comparing yourself to other people, you will almost always fall short, no matter what you do. I have had to keep that in mind and say, Well, I'm doing better than I was. I guess I try not to compete.'

For those families in large, overflowing city schools, it is hard to understand the limits of a small-town high school. In 2017 there were six Year 12 students sitting the HSC at Murrumburrah High. Depending on the electives chosen by the tiny group of students, there is often no two-unit maths class, let alone three-unit. Sometimes there is no physics or chemistry class, depending on demand. It is not unusual for students to undertake distance education classes for subjects that a city school would assume were core offerings. So it's a stretch to attend the required classes, never mind to get the marks. When Maggie-Kate went through, there were seventeen students in her year. By senior school, a number of teachers had recognised her dream and were pulling out all stops. They put on a two-unit maths class, a three-unit maths class, a two-unit chemistry class and an ancient history class. Maggie-Kate was the only one in any of these classes. Two, sometimes three teachers came in through the week to tutor her before the school day began. When she missed a class for a day, other teachers stepped in to explain the concepts. There were a couple of competitive kids in that cohort who pushed her along, but most of the drive came from her. The twenty-four-year-old Maggie-Kate calls it self-directed learning, and remembers how 'everyone there wanted you to do the best you could'.

As the HSC loomed, Maggie-Kate had to negotiate the business of the university application. Our local careers advisor was vital in helping her with the application process. She also spent a lot of time talking to teachers and looking online at universities, but she did not know anyone who had applied for anything other than early entry. Early entry is the best way for country kids to get into university these days: in New South Wales some universities offer a place to country students based on their assessment marks prior to the HSC exam. This takes the pressure off students by assuring them of a place; it also helps to give them a longer lead-time to plan the move from their home town to the university city.

The navigation of university entry is no small thing when your family has not done it before and I still remember the buzz around town when Maggie-Kate discovered she had made it into medicine. She scored the ATAR, passed the UMAT medical exam and the interview to qualify for a UNSW degree in medicine.

Kids get into medicine every year. Except if you live in a small town with one of the smallest high schools in the state. 'I never thought an old drover like me would have a doctor as a grand-daughter,' says Bernie. 'I don't know how she keeps it all in her head.'

==

I first met Maggie-Kate with Bernie at the local pony club. My daughter had fallen in love with a pony called Gypsy when she was six and pony club followed. That is how I found myself at a table, in a cold shed at the showgrounds, sitting next to Bernie Minogue. Stock carting was hard work and men like Bernie were regular visitors to most farms once the sheep and cattle were fat and grown for market. Carters know the economy of the rural communities because they know what is selling and for how much. Sale yards are places where stock carters, buyers, sellers and agents come together and chew the fat. They load in the evening or early morning to get to the yards, pushing animals on to their trucks. I have often heard Bernie's truck change down gears along the track to the yards below our house at 5 am.

Bernie and Cate used to bring Maggie-Kate to pony club with her little grey mare, Hazey. She would join all the other kids, trit-trotting around the showground, jumping over poles, and lining up for troop drills before sausages and fizzy drink at the clubhouse.

It was usually freezing cold or hot and dry, the sun bleaching the flat showground like an Instagram filter. Except it was real life. You had to squint without sunglasses. The little kids would rev up after lunch, fuelled on red frogs and musk sticks bought at the club tuck shop.

Years later, as Maggie-Kate made university, my own kids were getting near high-school age and I had a sinking feeling in my gut. The farmer and I had discussed boarding school, with its benefits of learning to navigate the city environment, greater subject choice and a bigger pool of friends than the twenty kids in the local Year 6 class. For his school years the farmer had travelled 350 kilometres to boarding school in Sydney. I went to the local Sydney suburban high school and then on to my mother's Catholic school in Year 11. On a farm, you spend most of your time with family, locked together in a tight scrum. The farmer comes in for morning tea, lunch and in the afternoon, all things being equal. Once, my life had been devoted to work, but that was before I had settled into this new life. The thought of separating from my children terrified me.

But these are the patterns – those animal patterns again, as annual as the harvest. From two primary schools in town, the Year 6 splits. Some to the local high school, some to the regional high school, some scattered across the four winds into Sydney and to other regional boarding schools. The pool shrinks. Our family also looked towards Sydney for a boarding school. My family was there. My helicopter tendency was tempered with the idea of those opportunities further afield. I wanted my children to be able to imagine a life larger than a town of 3500 people.

And out they went into big city schools. I cried and cried with grief. My hair started going grey. My neck seized up for the first term and I wore large sunglasses to cover my puffy eyes. I locked myself in the Sydney school dunny, unable to pull myself together on the first weekend visit. I called the farmer, bawling from school car parks. It had to make sense, this pain, because they would be fully equipped. They would speak the language of the city. They would be global people. And that's all we want, isn't it? Young adults who are comfortable in their owns skins in any setting. People who can up sticks and move anywhere for that great opportunity to fulfil their life potential. I could see the hurdles local kids face at our small school. Like many country parents with the means to do it, we were buying what Abigail McKnight, Associate Director of the Centre for Analysis of Social Exclusion (CASE) at the London School of Economics, calls a 'glass floor', hoping for a measure of protection for our kids on the economic mobility ladder.[2]

Associate Professor in Rural Education at the University of Canberra Philip Roberts believes this split in education outcomes can be deleterious to small communities because the children who go away can overly influence a town's leadership with what he calls 'city mentalities'. He says you can pick any regional town to see this.

'Where did the one hundred kids go? They didn't go to the school 60 kilometres away because that hasn't had a bump in numbers. So they are all heading off. We know, from qualitative stuff we do, they are the children who own the land or who own the local enterprises. They go away and are educated in city stuff, and come back to run the rural stuff. The rural class don't have any access to that, but they are being governed by city mentalities again because the town's dominant leadership have been trained in it from the schools and the universities. They don't have the same sensibilities with the people they are working with because they are the capital class. We rhetorically conceal that.'

Roberts pinpoints a valid claim here, though I think it would be equally prejudicial and self-defeating for small communities to cut anyone educated in a city out of their local leadership. It would seem more productive to ensure that influential community leaders consult widely with their fellow residents and be more inclusive in decisions affecting governance.

==

My small town has taught me that not everyone has the same priorities. We want our kids to be happy but we emphasise different aspects. The education divide was the thing that really helped rural political culture gel for me. For some fellow residents, place is more important than having an economically mobile career. For some, being close to parents and grandparents might be more important than being able to function in any setting. For some, history and connection might be more important than social mobility.

There was a time when I encouraged a local artist towards the Canberra Museum because the museum was looking for someone to teach their art workshops. I had it all mapped out for her. She could teach, meet a whole lot more artistically minded people, have the option of moving into a city if she wanted. But they were my priorities, not hers. She wasn't interested in my priorities. 'Why are you always trying to make people better?' she said plainly.

If I think about it long enough, I have always encouraged people out while at the same time I have worked on committees to future-proof the town. Certainly I have been worried that maybe all I have been working towards is a brain drain but I'll come back to that. Anyway, my anxiety has always reminded me of a line in *Wake in Fright* when the central character, John Grant, is explaining to the copper, Chips Rafferty, how education departments force teachers to country schools using a 'bonded slave' system. The policeman replies, narrowing his eyes with suspicion, 'You clever blokes never like to stop in the one place long, do you?'

So, another lesson. Not everyone wants the same outcomes. For some, living in global cities and jumping aboard the career rocket straight to the top is not desirable. However, if children from the smallest town do strive to reach those heights, we need to ensure that the hurdles are not so much greater than they are for children in metropolitan centres. I have learned that small towns are not stereotypes. That one woman's meat is another woman's poison. The most switched-on people in town want equality of opportunity for local kids, not equality of outcomes.

LESSON 6

White girl rural culture hits the city

Heading west to meet Dr Maggie-Kate after her final medical exams, I follow the railway line through Cootamundra, Bethungra, Illabo, Junee and then on to the city of Wagga Wagga. We meet there at the Thorne St General Store, a former corner shop turned café opposite a park to which mothers have brought their babies and toddlers to loll in the unseasonally warm spring weather. Coffee is served by young blokes with ponytails and it rates highly on my coffee index.

Wagga is a university town and though its local government is called Wagga Wagga City Council, it has the relaxed feel of the country. Wagga reflects the reality of demographic change in the country. While we often hear of small towns like Harden-Murrumburrah losing its youth to the cities, in reality country kids raised in small towns more often move to a regional centre like this one. The culture shock is not so great.

'It's quite incredible that I have finished uni,' says Maggie-Kate. 'Most people are like, "Oh well, yeah, we did it. It's taken us a while but it's more a personal achievement." And then the local [Harden] paper did a small piece, and everyone was like, "Mags wins cutest town!" They thought it was so cute that the town has just gone ballistic over having produced a doctor.

'A lot of people in my year have family doing medicine. Three of the fifteen people in my year alone in Wagga – their dads are local specialists; and there are more of them who have parents or aunties or uncles in the city who are doctors themselves already. So it's more of family tradition or sticking with what they know. Whereas what we know in Harden is smaller things.'

Though there are always exceptions, farmers often produce children who become farmers. Station hands produce station hands. Railway workers produce railway workers. So it stands to reason that doctors produce doctors. But it's sobering to realise that the track from small rural towns is so entrenched that to stray off it produces front-page news.

══

Maggie-Kate's graduation to medicine was a bit like the Murrumburrah steam engine trying to get up the hill from a standing start. Kids who go to larger, well-resourced city schools sit on the station at Harden with a downhill run in one direction and a flat in the other. Kids like Maggie-Kate have the hill to climb.

Life is nothing if not a series of peaks and troughs, and when Maggie-Kate qualified for medicine at UNSW, her journey to Sydney was only the beginning. She made plans to move to the university campus in the eastern suburbs of Sydney for the first two years, after which, if she was still passing, she hoped to move to the university's Wagga campus for rural medicine.

Maggie-Kate had rarely travelled to Sydney, save a few overnight stays, and she had certainly never driven in the city. So it was with a mix of nerves and excitement that her little family, Cate and Deanna, who had inspired the whole thing, as well as a close family friend, packed up two cars to move Maggie-Kate to the Kensington campus. They drove in a convoy out to the Hume Highway and headed north, the cars packed to the gunnels. Passing the 60 kilometres sign, she thought, Yep, this is it.

'I think it was too overwhelming, the fact that I was moving away from home. I think I was just focused on starting a new chapter in my life. I got a bit nostalgic leaving Harden.'

Maggie-Kate would share her new accommodation with four other students. She had chosen self-catering so she could cook, one of her de-stressing methods through the HSC year. She didn't want to take what was served up in college, and, besides, it was cheaper to buy groceries and make your own meals.

Financial support was always going to be tricky. Cate was determined that her daughter should not have the dual responsibilities of working to raise money at the same time as completing an academically arduous degree. So she supplemented Maggie-Kate's means-tested government Austudy. Bernie kicked in some of his wage earned while carting stock. Maggie-Kate was also supported by the Country Education Foundation. The family says that her medical degree would not have been possible without the foundation's ongoing financial support. Family friends chipped in donations of microwaves, printers and other necessary items.

Like a new skilled migrant, Maggie-Kate settled into her new surroundings. She studied, she cooked, she made new friends. From our very white-looking town, she walked into a lecture theatre with overwhelming diversity. It was mystifying and exciting. She met a lot of private school students. She met people with money. She gravitated to other new migrants, the international students. Many of her new friends had a Sri Lankan background. They asked, 'What's up with the questions?'

'I said, I have gone from a town where everyone is white to a uni where, among three hundred of my year group, ten per cent were Caucasian-looking, from the look of a full lecture theatre. This is so culturally diverse compared to where I am from, I have never had to ask these questions. I have never had to learn this or this.'

Maggie-Kate learned how to navigate public transport from her city friends. In most cities of the world public transport systems have similarities, but in small towns there is no such thing as a transport system, let alone an Opal card. In the early years, students had to visit teaching hospitals regularly and Maggie-Kate would ask her friends to wait for her. 'I would ask to tag along because I couldn't navigate public transport to save my life. So that was kind of isolating. I was like a lost little puppy, yelling, Take me with you.'

In the first few weeks, as a bonding exercise, the university threw all the students together for a long weekend – at med camp at Wisemans Ferry. There, Maggie-Kate shared a cabin with other girls, including a Muslim girl wearing a hijab and a Catholic girl from the eastern suburbs of Sydney. Maggie-Kate identifies as Catholic, she went to the local Catholic primary school, but she does not practise. While other cabins were playing drinking games, the three girls stayed up late comparing religions.

Maggie-Kate asked her Muslim cabin mate to excuse her because she 'actually didn't know anything' about the Islamic religion. The girl told her it was quite all right because she didn't know anything about Catholicism. 'It was this beautiful conversation where neither of us was judgemental, neither of us really cared about the other's [religious] beliefs,' she says.

The Muslim student was from the country town of Armidale in northern New South Wales, and had decided to wear her hijab in Sydney, when she had not done so in her home town. Maggie-Kate said her parents did not force it on this girl, though they approved of her decision. Her new friend came to the conclusion herself that she wanted to wear it. That very different perspective stuck with Maggie-Kate – the idea that for her friend it was her own choice.

In those conversations with her fellow students, she found herself defending country towns. Everyone asked her which school she went to. No one could imagine a school with just seventeen students in the final year. When she asked about Sri Lankan culture, one fellow student asked about 'white girl rural culture', which was as mysterious to them as their culture was to her. It reminds me of when a city kid at my daughter's school asked the country boarders whether they had toilets at home. Straight-faced, one of the country kids said, 'Nah, we poo in a can.'

Maggie-Kate learned what it is to be a minority. Another student would regularly point out she was the only white person in their group brimming with cultural diversity, featuring Sri Lankans, Bangladeshi and Chinese students.

'I was like, I haven't missed it but I don't care. Do you? I understand I am the minority right now. But I'm okay with it. You don't have to point it out.'

The link between country towns and racism was a given among her new friends.

'I would say, No, no we are not racist. We just don't know, we are not exposed to it. And trying to get that through to them that all we see about the Muslim religion is what we see on TV, which is unfortunately all bad.'

She and I talk about the paradox of race conversations. The migrant you know is always different than the migrant group discussed in scary ways on television and in the newspapers. For some, the Muslim doctor that provides a service is okay, but Muslims as a group are not okay.

'Trying to explain the lack of cultural diversity in Harden alone was hard,' she says. 'There's nothing – there's the doctors and there's the owners of the Chinese restaurant. Even with your cultural diversity,' she says to me, 'you blend in quite well.'

Maggie-Kate's friend lives in a nearby town where there is a practising Muslim doctor. Everyone loves him. 'They all say, Dr D., he's the greatest, and then turn around in the next sentence and completely bag out Muslims all together. How often do you see a positive thing about Muslims? You don't. You only see the bad stuff, and automatically you have this stereotype, because few people know anyone who is a practising Muslim.

'I think, Hold on, you know someone here who is a great person, a good member of the community and a practising Muslim. A lot don't seem to understand it's the extremists who are bad and not the majority.'

For many country students, if they get to university it is where they first encounter what Maggie-Kate calls a 'melding of cultures'. There are misunderstandings across the city–country divide on both sides. She laughs at the view of rural Australia held by some international students, as well as metropolitan students. An Irish exchange student asked her, 'What colour is your dirt?'

——

Just as city students rarely consider living anywhere but the city, country students often feel more comfortable in the country. That's why government policy has made universities draw at least 25 per cent of their domestic intake from rural areas. (UNSW is at 27 per cent.) There is also the consideration of ATARs. Country students are aware that their small cohort and their school's performance in the HSC exam will affect their final assessment marks because of the way the assessments are moderated and scaled. This education divide is recognised by some universities, which offer bonus points to students applying from regional areas to bridge the gap between their ATAR – or tertiary entrance mark – and the course requirement. For example, Macquarie University offers students from my inner regional area five bonus points for 'restricted accessibility of goods, services and opportunities for social interaction'. Students in very remote areas are offered up to nine bonus points at Macquarie. Other institutions, the so-called sandstone universities, tend not to bother.

Some metropolitan students resent the fact that rural students might be allowed into a course such as medicine with a lower ATAR qualifying mark, even though they still have to pass the UMAT general medical exam and an interview process. This was brought home to Maggie-Kate when she overheard a medical student representative complaining that rural students got a head start with the five-point bonus. 'He had friends who missed out who had higher ATARs than rural students. I thought, Stuff you. You can get in other ways, and rural students did not make the policy. Also, it's not just ATAR, it's UMAT, it's interview. You can't just blame those five points.'

After two years in Sydney, Maggie-Kate elected to go to the rural medical school in Wagga, a decision that horrified many of her peers. 'Going rural' are dirty words for a lot of ambitious young metropolitan medical students. Maggie-Kate had a preference for Wagga because it was ninety minutes from home. It felt like a country town with the benefits of a city. It was a joy for her, coming back to the country, and she moved in with a cousin until she found her feet.

'You notice people, you get to know people. Even working in a hospital has made Wagga seem a bit smaller. You walk around thinking, I know that face,' she says.

Still, her student peers did not get it. There is a view among young doctors that practising in a rural and regional area limits their opportunities. Most have not been west of Goulburn. Maggie-Kate was getting a lot more hands-on experience in Wagga, and defended her decision to fellow students, saying she couldn't justify travelling further away to get less experience. She compared her country medical experience with metropolitan training and explained she had completed a lot more basic medical procedures, such as cannulation, than her city peers.

Her lack of contacts in medicine made finding the path through the maze of career options more difficult. 'A big part of medicine is not just the knowledge but the networking, [like] any other career. People who have family in med have a bit of a head start in terms of networking. It makes that a little bit trickier to get your foot in the door, but once you [have] there it is really no difference. You just don't have that social networking they have; it's more a professional network.

'It's worth a lot, but at the end of the day the people with the social connections through family have to live up to a certain standard that family members have already set. It has that pressure as well – it's not without its cons. Initially it's a bit trickier, but after being here four and a half years I have got my foot in the door a little bit more.'

Maggie-Kate has had some rocky times, especially around exams. Why am I doing this? One achievement could realign her spirit and drive. This is what I want to do. It's fine. Then as the final exam pressure piled on, she was stressing out, wondering why she had embarked on this whole medicine thing. A friend likened her to James Tamou, a star prop with the Penrith Panthers rugby league team. 'He said to me, "You're just like James. You have trained your whole life for this. You've got it. Nothing can go wrong . . ." And I just kept saying, What if he gets injured? What if something goes wrong and they lose the game? But he goes, "It's not the point, you've trained for it." So I kept that mantra in my head. Yep, I've got this. I have trained for it.'

With her final exams out of the way, Maggie-Kate won an internship to Wagga Hospital for two years, and she is aiming to be a country general practitioner.

'I think I have more of an open mind than what I did have at the end of Year 12.

'I think I am very much a different person to what I was. I think I was quite a sheltered girl back before leaving Harden with my seventeen people in my Year 12 cohort. Definitely being a bit more confident and able to hold my own a bit better. It's a general maturing with moving away and looking after yourself.'

===

In our bakery I sit with local students who are finishing school and contemplating their life ahead – kids I have known since they were babies. Apart from worrying over their leaving results, key priorities are a gap year, jobs, or a good course. They are not all interested in university.

They have that teenage energy, and spend the afternoon wisecracking. We joke about silly things like the vocabulary of the talking parrot in the courtyard and the wisdom of eating a pie with chicken salt. Living here, they love having freedom as younger kids, not being chased by their parents.

I still remember walking out of the gates of my school in Sydney and feeling overwhelmed. You could treble that feeling for kids who have been to a small-town school all their lives. We want our young people to do what grabs them, and that means only two things if you live in a small town. To stay and find a job, or to go away, maybe do some study, and then find a job.

They tell me they feel like the town is declining, and given it has lost the abattoir and its railway employees in their lifetime, it has certainly changed, even if the population has stayed stable. They say it feels like it's ageing, and it is. In the 2016 census, it has a higher proportion of population in all the age groups over sixty than both the state and the nation. One girl craves anonymity. 'I like the city for the fact that you can make a fool of yourself and never see those people again.'

Molly and Evelyn are thinking of careers in science and the creative arts, careers that they acknowledge will be hard to pursue in a country town. After successfully completing their studies, a job is their most important priority, no matter where. 'Jobs and getting a job at home.' Evelyn wants to go to Sydney; the others talk of going to regional cities like Canberra or Wagga: they feel those places are more liveable because they perceive the living costs are cheaper and the quality of life is better.

Michael wants to do agriculture and will come back to this area if his family keeps the family farm going. Some want to buy into agriculture via farm work and management by working their way up and trying to save.

One of the isolating parts of living in a small town is getting a handle on your competition. Both at school and in the job market, you just don't know where the level is for kids your own age. The students I talk to in the bakery are also concerned that their prospects will be affected by coming from a small school. They mention the lack of competition. To see a local succeed gives everyone else a certain level of confidence, and Maggie-Kate and students like her are important mentors and role models.

'Seeing Maggie-Kate go off and do so well, we were like, She was able to go off so we should be able to do that too,' says Molly. 'Living here has made us harder workers because we know we have to work for it. Your own ATAR is affected by the people around you. Here we have fear of being brought down by [others].'

Likewise, the idea of finding employment in larger centres, including part-time university jobs, is daunting. These teens have had experience in local shops, supermarkets or within family businesses, but they are concerned that it will not be valued by a city employer. Like Cate and Maggie-Kate did, they worry about the cost of study for themselves in terms of the HECS debt and the living costs for their parents. But they are positive that they can bridge the gap from their little town.

'It depends on how persistent you are as a person and how you would strive to be, what you want to do and how hard you will work,' says Evelyn. 'That will influence the result.'

There is recognition that Aboriginal, Torres Strait Islander students and rural students do get places saved for them in various university courses, and they appreciate it. 'There is a lot done to help us out which is good because it is hard.'

Those last couple of years in high school can be critical for making decisions about the next step. Since university education was made free in the 1970s, a strong cultural bias towards university has dominated city and country schools, notwithstanding the hurdles facing country students. Most students here are encouraged to consider university over TAFE and trade courses, a fact that annoys local employers who are looking for trade-based skills such as mechanics. Within the university options, there is also a bias towards certain high-status professions, as Stephen discovered.

Stephen is a clever kid from a working-class family. His parents did not go to university but worked hard and taught Stephen the value of working hard. At some point the family conversation started to focus around what he should do with his academic success. There was no stay-or-go imperative. It was more a case of being mindful to do something with it. Stephen felt lucky not to face the parental pressure imposed on some of his friends. He wanted to be a teacher but says he was advised – including by some of his teachers at a school in the region – that he was 'too bright' for teaching and should instead aim for law.

'It was never my intention to do arts law, but I did it because I got in. Isn't that strange? It's still a thing every year. You see these kids who do courses they never thought of until they get their results and they think, Maybe I can. I was considering doing education at the end of Year 12 and the amount of teachers who said to me, "You are too good for that." Isn't it absurd? People working in the field. They talked me out of it and into law.'

There is a contradiction here. Maggie-Kate and Martin Parkinson had supportive families who enabled them to work hard and capture opportunities that are harder to see and access from small country towns. On the other hand, the more recent push towards university means that country towns lose young people like Stephen, who might be perfectly happy in productive, rewarding jobs such as teaching – jobs that are more likely to draw them back to their home towns. Instead, the obsession with not wasting your ATAR musters certain students into more high-status professions. This occurs not just in the country but is a feature of the education system more generally.

So, driven by his hard work and the number on the ATAR, Stephen moved to Sydney. Even as he began his law lectures, he knew he had no intention of practising. He lived on campus and partied for his first two weeks, like most other students. A family photo on Facebook is tinged with homesickness.

Apart from the physical dislocation, the political culture of universities was a shock to Stephen. His family are traditional blue-collar Catholic Labor voters and he has followed their lead. His father credits the unions for helping him through a workplace injury. Stephen knew the campus would be left-wing, but he was surprised at the gap between his own experience and the preoccupations of university life. Even for a self-proclaimed political tragic, campus posters on fascism and other obsessions felt oddly remote from his life in rural Australia.

'I think it's not common issues. The subject matters seem to be a bit beyond reality, beyond the scope of average life, which is probably the case with politics in general. It deals with extremes, and most of Australia exists in the middle.'

Even as someone who identifies with the left, he struggled to understand the unthinking criticism of any element of social conservatism. With a certain timidity, he says there was an intolerance of people with other opinions.

Stephen identifies the disengagement with political debate because of conversations conducted by people who have these extreme positions. Certainly we media often choose people who are unforgiving protagonists to represent views for a 'yes' case and 'no' case – the heads of lobby groups or people found by lobby groups when you haven't got time to chase down 'ordinary people'. Are we really surprised when those outside the system decide that it is not worth engaging?

But Stephen thinks it is not just media that is feeding the polarisation. 'The tertiary education system is feeding that. I think it's feeding those people who exist on the fringes. I don't know why people think Pauline Hanson is the answer, given that over seventy per cent of her votes have been with the government. But I completely understand why people are looking for someone who makes sense. Not to me, but I understand why people are looking. Pauline's base is not my age. Most of my friends are politically unaware, they don't really care. When she wears a burqa into Senate, they laugh.'

Stephen was observing and to a certain extent resisting the ideological straitjacket. Like all of us, he does not fit in a box. He is a country Labor voter but he is no left-wing warrior. While he supports more left-wing economic ideas, he is accustomed to being surrounded by more conservative social concepts. Like the majority of Australia, he supported marriage equality. That leaves him in the badlands of Moderatesville, like most of us.

When I was interviewed for a job as a copy girl at News Ltd in 1984, my interviewer said the company offered journalism cadetships annually. Usually, nineteen were school leavers and one was a graduate. 'Graduates come out too far on the left or right,' this man said. He might be right or he might have considered graduates too fully formed. To be fair, though, in those days journalism was considered a trade, which made a degree unnecessary given we completed a full three-year cadetship, rotating through the stable of newspapers from screaming tabloids like the *Daily Mirror* to conservative broadsheets like the *Australian*.

Universities have always been a cauldron of ideas and vociferous discussion, as well as a training ground for the political profession. Like politics, university debates are also polarised, and the extremes dominate with the loud megaphone of social media. In this, campuses simply reflect wider society. When Stephen mentions an intolerance of people with other opinions, he says he is thinking of the (admittedly milder Australian) version of the US and UK campus 'safe space' debate, in which students and some academics have called for 'trigger warnings' for confronting curriculum content. In some cases, academics with controversial ideas have been disinvited from talks they were to give. Monash University has become the first Australian university to start a pilot program in which academics will review fifteen courses for emotionally confronting material in order to trial trigger warnings. While Stephen totally gets why students might need warnings for things like sexual assault, vetting curricula worries him. He also thinks universities have become places where people with extreme views dominate public conversations, while people who mildly disagree with the strident positions are 'frowned upon'.

Political correctness is a much debated term, which came into public consciousness in Australia in John Howard's government. As a concept, it was picked up and rammed home by Howard's mentee Tony Abbott, who memorably urged Australians to vote against same-sex marriage to stop political correctness. Of course, it is not just a feature of the left. Try making a joke about Anzac Day and see what happens. It is a feature discussed more and more away from Parliament in my local community. There has been ongoing debate in the US about whether the rise in political correctness led to the election of Trump – an idea impossible to prove or disprove.

No doubt issuing edicts that some subjects are untouchable is a surefire way to make them attractive. For me, being told what not to say is a guaranteed way to make me think about saying it, though

I try to restrain that immaturity by assessing facts and coming to a considered conclusion. There are many people around me who feel that academics and journalists are all left-wing. Perhaps the word 'feel' is instructive, though, because some of the highest-profile, best-funded columnists and Australian publications are on the right.

Once he got into the swing of city living, Stephen's dislocation became easier, but he could not escape the idea that law was not really for him. The five years ahead seemed interminable. He worried about paying for the student loan for a course he didn't love, and the idea began to grow that maybe he should return home. Again, he felt the weight of expectation. His community had been rapt that Stephen was doing law. Still, he returned to the local supermarket to work out the rest of the year.

'It was like: Stephen is doing law and then Stephen is not doing law. Stephen is back at IGA. That was just a small-town pack. It's such a cliché that small towns talk and know everyone's business, but it's so true. And it was hard because I was exposed, serving everyone and having to explain every time what I was doing. So it was intimidating and I quickly learned not to give a shit. But when I was deciding whether to come home, that played a factor. Should I care what people think? Which is sad, isn't it, that you would decide your future based on the mentality of a small town?'

These are the things we learn as we navigate life – the balancing of people's expectations of ourselves while pursuing our own life goals. I worry about the pressure we place on the next generation and, talking to fellow townspeople, I realise I'm not alone. Emily Bowker is a young businesswoman who owns a local financial advisory firm, Cultiv8. She has primary–school-age children and she thinks about the difficulties for the young adults she sees returning home to a country town after a spell away. 'There is a stigma attached for the brains to come back. Some people see going away and then coming back as negative. Some people come back and resent having to come back. Some have obligations to take over a family business. There is so much pressure on the next generation. Kids have pressure to have it sorted, straight from school to uni, then marriage and on it goes. They don't notice that if you just kinda let life happen, you can change your mind and find your path and what you actually enjoy by experiencing different things. But because of this pressure, they don't experience the kind of industries they want to work in, or they think they want to be somewhere traditional because they haven't been shown other places.'

What I know now, which I did not know when my children went off to boarding school in Sydney, was I never really considered them returning to this small town in their adult lives. I assumed they would move on. It is a hard truth that I have been reluctant to acknowledge.

After Stephen took half a year off working in his home town, he opted for a more generalist degree to see where it took him. He has matured for the experience and tells anyone who is struggling that it is okay to take some time off, work in the supermarket, or try a few different things. An internship could be the thing, or a traineeship. Just chill. And ignore the gossip. Don't let it run your life.

Place was also important to him. He does not want to lose that connection. Like a nest, place can become crowded as you grow, but it settles around you as you move into the next phase. It holds you up and provides a safe place from which to view the world. Even as many young people struggle to throw off the binds of small town life, they recognise the comfort of home. Stephen and his friends recognise the two forces, pulling them in opposite directions.

'Most of my friends have said we would like to go away for work, but we always want to come back. They say, "If we have kids we will come back. We can't imagine raising them in Sydney. The lifestyle is too superior." Living in a big city now, I couldn't imagine being a child there.'

But he is one of a number of youth who think small towns are generally run by older people for a largely ageing population; that, therefore, community leaders approach issues without due consideration for younger generations. 'It feels like the town is not supporting us; we don't feel like we are being encouraged to stay.'

It is true that our town has worked actively to encourage school leavers into university and further education, but a number have gone away to get qualifications and returned after a few years' work experience in a city or large regional centre. They have returned with a stronger sense of who they are, and often that means they actively want to settle in or near home and raise their own children with the support of family.

Intuitively, it makes sense to give people a leg-up by pushing them into university to increase social mobility and expand opportunities for all young adults, no matter where they live. Except if they don't know what they want to do and don't know why they are there. Or if they don't feel convinced that university is for them.

LESSON 7

Not all kids want to go to uni

It is October and the town's yearly cycle is running down to harvest and Christmas. That means the annual picnic race day. The races are a feature of most country towns, a day when people dress up, have a drink and bet on a horse. Some people hire a tent to entertain for the day, others just turn up. Kids I knew when they were in preschool are dressed to the nines, blossoming into adults with their own lives, jobs, and some with their own preschool kids now. I haven't been to the local race meeting for years, not since returning to the press gallery.

We park in the grounds, where committee volunteers check tickets and wish us well for the day. As I get out of the car, balancing a cheese platter on my lap (ladies bring a plate), the band has already started up on Cold Chisel's 'Flame Trees'. Kids out driving Saturday afternoon really did just pass me by.

Friends have hired a tent for the day. Darren Sargent calls himself 'just a truck driver', but he and his brother run a large quarry business, built in one generation from scratch by his parents

John and Barbara. Their company is one of the largest employers in town. It has eighty-five staff, and of those one employee has a university degree and five have Year 12 HSCs. The rest were educated to Year 10, have a strong work ethic and a great skills base.

Darren sees it as the company's job to expand his employees' skills base in areas that interest them. As an employer, he has three gripes. One is that the education system and the professional class are pushing all students into universities to complete expensive degrees which don't necessarily provide a career path. The second is that, in doing so, the same system has diminished the role of skilled manual workers, who do important jobs. His third complaint is that some kids – not all – don't want to do the crappy work in order to qualify. I have heard all of these points made repeatedly by others, too, in my town.

The subject's not one I expected to discuss when I embarked on this project, but the hollowing-out of vocational training remains one of the most talked-about aspects of government policy on the main street. And there is, again, a mismatch between political rhetoric and experience on the ground. Tony Abbott's government made a big song and dance about 'Tony's tradies', who benefited from the $20,000 small-business tax breaks in the 2015 budget. Ministers sold the tax breaks to me as a journalist on the basis that those trade voters were in the marginal seats and would cement support for the Coalition. The issue was viewed by politicians through the political lens, when the question they should have been asking was not whether those voters would go for them, but who was the next generation of tradies?

Darren quotes a news story that says many graduates are now driving for Uber. It comes from a speech by the New South Wales TAFE boss Jon Black. 'Why is it that every Uber driver I speak to has a communications, business or law degree?' In October 2017 the Productivity Commission reported that university students were struggling to find employment relevant to their studies. '[So] would you rather finish with a $4,000 debt or a $30,0000 debt? With strong job prospects or weak job prospects?'[1]

Darren agrees. 'In the 1970s and 1980s we had a compromise. If you knew you wanted to be a doctor, you knew you were going to university to be a doctor. If you were going to be a builder, you knew you had an apprenticeship where you started at the bottom and worked your way up. You bought your first tools, you bought a second-hand ute and you worked your way up, and then you built your own house and you went out on your own. And parents endorsed that. They didn't have this bloody hang-up with what is in fact incredibly expensive education for a parent. Because you come out of a school phase and you've got to take them through the university phase.'

Darren refers to a Year 11 student he met earlier that day. She is keen on agriculture after being in her school's farm club but she doesn't know where to start. She wonders aloud why all the teachers want to push her into university when she would rather find a job. Darren took her aside. 'Those studs that are now selling bulls for $12, $15, $18,000, $25,000, little lady,' said Darren. 'One bull pays your wages for the year. I will find her a job. I said, pick your mark, give it some thought. Now all the way through her area in the Southern Highlands, there are cattle studs up there funded by external businesses. She started to list them off. I said, that's where you want a job, because they have got an umbilical cord that keeps pumping blood into them. These off-farm or high-wealth farmers can't find staff with passion, particularly for livestock. They have the ability to pay big money for skill and passion.'

Darren explains that while her starting wage might be low – $24,000 for an eighteen-year-old on a minimum wage – she would learn the industry and get a bit of confidence. By contrast, he argues, if you push a kid into university before they are ready, or before they know why they are there, they will most likely fail.

'If she can go and work in that industry for four years then she may say, Now I have a passion and a drive and a confidence to go into university, and there are the goalposts. There's the checkered flag. And you just wish that kids could bump into someone that says, "Little lady, don't you give up. But please don't sit at home and tell me how hard it is."'

He also gets frustrated that some kids won't start at the bottom, and he tells the girl to pass on a message to her bloke, who is standing right there, watching. The young bloke is what Darren calls 'a diesel burner', a natural driver who can do anything with a header or a windrower and is well ahead of his years in mechanical ability. He has the drivin' in him. Darren was keen to get him into an apprenticeship, but he wouldn't start at the bottom because he had been working on big machinery for years. Then he got stuck in a parks position in a larger regional city, pruning roses. 'You are never going to get peace of mind pruning roses, mate, if all you want to do is drive heavy machinery,' Darren told him.

'The problem is you're with your bloke and he has the shits because he won't accept an apprentice's wage, so tell him to get his head out of his arse so he starts at the bottom in order to make his way to the top. He doesn't listen to me.'

The bloke makes a mild protest. 'I do a bit.'

==

My mother dropped out of university at nineteen when she got pregnant. My father, a fellow uni student, completed his science degree and worked long shifts while my mother looked after three young kids. She went back to university when we were teenagers, first to do an arts degree with a diploma of education, then to do a masters in literature and another in education. Notwithstanding her late start, it was always expected that we would all go to university, which I did – for a year. I left after that first year with a great sense of relief, and did not return until I knew what I wanted from it. History and politics part-time while working full-time in the New South Wales press gallery.

The university sector has boomed since then, as have the numbers of places and courses, providing more opportunities for kids in regional areas. But, as someone who understands the educational hurdles for country youth, Martin Parkinson questions the rush to change existing institutions such as technical colleges into universities and expand places.

'I think in many ways we fell into a bit of a trap in thinking we would fix a lot of [the hurdles] by expanding the number of university places. So we had a whole pile of institutional structures which were really quite good for delivering what they delivered and then we tried to turn them all into universities,' says Parkinson.

I was unaware of the strong feeling on my main street that the concentration and expansion of the university sector has devalued skilled jobs like trades and other manual work. With that devaluation, people tell me, there has been a drop in the numbers of school leavers considering such work. It bothers Darren. 'No one is saying you don't need a good education or you don't need to train for a job,' he says. But it worries him that technical careers are being undersold because they are considered jobs on the 'lower' rung in a social sense.

'They are telling everyone they have to go to uni. To achieve what? We are looking down the barrel now where it's $130 an hour to get the exhaust system fixed on your car and $80 an hour to get your computer fixed.

'We have got a real issue in our education system that our high schools are now pushing so hard for educational supremacy that we have lost sight of what we are on the planet for. How about we go and find an occupation that we enjoy that pays the bills?'

While jobs might be thin on the ground in a country town, if you are trained as a carpenter, plumber, hairdresser, beauty therapist, butcher, mechanic or electrician, you will always be able to hang up a shingle. Yet successive state and federal governments' vocational education policies in the technical education sector have made it much harder to get training in these areas if you live in a small town. Kids have got the idea that a university education solves everything.

Parkinson says the focus should be on opportunity. 'I think there is a real tension between credentialism, that is trying to send people off to do particular types of training through big institutions. I can see why you might get better training – might – from big institutions that have scale, but to the extent that the focus is on getting credentials rather than the focus [being] on getting opportunity, I think that's potentially counterproductive.'

Parkinson would like to see more differentiation among post-secondary education providers to allow pathways to open up to young people from regional areas, rather than regional educational institutions trying to copy the group of eight elite universities.

'The model was [that] they all had to look like the G8 [sandstone universities], and only now have they started to morph out into different models, and I think that is really promising. I am not disparaging any university, but why should a university in a regional area think that it needs to teach economics and business in the same way as a Melbourne uni or Macquarie does?'

Allowing educational institutions to develop their teaching from local industries would not only allow students to see its relevance to regional communities, but also create a pathway. Students could see the reason for studying. Parkinson thinks it would allow students to have the definitive choice of going to a rural and regional university 'which is not second best, it is different in its focus'. '[It's the same choice as] do I go to an institution that focuses on teaching, or do I go to a university that focuses on research?'

Watching the twists and turns of vocational education policy in the past two decades as a political reporter, it has been hard to keep up. Heaven help the students and the employers. The commercial imperative was introduced to the technical sector in the 1990s under John Howard's Coalition government before the Rudd–Gillard–Rudd Labor government introduced the VET student loan scheme to extend loans to vocational education students in the same way that university students are covered by HECs.[2] In the process the scheme ballooned, with the entry of a number of dodgy private training providers offering low-quality courses with no employment prospects, and using inducements like free laptops to gain enrolments. Students were left with debts, and the problem lingered through the Labor term and then the first term of the Abbott government before there were some reforms under the Turnbull government.

At the same time, state governments such as New South Wales' continued to take funding out of the technical system, leaving enrolments in freefall and staff being cut. For example, New South Wales TAFE devolved to ten institutes that competed with each other, and whose fees were raised significantly, in some cases quadrupling.[3] The rationalisation within an institute over a large region has meant that while your local or nearby town might have a campus, you don't get courses offered in every campus. So smaller campuses that are within the one TAFE institute have to compete with larger campuses to conduct a course. Small-town campuses have suffered, and as a result, a course like hairdressing might only be offered at a college ninety minutes away, as has happened to our local students. So a teenager who wants to combine a VET course with senior school cannot get there in the school day without major disruption. Usually they are not old enough to be driving, and even if they are they can't afford the fuel to travel every week, and rarely can their parents, who most likely have commitments around their own job, drive them there, hang around for a day and then drive them back.

Associate Professor Philip Roberts says that it's all very well to tell kids to get a technical course, but a local campus does not mean it is actually local.

'For example, a large regional New South Wales TAFE institute might have all these campuses, but one town campus might offer hairdressing and plumbing, and another one three hours away in the same institute teaches accounting, while a third, a few hours again, teaches butchery. They might be the same campus but the courses are actually not there in the local area.'

In 2016, TAFE amalgamated back into a single education provider.[4] The unending change has broken down relationships between campuses and local businesses, to the point where business owners who might be prospective employers don't know who to contact in the system. As a forty-something small-businesswoman told me, when she and her husband left school there were apprenticeships for most local students who wanted them. It was the same in my public high school in Sydney. In Year 10 many left and anyone who wanted an apprenticeship as a plumber, electrician or a carpenter found a job. Now, as Stephen, the university student, told me, 'University is now the default path. It's not a fork. One's a highway and the other is a backroad.'

There are other considerations for country students. If you pursue a trade, you lock yourself in for four more years on the minimum wage. To chase a trade in a larger centre away from your home town means you are on a minimum wage away from family support and accommodation. It can also be challenging for apprentices who watch their peer group go off to university or travelling. Some people specifically choose university as a way out of town. These are the decisions facing teenagers in my area.

For employers, vocational education policy disruption at a state and federal level has meant that some bosses throw their hands up in the air in despair. Other local employers tell me they don't want apprentices because they are moody, their expectations are too high or they leave as soon as they finish their apprenticeship. 'They don't want to do the shit work, and then they leave.' Then there is the cost to employers. Qualified tradespeople complain that the government provides no incentives for employers to train new apprentices, and that apprentices see the lower wage but not the outlay for their potential employer.

In our town, young school leavers often travel to larger centres and get placements through industry bodies, which provide training and organise jobs with employers. Says a former TAFE teacher, 'For employers, they don't know what the incentives are; the names of government departments change all the time; contracts come and go and there is a real disconnect between business and departments. It's all too hard.'

There needs to be ongoing contact between the education provider and the employer to change this so that everyone knows what courses and what training assistance from government is available to both prospective employees and employers. If the complexity of the system is too much to navigate, no training occurs. So a supermarket that might have a high number of young staff who would benefit from small courses goes under the radar, and their young employees don't get the benefit of building their training and their resumé while they are getting work experience.

This has not been ignored in the political debate. In the past few elections, there has been a growing outcry at the loss of apprenticeships and traineeships. Apprenticeships refer to the more traditional trades such as plumbing and electrical, while traineeships are service-based jobs with formal training. The Australian Council of Trade Unions (ACTU) and the Business Council of Australia have both claimed there have been declines in apprenticeships. The NSW Business Chamber chief executive Stephen Cartwright's comments are typical. 'Young people, their parents, and all too often career advisors at school, do not see an apprenticeship as a desirable career pathway. What is missing from the careers conversation is recognition that the skilled trades are the backbone of our economy and will continue to offer great job prospects in the years to come.'[5]

In the push towards university and away from trade-based skills, a TAFE teacher explains that students are being encouraged to choose courses not aligned with jobs in regional areas. So there again are the two competing tensions in a small town: encouraging students to be the best they can be to improve their lives with economic security, and the fear of pushing our children, and their brains and skills, out of the place.

Roberts argues for the need for rural education specialists to juggle not only the context of learning in rural areas but the social factors at work as students start to think about their career choices. 'When I talk to parents, they don't want their kids to leave town; they want them to stay because it is family and community. But they also want them to get ahead. The implicit message of all of these university outreach programs is you are bad if you don't go to uni, so a lot of the parents we talk to are really peeved off at the universities coming in and selling the message. The universities don't understand all that. They are there for market share, essentially, so it's this whole disconnect.'

=

Shiralee and Matt work seven days and their three boys, Will, twenty-three, Beau, twenty-one and Michael, nineteen, have inherited their work ethic. They are not the type to linger inside, and anyway Shiralee says that if anyone tries to sleep in they get a boot up the arse.

The farmer and I met the family when Beau came to work on the farm. He is well skilled in farm work, having been taught by his parents since he was a little boy. He's the only person I know who can chop wood sitting down. Shiralee and Matt also have two girls, Jess, eleven, and Isabella, seven, who are still at school. The whole family often goes out on weekends as a team, chopping firewood for sale, fencing and contract mustering.

Like Matt, the three boys all left school early, eager to pursue paid work. Matt said he got the citizenship award at school pretty much every year because he spent more time gardening than in the classroom. He says he didn't learn to read and write very well, and still gives any reading to Shiralee. She is a keen reader, who loves history, especially anything about the Second World War.

Since 2010, under New South Wales law students must complete Year 10 and then continue in either full-time school, training, paid work or a combination of these until they turn seventeen. The school allowed Shiralee and Matt's two older sons to leave school to move into the family contracting business, and when Michael wanted to leave in Year 9 to chase farm work – he had got a job lamb marking – he talked to his mother about the possibility of leaving and Shiralee agreed. She told him, 'Mate, you're not learning anything at school; you're in with the wrong ones anyway. Every day . . . you're in trouble for something, even if you're not there.'

She approached the principal, who refused to sign Michael out because he was under seventeen. Shiralee could see no reason for the reticence, given that Michael had more than thirty hours a week of work on farms, but the school kept sending letters. She just let the letters go. This is the reality in many schools. Rules on leaving age cannot be enforced. A year down the track, a new principal made the decision to sign Michael off the books and, like his brothers, he has been in continuous work ever since.

But Shiralee is telling her girls to give school a chance. On the eve of high school, Jess talked about getting out. She was impatient, like Shiralee was. Like I was. Like many of us are. Shiralee told Jess, 'Wait till you go to high school and then we will see how you're going, and then you might end up going through to Year 12.' Jess's retort was that her brothers had got out in Year 10. 'That was the boys,' Shiralee told her. 'They had no interest in learning. All they wanted was to get out and do something. They left to help your father and then after that they got their own jobs. The new law is you can't get out in Year 10; you have to wait till you're seventeen.'

The key to education is about having the capacity to make your own choices regarding your job and your life, with the right guidance. Maggie-Kate and fellow high achievers throw a long shadow in a small town, and I am in awe of what they have done. But it pays to remember that not everyone wants to be a doctor, and we must not forget the kids who aren't interested in getting on the superhighway to university or any formal training. My hope for small-town children comes back to equality of life chances. My community works hard to augment the opportunities for our kids so they can bridge the divide from their small school and obtain a job they enjoy 'that pays the bills'. We don't expect governments to solve everything and we acknowledge city people have problems, too, but we plead for state and federal education and employment policies to enable geographical equality.

LESSON 8

You can lead a small town
(or country) up or down

In 2006 I went to work for my local newspaper, having spent almost two decades at metropolitan papers. My kids were in primary school so I was looking for something that would keep me close to town for school drop-offs and pick-ups. I also wanted to understand the way small rural towns operated, their unwritten rules and ingrained culture. Every town has a history and a culture. They are not exactly the same thing, those two elements, but they are intertwined like the wisteria and the ivy behind our outdoor dunny. You wouldn't think of spending time separating them because it would be an impossible and unrewarding task.

The *Harden-Murrumburrah Express* was part of what was then the Rural Press empire. It had a readership of around a thousand people, and eight to twelve pages of local content, plus an insert with wider southern New South Wales content to add more weight. In 2006 – the year before Rural Press was swallowed up by Fairfax Media – it had a staff of two and a small office in a shopfront on the main street of Harden. In a sign of the media times, that office has since closed down, though the newspaper still exists. The single room was about 3 by 4 metres, with a tiny toilet off the office. I was the editorial department, my friend Jody Potts was the advertising department, and we had twenty hours' pay each week to produce the paper. In metropolitan papers probably seven or eight sets of eyeballs had been laid on a story by the time it got into the paper. At our local paper we went without subeditors or check subs, but it is virtually impossible to edit your own copy so I gathered a small group of avid readers to proofread pages before they went into production to cut down the possibility of errors.

My first lesson was the newspaper itself. If a local issue did not get a run in the paper, there was usually little chance of it running in a larger state paper such as the *Daily Telegraph* or the *Sydney Morning Herald*. Local newspapers play a very important role in a small town, providing information to a community that is unlikely to find it anywhere else. Certainly this was reflected in the views of one of the world's most successful investors, Warren Buffett, chairman of Berkshire Hathaway, when he began buying smaller local American newspapers in 2012. Buffett maintained that readers eyes may 'glaze over' when reading international news, but people always read to the end if a story is about their neighbours or themselves. Though recently Buffett has cooled on newspapers – 'circulation just goes down every month' – in my experience no one reads a story so carefully as when it is about someone they know.[1]

In 2018, the challenges for larger media companies are disruptive technology and fake news. For small communities, if we have no source of local news we have no facts. Or at the very least, facts become difficult to find for the average resident, and rumours on Facebook feeds fill the void. Rumours need to be scotched, preferably in print, because in 2018 printed local newspapers still have a measure of authority and loyalty, the likes of which are fast disappearing in their bigger city media cousins.

Back in 2006 I had no experience editing a local paper, but what I craved as a reader was unvarnished facts on services, local council, community groups, schools and sporting clubs. I wanted to have a complete report, for example, on the monthly local council meeting. I wanted to know about the more controversial development applications that might affect how the town looked and the way it changed. I wanted to have a local angle on federal and state government budgets and other initiatives. I wanted to see how my neighbours felt about current issues affecting the local economy and local industries, either in the form of comment or letters to the editor. I wanted to see pictures of local kids and read funny, quirky or historical facts about the area. Above all, I wanted to see some investment from the community in its future. Here I am talking not just financial investment but also emotional investment. What is it that we want this town to be? How do we envisage this area in ten, twenty, fifty years' time?

The projection of my own needs as a reader became the recipe for my approach as editor and chief bottle washer. The lesson for me as editor was that the way information is presented can lead a town up or down. Editorship in a small community is a balancing act between optimism for the future and the seductive narrative of rural decline. It is the pull of sad songs. It would be easy to create a newspaper riff of the Bob Dylan song 'Hard Times' and we could all sit around woe betiding. The high-wire act is finding an upside while not ignoring the challenges of the downsides.

No two small towns are the same, but elements and themes emerge. Back in the day, our town was a railway town, and it serviced the farms surrounding it. While the abattoir was once a big employer, the railway has been the long-term employer throughout the town's history. State government was the main supplier of jobs on the railway, so it was a central part of our town. Local government was the other big employer. These two employers kept locals in work and kept the footy team well placed for players. There is nothing like hulking wheat bags to build your front row. Ours was a trade union town and a league town.

Tom Apps was in the front row for the Harden Hawks in the southern New South Wales Maher Cup glory days. The railway and the football club were the twin pillars of his life. He remembers the band greeting the Hawks as the boys drove back into town after a win. The footpaths outside the pub were full with people celebrating the local victory. The Hawks loved playing a home game, and if they won the toss they would choose to run towards the pub in the second half to give them extra push. Tom speaks of an era that is difficult for newer residents like me to imagine. In 1959, for instance, the Maher Cup gate (that is, the total value of tickets sold) was 800 pounds and it was three shillings to get in, he says, incredulous. That is more than 5000 people turning out.

I first met Tom when I was working at the *Express*. He used to bring in the bowls report of the weekend's games, handwritten in capital letters on a piece of paper. I typed it up for him and put it into the paper. Our friendship developed over those weekly exchanges, when he'd reminisce about the glory days of football. Tom loves to remember.

'We played thirty-five games a season, Saturday and Sunday. And to hear these footballers today whinge about playing too much football, we did that for a whole season – twenty-six straight wins, and we broke Gundagai's record.'

All the local towns had their turn winning the Maher Cup competition, and it remains a proud part of the region's history. Sport in country towns holds people together and forms bonds across classes. The stories of getting players back from working shifts around the region so they could make a game are legend. There was a five-eighth who was flown to Temora after work, picked up by the garage owner and driven to West Wyalong, an hour away.

He arrived just as the Hawks ran on. Well, he wasn't there for five minutes and scored a try, says Tom.

We are sitting in his cottage kitchen, one of the original rail cottages, which backs on to the train tracks. You can see old rail buildings and depots, and it's pretty close to the brick bridge that takes the railway line over the road. As the XPT travels north to Sydney just over the back fence, Tom tells me he is one of nine kids. His dad was a fettler on the railway, looking after the state of the tracks with a pick and shovel. Tom's mother gave him permission to leave school in 1950, when he was fourteen and a half years old, to start work on the railway: there was a job and, by his account, he wasn't doing well at school. Or, as he put it, 'I probably wasn't real bright at school at that stage.' Tom was the oldest kid and it would have helped being able to bring in a bit more money for a family of that size. 'Things were pretty tough in those days.'

So that Christmas, 1950, Tom started in the refreshment room at Harden railway station. The elegant old Federation station remains essentially unchanged, but its rooms are all locked up these days. Somewhere inside the stationhouse there is even a flat for the railway manager and his family. The highly polished timber and brass bar with its foot rests and overhead shelving has been moved down to the Historical Society as a relic from the past. Refreshment rooms are so last century.

Tom's voice must have only just dropped when he joined eight to ten women serving customers while the train stopped for twenty minutes at Harden's station. His first job was a 'junior useful', cleaning up around the place. He helped serve at the counter of a night-time. He made the toast, watching as one of the 'old ducks', Mrs Lawless, made the pies. Other food was brought in on the trains from Sydney, the carriages packed to the gunnels with baskets. There were piles of cold meat for sandwiches and ice blocks for the bar, which were coated in sawdust.

It was the post-war boom. Wool was going gangbusters so the cockies were happy as pigs in shit. Migration was in full swing, not that you saw much of it around Harden. The town was thriving because of the railway. There were hundreds of people working there – the biggest employer by a long shot. Tom can still rattle off all the jobs: clerks, drivers, firemen, fettlers, traffic men, yardmen. Station staff worked around the clock and the station master had two or three assistants, as well as porters and guards. Yardmen cleaned up around the place, signalmen, or boys, manned the boxes.

All the goods for the shops, and the beer for pubs, used to come by rail. 'I used to load it, that's how I know,' Tom says. He loaded everything in his day, including wool bales, which are chest height, packed tight by a wool press and heavy as lead. There were times, says Tom, when he would go to work of a night as a senior shunter and it was flat-out. The yard would be full of stuff. Trains going to Cootamundra, to Cowra, one to Goulburn. We'd get a great string of traffic, an engine, a dozen trucks, working by lamplight. The union was strong.

'They say you didn't work hard on the railway. I tell you what, they don't know. But it was great in those days. It was different.'

As though he's playing a memory game, he lists off the shops in the main street. He describes a landscape I cannot see now. A couple of butchers, a Police Boys' Club, two drycleaners. There is not even one now. A clothing factory. Can you believe it? Thirty to forty women working there from town. It's all gone. Clarky's bakery. Tom Jones' fruit shop. 'Yeah,' Tom sits back, 'ole Tommy Jones. I'm told he had an eye for the ladies.' There was a café, another bakery, a pub, the Calypso café, Grainger's supermarket, Prosser the tailor, a dress shop, another drycleaner. Then there was Guilty Macdonald, the solicitor. 'A bloody good bowler, ole Guilty.' Five pubs in Harden alone. All doing well.

He saves the greatest affection for the Greek owner of the Paragon café – epitomising the town's embrace of European migration. Nicky

Flaskas easily had 'the best café in the group nine [football competition]', says Tom. There were booths down one side and a milk bar down the other, and little jukeboxes down the end of the table.

The café was intertwined with football and the war. According to local sports historian Paul 'Wings' McCarthy, the Harden footy team won its first Maher Cup on 12 June 1940.[2] The Flaskas brothers' café was officially opened on 6 July that year, and the takings that day were donated to the district hospital and the Patriotic Fund. Nick Flaskas was known for handing out cigarettes and chocolates at the local railway station to troops travelling past. He was given a honorary membership at the RSL for his efforts.

After the new Coalition New South Wales government swept into office in 1988, Liberal premier Nick Greiner set about overhauling the state rail system, which was losing $1 billion a year. In Canberra, the Hawke government was deregulating the financial system. The winds of economic rationalism were blowing down the main street of the town as it was trying to recover from the early-1980s drought. As successive governments continued to overhaul the rail system, its jobs slowly but surely disappeared.

'I drove a coach for six and a half years,' says Tom, 'and when they privatised the coach, I went into the booking office. Then they cut it out. Everywhere I went, they cut the jobs out. I ended up in the signal box. It was the best job I had, pulling a few levers and letting the trains go by, and in out of the weather.'

Tom and his wife Robyn got a chance to acquire their cottage in the 1980s because the railway started selling off assets. They bought it for $22,000. Tom said it was a scary time, not knowing whether he would keep his job. He received a gold watch at thirty years' service, and retired after forty-five years, with a good send-off.

We talk about the death of the rail and the corresponding increase of trucks on the highway. The Sydney–Melbourne XPT still comes through the town twice a day, in the middle of the night and the middle of the day. The possibilities of opening up the town would be endless, if, for example, there was a train from Canberra to Harden-Murrumburrah, a ninety-minute drive. It would be the equivalent of commuting from the Blue Mountains to Central Station in Sydney. It would provide cheap housing for young families in Canberra. You can buy a house around here for $200,000. Alas, while there is a station in both towns, there is no track to connect it. 'It's too expensive,' says Tom. 'Imagine the stuff they cart on the road – Woolies, Aldi at Young. Imagine if that could come by rail like it used to. When it used to come by rail, it would leave Sydney and they would have it all in the shops by nine am. Nothing now.'

Tom can't see another big employer in town ever again offering a couple of hundred jobs as the railway or the abattoir did. In their bones, many people know the big-employer days are gone in small towns like ours. But in understanding the town's history, it is easier to comprehend the wistfulness about the big employer, and the tendency in small towns to look back with nostalgia. Who wouldn't want to get back to the days of the bustling footpaths, celebrating the local footy team's win?

Robyn says, 'I suppose ... you've got to go with the flow. We could whinge and vent our anger but that is the way it is.'

That acceptance of change represents one group in small communities. They feel powerless to change larger forces such as the economic rationalisation of government services; globalisation; political instability. So the focus for change moves inwards. In Robyn's case, she concentrates on raising money for the local hospital auxiliary, which has been enormously successful.

There is another group, though: people who are actively angry at the larger forces of change and what they see as a failure of the political establishment to pay attention to their needs and deliver on their promises. They feel they have nothing to lose by voting for outliers, because they do not believe the major parties will follow through with their commitments. They are the disrupters who are seeking to change the political status quo.

===

If there was a consistent theme at the local newspaper, it was, and remains, the need for economic development in order to return the town to a more prosperous time. In 2006 one of the town's biggest employers was going under. The abattoir, which employed 140 people, was crippled against the backdrop of the 2000s drought, dubbed the worst in a hundred years. Jobs disappeared overnight. Bernie Minogue, the former head stockman at the abattoir, says that in his time it had employed 180 people. 'It was a terrible shame to see it closed, and a real blow to the town. It affects everything in a small town. When that closed, it pulled a hundred and sixty to seventy people out of a town like this.'

Around that time, one of my first stories for the paper was to report on a public meeting held by the local council. It was the follow-up to a community survey that had asked for comments and suggestions for the council. Residents were offered free beer to attend. Comments focused on the perceived lack of economic action being taken by our closest level of government – local government. The arguments centred around the lack of work on planning regulations, or slow approval rates – things at the back end of local government. They are the bits voters cannot see so it's hard to comprehend the hoops that need to be jumped through. Conversely, there was plenty of praise for people at the front end of local government, employees who had no power to change things themselves. The garbo man on the local street, the person weeding the patch in the median strip and the front office staff taking a bill payment. In a small community, they are us.

Herein was a lesson for me. People directed their anger at the government machine, the slow-moving behemoth that has to comply with the regulations imposed from the next level up.

Anger was particularly directed at experts, the decision-makers in council. When one level of staff was blamed, that level blamed the one above. For example, facing angry ratepayers, the then mayor blamed the state government for moving the goalposts on local planning. It was reminiscent of state governments blaming federal governments for GST revenue shortfalls. And federal governments blaming state governments for locking up land and causing a gas crisis.

Note to politicians: the main street thinks of Government with a capital G. The main street doesn't care which level it is, they just need a point of contact and a response. They want signs that government has listened and that government has responded.

On the council itself, which has since been amalgamated, controversially, into a larger regional body, there were many fractures and factions. As in federal politics, there were two identifiable groups of councillors from the Harden-Murrumburrah shire: those who tried to work with the system and those who were more critical of council decisions – the latter being closer to 'outsider' politicians such as those in the Senate's minor parties. Both sides had their supporters and loud critics. The outsiders presented as if they were no different to the person on the main street, notwithstanding their access to the inner workings of the council. Laid over those fractures was the divide between farmers, small business and ordinary citizens, which were less easily identifiable.

On the sidelines were the town's voters, interested observers and journalists like me. All of us were lining up with one or more of these groups, offering plenty of free advice as to 'what you should do'. What I saw in covering councils and main-street politics were competing expectations over what council could or should do. This has been best enunciated by political journalist Laura Tingle in her essay 'Great Expectations'.[3] She argues that in Australia we have not worked out exactly what we expect from governments, partly because political parties have long been telling us they can fix everything if only they get into office. This much was clear from those early council and town hall meetings. There was concern there was not enough support from local government for local business, though it was unclear what council *could* do in this regard. Suggestions were also made for new local industries – a sausage factory or a rabbit farm, industries that might offer jobs. When pushed, it was, again, unclear where the investment would come from to create these businesses and by whom.

At the same time, when governments and communities do get active, implementation of change is still tricky. At that same 2006 meeting, some residents complained that not enough had been done for the look of the town. Then, years down the track, when a group of us planned a street beautification, with significant council investment, to attract more small businesses and tree changers, there were major complaints about the architect's recommendation to change the parking arrangements in the main street from rear to nose. It was one of the most divisive debates I have seen in the place. People complained that accidents would be caused by loading groceries into car boots and children would be injured. Eventually the change was made and, apart from the occasional niggles of losing some car spaces to trees, the vast majority are happy, and compliment the garden staff on their work with the landscaping.

One of the biggest issues of many small rural communities remains – attracting and retaining doctors. We were lucky enough to have two constant doctors for more than thirty years, but when they retired there was much debate about the succession plan. There were fears that our local hospital may close, as services such as obstetrics had long ago been rationalised and sent to larger regional centres. Local government had begun planning a medical centre with a mix of public and private funding, which constituted a foray into health services, traditionally the role of state government.

(There is often confusion over which government is responsible for what service, though if people are actively angry over an issue they usually work out which to blame.)

While the debate raged as to how to develop the town, many, newly unemployed, were being driven out by fewer jobs. In the same year, pressure increased on the last of the railway workers in town. Signal jobs moved elsewhere and the railway lost its last three workers, including one lifelong employee who had joined his father, grandfather, two uncles, a nephew and a son on the railway. Times were changing.

In the town's other key industry, agriculture, the Australian Bureau of Agriculture and Resource Economics was forecasting a collapse in farm income of 72 per cent in the financial year. At the same time, the services sector marched onwards and upwards. The Fairfax economics correspondent Peter Martin wrote at the time, 'For many farmers the collapse will be devastating, but for the rest of us the official forecast suggests we won't notice much.'[4] When you are in a small town, though, the effects of income collapse can be seen everywhere. This is where farmers' income is vitally important, not just to them but to the whole town. Down at the schools, we fought to keep our teaching staff. When a big employer closes, a certain percentage of families move on, taking their kids. The classes shrink because the school staffing numbers are based on the enrolments. At the P&C and the school council, we scrambled to ward off cuts. Within weeks, my front pages were proclaiming there would be no first-grade rugby league team in the local competition, for the second time in three years. Under the rules, the junior teams could not play without a senior team. The club president told me there was not enough work in town. It was hard to play without a job, while paying for the cost of insurance and travel. On a winning streak, the local team could pull 1000 people to a game on the weekend. You can sell a lot of pies and coffee to 1000 people.

Rampaging Roy Slaven and H. G. Nelson used the local club as an example of the impending death of country rugby league. It was 'just another boot up the arse' for country towns, Roy said. That is exactly how it felt.

There is nothing like a dry time to focus communities and governments on climate change. John Howard was locking in federal government control over the Murray–Darling Basin, something Malcolm Turnbull said should have happened in the 1890s.[5] Then Labor opposition leader Kevin Rudd called climate change the greatest moral challenge of our generation and called on the Howard government to convene a climate summit. In response, a local group organised a screening of the Al Gore movie *An Inconvenient Truth* at a town hall.

On the ground, I watched the state and federal elections roll in like summer storm clouds in 2007. Covering the elections for a small-town paper was very different to covering it at the state or federal press gallery. My priorities had shifted and my scrutiny of policy was filtered through a small-community lens. From a press gallery, I took a helicopter view, but on a small-town paper the view is from the grassroots. Policy areas that are rarely covered by the press gallery received a lot more of my attention in the local paper. The Labor New South Wales government handed over $200,000 for an upgrade of the town pool, a grant that would not have rated a mention in a state or national paper. The New South Wales Coalition opposition used the provision of water as a point of difference between the major parties, including the Country Towns Water Supply and Sewerage Program. I would not have given the policy a second look in the press gallery, but it rated a big mention in my local paper. Even the New South Wales National Party leader was talking water recycling, carbon trading and biodynamic fertilising. Andrew Stoner said the National Party's changing demographic on the north coast forced him to be 'across a whole lot of issues that are not the old Country Party issues'. (This was in stark contrast to the federal National Party policies at the time and ever since.)

Speaking to the stream of people coming through the tiny main-street newspaper office around the time of the New South Wales and federal elections, it became clear that rural people voted on a much more local basis that city voters. The country will embrace a good grassroots candidate, and then they will not shift loyalties easily.

To check my view, I spoke to the ABC's election analyst Antony Green when I was covering that 2007 New South Wales election. He told me, 'In rural and regional electorates, politics is much more about place – about where you live and the local services in the area. In the city, voters don't generally make decisions based on where they live, but more about the general level of services, and they vote more along class lines, education and background. Class solidarity is much more a feature in the cities. A blue-collar worker in Newcastle will vote along class lines, as opposed to the blue-collar worker in rural New South Wales.'

A newer resident, a working-class man, told me that he had changed his lifelong Labor support to the Coalition a few years after he moved from the coast into the town. It happened slowly. He met the local member, who helped him on a number of occasions with his local community groups. He saw the MP more often than he ever had seen the incumbent who'd been in his former coastal seat, and it cemented his support. Voilà. A voting habit was changed.

Intense, honest conversations with readers like him were incredibly important to understanding the differences between the city and country political culture. If local councils are the first port of call for frustrated citizens, local newspapers are often the second. (It helped that our office was 20 paces from the local council.) I had heard a few horror stories of local editors and journalists being hounded over coverage, threatened if court stories appeared, and generally harangued for making a stand on more controversial issues. I never experienced bullying, though a property owner got close after I started writing about the rundown state of several properties on the main street. There was also a very well-dressed woman who threatened me with dire consequences if I printed a story about her down-town bingle that had resulted in a dented bumper bar. (I assured her it was not that exciting.) Generally I found people were happy to vent in a letter to the editor and leave it at that.

The reporting I did for our paper showed me the connection between influence in small towns and political parties. Agriculture has dominated areas like mine so completely that it has often crowded out the rural political agenda, which has fed parties like the National Party. It has also left a large proportion of rural and regional communities – not involved in agriculture – without a direct line to parliaments. It is those people, without a stake in industries like agriculture, sandwiched between groups of influence and those below the bread line, who feel political representation has let them down.

If working on the local paper taught me one thing, though, it was that small towns can be led up or down. By editing a local newspaper, you curate the narrative for the main street and it comes with immense responsibility to report fairly and accurately, as well as with some vision for the place. I am not saying I always achieved that, but that was the aim of the exercise. If the editor concentrates all coverage on sad songs, that is where the town will focus. If information is brought to the readership that can help the town develop, it has a chance to move in a positive direction.

LESSON 9

Small town life is not all sad songs

It was via an American jukebox that I first heard the maudlin songs of Patsy Cline. I may or may not have been falling to pieces at the time – perhaps it was the Long Island Iced Tea – but the songs still strike a chord with me. The narrative of small towns is a bit like the sad song from the corner of an empty bar. It is a song of decline. If you follow the debate, it is all about loss and past glories. At the same time, not a single person I speak to around me who might complain long and loud about the economy or the government or the state of the world would ever countenance moving. It is the country conundrum in sharp relief.

The decline narrative reflects a lot of the international discussion about the regions in the US that voted for Donald Trump and the regions in the UK that voted for Brexit. People who examine and advocate for country communities for a living, people like Jack Archer of the Regional Australia Institute, have the narrative down pat.

'There is this national story about rural Australia that really misses most of the stories. They come with quite a pejorative [angle].

These are people in rural decline. Towns are populated by people who aren't well educated. They are populated by people who aren't good enough to make it in the city. There are a lot of deliberate or implied perspectives on people who live there, which either leads to a dismissive attitude – this is old Australia – which doesn't add up, or a patronising victim perspective of those poor people: someone should go out and save them. I think that colours the whole discussion of our regions. When we look at regional Australia, it does not match the public discussion of regional Australia and what it is and what is happening.'

Archer argues that the right story is the story of growth, that regional Australia contributes 40 per cent of our economy and that while population growth is much lower in regional Australia than the exponential growth in Sydney and Melbourne, it is inching up. (According to the Australian Bureau of Statistics, the combined population of state and territory capital cities increased by 315,700 people, or 1.9 per cent, between 30 June 2016 and 30 June 2017. This accounted for 81 per cent of the country's total population growth.)[1] The story for Archer is about understanding different places and what their challenges are, and being able to respond to those challenges. 'We do ourselves a disservice by trying to lump it all up into a single perspective.'

Like city communities, rural communities are complex, and it is important to acknowledge that complexity and respond to it in a policy sense, in order for people to stay in their place of choice. It doesn't mean handing out crutches in the form of buckets of random money. It doesn't mean propping up dud farmers who need an exit plan rather than another loan. It means acknowledging that the towns that get off their arses can, with a small amount of targeted government help, rewrite their futures. In most cases, people actively choose to live in place. The decline narrative butts up against research from an Australian Bureau of Statistics general social survey in 2014, which found that the number of people involved in social capital activities rises the further you get from the central business districts of the capital cities.[2]

Human contact is important. When it comes to things like volunteering, participating in a community group, or face-to-face contact with family and friends outside your own household, outer regional and remote people have greater rates than inner regional people, who have greater rates than those in major cities. This comes against a backdrop of an overall decline in volunteer rates since the ABS started measuring these things in 1995. Every week on our main street a couple of volunteers from the hospital auxiliary, the football club, the show society or myriad other clubs sit at a card table selling raffle tickets. This town loves a raffle.

In the Australian Unity Wellbeing Index 2016 conducted through Deakin University, rural areas had higher self-reported levels of personal well-being. Broken down by federal electorate area, seven out of the ten electorates with the highest levels of personal well-being were in rural areas. A 2015 survey on Wellbeing, Resilience and Liveability in Rural and Regional Australia adds weight to this evidence.[3] It represented the difficulties and the benefits of living in the country. The top line was that most rural and regional Australians (70 per cent) reported being highly satisfied with their lives. More (73 per cent) felt positively about their community's well-being, and even more (79 per cent) felt the things that they did in life were worthwhile. They were generally satisfied with their standard of living, sense of safety and personal relationships, though the lowest satisfaction levels were reserved for health and future security. Younger people and the unemployed reported lower levels of satisfaction. Women were more likely to consider their life was worthwhile compared with men, as did those over sixty-five compared with younger people. Farmers were more likely to feel their lives were worthwhile than non-farmers. It was very different to the sad song we hear most of the time.

The findings gel with my impression of rural life, particularly in relation to agriculture. Growing food, one of the basic needs in life, provides a fundamental sense of self-worth, no matter what others might think of you. Giving someone something to eat holds a special attraction, as evidenced by growing city farmers' markets. This is in spite of the onward and upward march of the service industries compared to agriculture as a percentage of the Australian economy. It is also in spite of the same survey in which farmers reported more financial stress than those residents employed in other professions.

Although nearly half (44 per cent) of all residents reported some form of financial stress in the previous twelve months, including skipping social events and not spending on anything but food, more people agreed than disagreed that their living costs were affordable, even if they were pessimistic at how well their local businesses were faring and the supply of jobs in their regions. While 42 per cent felt their economy was worsening, a high number (73 per cent) would recommend their community to others as a good place to live. Here, the state economies come into play, with Victorians most likely to recommend their towns, followed by New South Wales. Those in Queensland, which has suffered badly from drought in recent years, were significantly less likely to recommend their communities. It is also true that, according to the numbers, rural and regional areas have lower levels of education, health outcomes and lesser access to services that are taken for granted in the cities. This is an indisputable fact and one that is updated regularly.

So it is messy, but my point is that one side of the story is being played up and the other is played down, and that causes a disconnection between what metropolitan people hear about small towns like mine. Yes, we complain (who doesn't?) but there is a sense of pride and belonging in the community that is often fierce.

Who is responsible for the sad songs? Historically, this over-simplified story of country towns has been driven by rural politicians, journalists and rural communities themselves. We all have motives, whether conscious or not. Rural politicians are advocates and therefore seek to maximise the benefits for their local areas. The decline story provides leverage to argue for better resources in a Parliament where 149 other MPs are trying to do the same for their own areas. Journalists are bound to find a lead to our stories, and invariably it is the most contrasting or shocking part of the story. That in turn drives the debate.

As a result of these two drivers, a cargo cult mentality has grown up in some of our rural and regional communities. Some-times our communities are insatiable. We are not alone here. In the current political climate, everyone has their hand out: major industries, business, unions – rent-seeking is a national sport. But are we charity cases singing sad songs? Or is there a fundamental importance in producing local food, caring for land and maintain-ing regional communities?

The Coalition government has named agriculture as one of the so-called five pillars of the Australian economy; also manufacturing, mining, education and services. The Agricultural Competitiveness White Paper says it is because agriculture is part of our identity. Because our history and economy was 'built on the sheep's back'. And because agriculture plays a 'pivotal role in building the wealth of Australia.'[4]

To government and to many Australians, farming is like an old lover. Yeah, we had a thing with it. Hell, it was our first love, riding on the sheep's back. Now, well, we think about it every so often and we still feel that same nostalgic pull. Should we go there again? It's enticing but it always ends up being vaguely unsatisfying.

Australia has moved on to more exciting lovers now. Service industries that are taking the economy by storm. Those big banks are way more sexy and sophisticated, shaving decimal points off trillions of transactions and making a motza without raising a sweat. Not to mention the share price. Farming seems, well, a bit daggy and last century. Just a little bit poverty-stricken, even though there is a rising optimism within the agricultural industry.

This public equivocation over agriculture in turn drives rural politicians back to the same sad songs about old lovers and better times. Remember when you used to love me? And this, in turn, drives metropolitan Australia further away. Oh god, have some self-respect, will you? Now you're just pleading . . . it really is pathetic.

I would argue that this whole cycle, the sad songs and the old lovers' tiffs, stem from a lack of imagination on the part of a fair chunk of rural advocacy – mostly inside the Parliament – and a lack of long-term consideration on the part of government and metropolitan Australia about how to think about rural Australia.

My song is more upbeat and it would go something like this. Farmers grow food and fibre. Significant and influential metropolitan constituencies are obsessed with food – its purity and its story. Some of those voters are seduced by the very idea of country life, and many are moving to rural areas to beat city real estate prices, grow their own vegetables, raise their own chooks and slow down their pace. The essence of country life is the foil to a harried city life, and its foundational underpinnings are space, fresh air and the open road; this market – a largely middle-class and aspirational tree-change constituency, including a big chunk of millennials – would choose local produce as their ideal because these people have the luxury to make that choice. For farmers who are seeking to add value to their produce, this is a valuable market.

And if rural communities, and urban ones, hear a different song, a more positive song, they may look at agriculture, and rural issues generally, in a different light. They may look at global politics, where they can see countries like the United States raising protection barriers, and they may understand that the power of the story of locally produced food is growing. Who knows? They may see that ensuring a strong agricultural industry is not only essential but has strategic significance for Australia's future. It's the food, stupid!

That influential metropolitan constituency is evident in the two towns closest to the farm on which I live, Harden-Murrumburrah and Jugiong. Harden-Murrumburrah is on the Burley Griffin Way, the main route west to Griffith. Jugiong is more or less halfway between Sydney and Melbourne. In both, as in small towns across the country, the past two decades have seen transformations most visibly measured in the strength of their coffee. In the early days, takeaway coffee involved a caterer's tin of International Roast and, in the more innovative cafés, a bit of frothy milk spooned on top. The demands of travellers, the increasing sophistication of tastes in small towns, and an influx of new blood, combined with old understanding, has brought with it decent-strength coffee. And coffee is so often the harbinger of a gear change in a small town.

Jugiong is the most obvious example of this phenomenon. Twenty years ago, when I arrived in the district, there was a service station, a motel and a mixed store-cum-post office. Population varied between 200 and 300. The Hume Highway used to pass through the town and it was a significant blackspot – the place where you started to get sleepy on the drive between our two biggest cities. When the federal government announced the town would be bypassed, the community was terrified Jugiong would die altogether, losing the last travellers who stopped for petrol, a slash and an instant coffee.

Driven by an entrepreneurial local farmer, the late David Power, Jugiong residents got together to think about what they wanted for their place. They agreed on a vision statement and got busy. Individuals contributed according to their strengths, ranging from negotiating government processes to planning and planting trees and gardens. Fellow farmer Tony Willsallen hounded ministers, as well as the Roads and Traffic authorities, and Jugiong was designated a rest stop on the highway under the federal Labor government. That decision allowed the town to press the incoming Nationals MP John Sharp to ensure the bypass came with an on-ramp and an off-ramp to overcome drivers' psychological aversion to backtracking to the highway. Sharp, who came into Howard's government as transport minister, joked to me at the time that so persuasive were the locals, he had no choice but to give them something. After their relentless pushing, the federal government provided funding for the ramps and the state government funded an amenities block and a park for the travellers and trucks who camp overnight.

Once the infrastructure was laid down, the Long Track Pantry was established, with the skills of a young local foodie, Juliet Robb, and the financial backing and design skills of tree changer Jo Miller. Juliet, as business operator, concentrated on a good, reasonably priced café menu, speedy service, strong coffee and her own brand of deli goods, jams, dressings and condiments, while Jo got the look and the vibe of the place right. This combination of local and new blood is often the recipe for laying the strong economic foundations for small communities.

Next door, a local couple, Jenny and Gino Polemini, opened a fresh fruit and vege store to supply the café and other customers in the region. At the same time, David Power opened a cellar designed to concentrate on selling and marketing local wines to the passing trade. The Jugiong Motel provided accommodation and a beer for those who wanted to stop for the night, and suddenly there was the beginnings of critical mass and a destination food and retail experience.

In 2017 the Sir George pub, built in 1852, was bought by Liz Prater and her daughter, Kate, after Kate married local farmer

Charlie Hufton. The mother and daughter team extensively reno-
vated, with an eye to taking advantage of the rising traffic already
streaming through the little town. Liz's partner, Western Australian
restauranteur Kim Gamble, had previously developed a number of
ventures, and the Sir George has become a formidable outfit. The
Miller and Robb families then joined forces again to build a stylish,
rammed-earth shopping complex to attract more businesses. The
new shopping complex houses a homewares boutique owned by
a fashion and interiors stylist, a florist and artist's studio, and a
recycled timber trading shop. As a result, the traffic stopping in
Jugiong has skyrocketed. Locals happily remark on how hard it is to
get a parking space.

Things change slowly until you notice one day that what
is in front of you is completely different to what was. Jugiong's
makeover was like a child growing, imperceptible at first until you
look up into their eyes. Self-evidently the little town is an example
of the possibilities of an economic makeover. Its new shops, café
and pub are employing locals and bringing much-needed income
into the area.

'It takes an individual and it takes a bit of leadership,' says Tony
Willsallen. 'Unless there is someone motivating people, nothing
seems to happen. David Power was brilliant. He empowered people.
He wasn't always liked for it, but he had a vision and we all signed
up to it.'

Jugiong also represents what is a definite movement into rural
areas of #countrylife aspirational or financially secure tree changers,
who are focused on rural lifestyle for the sake of it. Magazines like
Country Style typify the new country aesthetic, an idealised rural
life with designer rustic interiors and beautiful, tanned people in
pale-blue linen shirts and appropriately scuffed boots posing in
front of styled houses covered with rambling roses and bordered in
box hedges. Their houses are the reverse of the old farm homesteads

which were dour and closed. In the country houses of these new city escapees, bathtubs sit in front of feature windows with views of forever.

Meanwhile, city audiences gorge on shows such as SBS's *Gourmet Farmer* with former restaurant critic Matthew Evans introducing you to his lovely piggies that he will soon roast. Or *River Cottage Australia*, where you will learn how to trap rabbits for stewing and build a chicken coop, before sitting down to a hearty frittata made with your own eggs. It's all so seductive and it provides a key to rural politicians out there. Small-town life is not all sad songs.

Jugiong started with some advantages. Its proximity to Australia's main Hume Highway makes it an easy travellers' rest stop. It's located fewer than four hours from Sydney and is a day trip from Canberra. The village atmosphere certainly helped its revival, in that it was under-developed so it retained its small-town charm. It had a supply of local talent, with funds, who could start and maintain businesses.

Other towns, such as Harden-Murrumburrah, have a larger base and have historically survived on more industrial income such as railways, pipe works and abattoirs fed from the local agricultural base. In towns like Harden-Murrumburrah, where the population is in the thousands rather than the hundreds, the imperative since its former industries closed or were rationalised has been to find a replacement industry. The town wants the security of more jobs than a café or a pub can provide though we will take all comers. Its shops are geared to provide items less attractive for tree changers: fertiliser and agricultural chemicals, hardware for stock troughs, widgets for spray rigs and ear tags for cattle and sheep. If you can get a good coffee at the same time, all well and good, but it is not the main priority.

In fact, there has been a constant tension between those who believe tourism – passersby drinking coffee – will economically vaccinate the town and those who believe the only saviour is big industry. These debates happen locally and across the country, and in most cases the answer must be delivered by the locals. These days Harden-Murrumburrah does in fact sit highly on the coffee index. It has specialty produce stores for honey, local duck products, life-style goods and boutique accommodation. But the priority for the townspeople remains larger industry. That is because in towns like these, which sit in between bespoke village destinations such as Jugiong and larger regional centres, there is a feeling of being left behind by economic change and outmigration. More than the luxury of good coffee, the townspeople I speak to want the luxury of a good job.

PART 2

The politics of country

LESSON 10

The gulf between the main street and Parliament

When the children were very small and I was no longer working from the press gallery, I started yoga lessons at a monastery near home. I loved the physical nature of the practice but hated the discipline of mindfulness. I considered meditation a waste of time. There were a million jobs at home and yet I had to sit still with my mind as it fidgeted and fiddled, jumping from problem to problem. But when my yoga teacher left the district it left me strangely discombobulated. So I learned how to teach myself. The journalist in me approached training in a studious but cynical way, snorting at various hippy notions of consciousness and letting go. But the things we need creep up. Gradually my brain slowed down, expanded and settled into a more comfortable cradle.

The British psychiatrist and neuroscientist Iain McGilchrist has long pondered the question of why the brain is divided into two hemispheres. He goes past the usual definition that left brain equals analysis, right brain equals creative.[1] The left brain, he says, is the part that understands and wants explicit rules and procedures, while the right brain is the bigger-picture side, which understands meaning and context. The brain that stands back and considers. McGilchrist's broader point is that the left-brain functions of detail, technology and laws are dominating the Western world, to the detriment of right-brain functions, which perceive a bigger, more complex picture, appreciating nuance and subtlety. We need both sides to operate in tandem, but the modern world is requiring too much of the left and not enough of the right.

While it may be wishful thinking, it was my perception that the whole process of slowing down and away from the speed of the daily news cycle – as slow as it was in the early 2000s – changed my brain. I went whole weeks without reading the news or caring about whether the latest government statement contradicted the previous one. I would catch glimpses of events if a bulletin came on between the children's shows. The only times I would really focus were for big events, such as 9/11, which happened when my children were preschoolers.

My lived experience during that time away was much as I imagine that of the larger Australian populace who are not involved in politics. Life was punctuated by short news items, much like the old Sunday night movie was punctuated by ads.

It was in this frame of mind that I returned to the press gallery during Julia Gillard's government. I would drive in for the weeks Parliament was sitting, coming home each Friday. This changed life meant less time in my old routines, less time in a settled environment, less time in the natural world and more time analysing detail, endless legislation, assessing government process and looking for semantic differences to divine political shifts.

Something cracked in that Parliament. It was when politics lost even the artifice of attempted justification, when politicians started focusing squarely on the so-called base. I don't kid myself that politics was not always a bit of a circus, but in debate there was an attempt to answer a point and return volley with an agreement on basic facts. Sometime in the Rudd–Gillard–Rudd era that system broke down. Tony Abbott as opposition leader sounded the trumpets on this new era. During the forty-third Parliament, from 2010–13, certain politicians began saying things that were factually incorrect or fundamentally dishonest in their framing. For example, as a lamb producer's assistant, I was waiting for Barnaby Joyce's $100 lamb roast under the short-lived carbon price. It never arrived. In the forty-fourth Parliament Tony Abbott repeated the claim that the Adani coalmine would create 10,000 jobs, even after Adani's own economic consultant told Queensland's land court that his modelling had corrected that to a total of 1464 jobs, which included jobs related only indirectly to the mine, over thirty years. In the forty-fifth Parliament, Labor, as the originators of the Gonski education policy, opposed the Coalition's Gonski 2.0 policy, which delivered a clearer, needs-based funding policy architecture, because, Labor said, there was inadequate funding – even though a subsequent Labor government could ramp up funding while keeping the fundamental formula in place. As of 2018 the Labor opposition has also promised to reinstate the special deals for the Catholic school system, which casts aside the concept of students receiving the same amount of funding based on their need. By discarding Labor's own promised policy principles, the decision will simply allow the party to create a scare campaign in schools that desperately need certainty of funding.

As a journalist who cares about truth and accountability, it makes you feel like bursting a valve. Apart from writing the correct figure ad infinitum or rehashing the policy history in every story, what do you do if politicians keep disseminating tricky or incorrect information in the face of evidence to the contrary, in some cases aided and abetted by an increasingly partisan, hollowed-out media?

When us journalists were in the rip of the hung Parliament, we told ourselves that the pace would slow back down again once a government with a majority had won power. Yet Tony Abbott's prime ministership continued the frantic pace. That government fed the news cycle while increasing the constraints around media. Information was harder to get because it was controlled. It was harder to get on to government distribution lists, for example, if you were not a chosen outlet. Abbott had elements of Trump before Trump. He loved nothing more than throwing red meat to his base.

Stories were old in a few hours. Reaching back into those stories, a typical news day might be 27 October in 2014, a normal parliamentary sitting day. That day Tony Abbott wanted a 'mature debate' on tax revenue within the federation, including a look at the Goods and Services Tax. Barnaby Joyce was apologising to Parliament for his office making changes to the *Hansard* that did not reflect his answer. A burqa ban in Parliament was being argued between Tony Abbott and the then speaker Bronwyn Bishop, pertaining to who had said what to whom, at the same time as three men dressed in a burqa, a motorbike helmet and a Ku Klux Klan outfit tried to enter the building to make a point. Oh, and Liberal Indigenous MP Ken Wyatt and Labor Indigenous senator Nova Peris delivered a progress report on constitutional recognition. Each of those stories represented major issues, but we were so busy nailing down the most basic details on the run that not many journalists in the gallery had time to address any of their substance properly.

At that time I was learning the ropes of writing the live politics blog with *Guardian* political editor Katharine Murphy, who emphasised a recipe for getting facts right over speed of delivery, while lovingly sprinkling the whole dish with detailed critical analysis. Detail is everything in that world. Indeed, being a political journalist is in many ways being the left brain. Process, procedure, regulation and consequences are the stuff of our days. We scramble to report, repeat, analyse and consider (or not) all of these details, ad infinitum. We study the black letter law meanings and then divine hidden meanings. We impose these details on the voter, and the voter is often confused. Mostly, the voter has a life and no time to watch the detail. The broader Australian populace, the people both politicians and journalists serve, is like the right brain. Commonsense tells the voter that a lot of political outcomes don't make sense.

In 2017, some MPs discovered they held dual citizenship and were therefore ineligible for Parliament: this fiasco was a case in point. Section 44 of the constitution, which details the rules on parliamentarians and dual citizenship, was clear. Politicians, journalists and lawyers were busy working through the implications of the detail. The public was broadly confused by the constitution. As a friend said to me over a drink, 'Why don't they just have a moratorium and let everyone get their papers in order so they can go back to governing?' Indeed, that's what we would do if they were kids. Time out, get your tickets sorted for the merry-go-round and then we will get back in the queue in an orderly fashion. Here was a solution that spoke of commonsense, but our system, our laws, our very constitution, would not allow such a solution. My instinct was to bombard her with the relevant constitutional section, the difficulties of prosecuting a successful referendum, the fact that the High Court was the final arbiter for those politicians who were unsure of their status; overlay the political difficulties for government, given the finely balanced state of the Parliament, Malcolm Turnbull's internal problems in the Coalition party room on his right flank. But I just shut it and took a sip of wine.

It underlined to me that, as a voter, she saw the bigger picture. She just wanted this problem fixed so the government could go back to the business of issues that affected her family's life. In the midst of campaigning in the by-election forced on him by his parliamentary ineligibility due to dual New Zealand citizenship, then deputy prime minister Barnaby Joyce picked up that voter sentiment and ran with it. He spoke to Katharine Murphy on the hustings in New England, where he had to win back his seat. At issue were some of the ministerial decisions he'd made while ineligible to sit in the Parliament.

'Look, argue whether you have a road here or here. If you argue about things which actually matter in people's lives, rather than saying, "Mate, I think we've got you on subsection Q4 part B Roman numeral two," people say, "I haven't got a fucking clue what you are talking about – but all I know is you are a dweeb."'

This is not to say that the voter is the ultimate receptacle of commonsense. A ride in the ute with the radio on is proof enough. A bloke rings John Laws, the man with a $10,000 golden micro-phone.[2] The guy starts railing about hopeless politicians and how they don't understand the real world. 'Now, if we had blokes like you and Alan Jones running the country, the world would be a better place,' this man says. So I am not arguing that the voter is the oracle, holder of all knowledge. But it pays to consider why the Parliament is considered so far removed from the people it serves.

Obviously the pesky details that frustrate voters do matter. Like the brain, both kinds of detail are required for the human to function properly. You cannot change the constitution just because a lot of voters have no patience for the letter of the law. But if voters in my town are any guide to future elections, Australia will keep turning over political parties until its people find a team that gets it right, and I would argue that this is because something fundamen-tal has broken in the relationship between government and citizens. By citizens, I mean casual observers rather than active participants.

'The major parties, the people who are running the country and keeping things going, they have lost contact with the local people,' a sixty-something man tells me. When I ask him if he thinks it will change, he says, 'When my grandkids are walking around with walking sticks.'

A third of the population, or thereabouts, now votes for minor parties. Nowhere is the diminished trust in the major parties more clear than in the Senate. After the 2016 election, the Coalition went into office with thirty senators. Labor had twenty-six, and the crossbench – if you count the Greens, as the parliamentary library does – had twenty senators. And if there was one thing that united those twenty senators on that crossbench, it was that they appealed to the voter using the old Democrats' concept of keeping the bastards honest. If these senators could not get their hands on government itself, they could act as a check against major party power.

The crossbench agrees that voters have lost faith in governments. The crossbench mostly agree on policies such as the financial services Royal Commission. (Labor came to this policy much later than the Greens and other crossbenchers.) The crossbench mostly agrees on the need for a federal anti-corruption body. Labor came to this policy in January 2018, at which point Malcolm Turnbull made comforting noises.

More than anything, the ideas that unite the crossbench represent my main street. Conversations centre on lack of trust and the sense that clever political advocates have changed the system to suit themselves. Here is Ken, the former abattoir worker and history buff: 'The major parties are there to see how they are going to fight to win the next election. It's like a business. They are trying to outdo the other one. They aren't worrying about the people out in Australia, they are just looking after themselves in one little corner. Bugger the ones outside.'

The people out in Australia. The separation is not just considered metaphorical. It is considered physical, like another country. There is Australia. Then there is the land of Parliamentalia – a castle surrounded by a moat. In Parliamentalia, anybody can argue any stance and make it sound credible. These skills, learned in school debating teams and university competitions on the road to a political career, have become the very things voters despise. Ipso facto, they don't trust anyone who sounds polished. No one in their world speaks like a politician, which explains the attraction of the anti-politician politician.

The divide between the composition of the Parliament and the people it serves continues to widen. The 2016 parliamentary handbook lists 226 members and senators, of which ninety-one describe their occupations as having been political consultants/ advisors, state and local politicians, party and union administrators, union officials, researchers and electorate officers, and public service/policy managers. Another fifty were in business as executives, managers or full-time company directors. Another twenty-four were lawyers and six were from the media. Of the recognisable jobs outside the extended political system, there were eight farmers, five military or police officers, four doctors, one teacher, one in real estate and one a psychologist. Thirty-two per cent of the Parliament is made up of women. This is our representative body.

Politics is driven by human nature. It makes sense that people with an interest in politics spend time in the offices of a politician. But when the Parliament fails to reflect the people it serves, it is bound to increase the actual and perceived divide between served and serving. Then there is the nature of our meritocracy. Are these people preselected because they are the best candidates, or are they preselected because they know people in the game? As a result, are good people with more diverse life experiences being shut out?

State and federal Liberal member Alby Schultz, our local MP for much of my early time in the country, told me once that his great advantage was he never wanted to be a minister, which allowed him a wonderful freedom to say what he thought. Ambition creates a ball and chain for the modern politician, and the main street recognises that.

Sitting in her drapery shop surrounded by bolts of fabric, buttons and bows, Lorraine Brown explains how she feels that politicians have moved so far away from our main street. 'Our politicians basically go from school to university, and do law, and go into politics, and they don't actually live in the real world and particularly at grassroots levels. I've said that to [a wealthy local businessman] over the years. He gets a bit carried away with grandiose things, and I say, "You have lived with money too long. You have forgotten what it's like down here for us because you are not attached to it. So you forget how difficult it is down here trying to make ends meet." They never actually touch it. If you go back to the early Labor Party, they were coming from grassroots like Alby Schultz.'

Lorraine can see the constraints placed on members by their parties. There is a recognition that members can go into the Parliament for the right reasons, but then are weakened by a rigid party structure and a thousand compromises.

'Unfortunately, even our local politicians are restricted by parties. They are restricted from speaking up. They are restricted stepping forward because it is not what the party wants them to do. I think that is wrong, again. I think we should go back to: if it doesn't fit with your electorate, you should be able to cross the floor and make a point of it. Those [major party] politicians are gone now. Alby was probably one of the last of them.'

If there is no trust and if there is perception that the political system changes people for the worse, then there can be no faith in political outcomes for the voter. Donald Trump exhorted black voters to give him a go because, hell, it couldn't get much worse. 'What do you have to lose by trying something new, like Trump? You're living in your poverty, your schools are no good, you have no jobs, 58 per cent of your youth is unemployed, what the hell do you have to lose?'[3]

That could equally apply to small-town Australia, not because of the gap so much as the view that politics bears no relation to many people's lives and cannot deliver for them. A fair section of the community – mostly the ones breaking away from the major parties – feel they no longer have a stake in the outcome. For them, choosing a politician is as life-changing as voting in *Masterchef*. And most of the time a *Masterchef* contestant sounds more convincing than a modern-day politician. Plus you finish the day with a decent feed.

'Locally, I always voted for Alby, but when it comes to the Senate I would find all the silly ones and vote them in,' says Ken Pearsall. 'When Pauline Hanson got in, over at the Men's Shed didn't they go right off? I said she is going to get in [to Parliament] and stir the others up. Now they are listening.'

Lorraine thinks that if voters support outliers at either end of the political spectrum, government is dragged back to the centre. 'The only way people can protest is to vote for Pauline Hanson and those ones. I think a lot of people went towards the Greens Party but I think the repercussions of that weren't good. But I think in many ways they were disappointed and the Greens have lost ground a bit now.

'So they are going to all these other little parties. I believe that is why Trump is . . . president . . . Because the Western world political parties – and, let's face it, there is not much different between Labor and Liberal here – they are almost the same, [so] where do you go? If you are disillusioned with those two parties, where do you go?'

Trump has been president for the better part of the year when Lorraine and I sit down for a series of conversations. She is a fan of Trump because he says it like it is. Saying it like it is. This is a big plus for politicians, as I hear again and again. It almost counts more than what the politician actually says.

'I love the man, I love him because he actually says what the people are thinking and saying. That's what people want. They don't want things to be covered up all the time with lots of political reasons. Not saying the things they should be saying. He is standing up.'

Lorraine's example, relevant at the time, was Trump's stance against the United Nations. 'What I am seeing now is Trump standing up against the United Nations. What have the United Nations done in recent times? Bugger all. Let's face it. They are highly paid people doing bugger all over most situations in the world. He stood up and said that, basically.'[4]

Lorraine notes that the UK prime minister Theresa May came out in a less blustery way and backed him in. 'Again, I believe that is part of the reason for Brexit, as well. So I think this is happening as a protest against the fact that the major parties are not doing anything. They are there but they are not doing anything.'

The modern political relationship between politician and voter has stretched thin, with a complexity that is hard to pin down. Substantial longitudinal studies such as the Australian Electoral Study find that trust in politicians is low.[5] In 2016, 26 per cent believe people in government can be trusted, compared with 74 per cent who believe people in government look after themselves. According to the same study, nearly half of us, 40 per cent, are not satisfied with democracy.

In the main street, voting has become a hopeful act. Each time people vote, they hope for better things, but they do not expect better things. They are looking for authenticity, or a bright and shiny policy idea that might catch their imagination. Or just a brand-name outsider. In thinking about politics, we tend to consider our priorities, add them to our values and then look for a candidate to fulfil the criteria. When we find someone we prefer, we feel that sense of hope and we are prepared to hear them spin a story. And while a little voice is saying, 'Yeah nah,' we largely swallow the candidate's story because it may align with our own beliefs and values. Talking to my fellow residents, I am reminded of the elephant and rider analogy coined by the US social psychologist Jonathan Haidt, who sought to answer the question of how our view of morality guides our views of politics and religion. He contends that the rational brain is like the rider, but our emotions are like the elephant beneath. We think we are coming to our decision based on rational evidence, but our emotions play a bigger part than we think.

So with the elephant in charge we are vulnerable as segments of the media amplify emotions like fear and loathing if they disagree with certain policies. With an eye to the polls, the politicians panic and we can smell their desperation. Policies are hurriedly rewritten and formerly high principles get thrown out the door, leaving politicians to argue the exact opposite of what they had so earnestly argued previously. Think of the 2018 reversal by the Coalition government on the need for an increase to the Medicare levy to part-fund the National Disability Insurance Scheme (NDIS). In 2017, Treasurer Scott Morrison brought in his brother-in-law Gary, who suffers from multiple sclerosis, to Parliament the day after the budget to argue the tax increase was about 'helping your mates'. Until it wasn't, because the government had it covered. As Morrison prepared for the next budget, he said the government wanted to deliver the NDIS in the 'most efficient and effective way possible'. Or recall Labor arguing for sector-blind school funding for every student based on need as recommended by Gonski, until they promised an extra $250 million to the Catholic sector to wedge the Turnbull government in 2018. Like good high-school debaters, modern politicians appear to get their topic on the day, follow the coach as to whether to argue the affirmative or negative, and flip it when they need to. This can only feed cynicism.

In some cases, governments get the macro policy right but fail to translate it for the voter in a micro way. My kids were still at the local primary school during the Global Financial Crisis (GFC) when the Rudd government rolled out its 2009 stimulus package.

I was a long way from the press gallery, still ensconsed in school council doings, teaching yoga to kids and driving around southern New South Wales to various school competitions. I had only a sheep's eye on national political proceedings, but it certainly came across the school agenda when Kevin Rudd announced at the start of the school year there would be a bloody great infrastructure package worth $42 billion. School infrastructure was at the heart of the package, with schools to receive $14.7 billion for halls, libraries, sporting facilities, science and language labs; they could also apply for capital expenditure grants and maintenance grants.

In June of that year Treasury outlined the logic behind targeting schools: school land was readily available; there was a supply of standard building designs already approved; there is a school in almost every town, which would spread the effect of the stimulus; the stimulus would supply jobs and a physical legacy. Treasury officials said at the time, 'This [is] important because the slowdown in Australia is not expected to have an especially strong geographic focus. That is, the economic weakness is expected to be geographically broadly spread and therefore it is useful if the stimulus is geographical broadly based.'[6]

Conventional wisdom and hindsight shows that Australia did escape the worst effects of the GFC because of the stimulus. 'From an economic point of view, the public spending sealed the Great Escape from the GFC,' George Megalogenis has written.[7]

For me, the fascinating thing was watching the response on the ground in a small town to a multi-million-dollar government investment. I was intimately involved in our local primary school at that time. I knew the kids, the parents, and spent time reading to infants and teaching sun salutations to the older kids. The teachers struggled daily with classes that held a wide range of abilities. Resources were stretched for students who needed particular attention. I saw classes trashed by kids who had desperate family circumstances. A $50,000 teacher's aide in each classroom would have been a great start. What parents in our school saw was the government handing over a couple of million bucks to a construction company, which was overseen by another level of government (state), to build a school hall next to the older school hall.

Of course, the government and Treasury were watching the GFC barrelling down at them and needed to survey the whole landscape and act to stop the country facing a 'shitstorm', as Kevin Rudd called it.[8] This does not mean those decisions are understood on the ground. People were genuinely confused about the priority of the spending and it was particularly so among those parents with tight budgets or small businesses, who had to watch their bottom lines closely. Of all the things we need, they said, a school hall is not one of them. The decisions appeared illogical and inexplicable no matter how successfully the economics lined up.

You don't even need to go to the more contentious issues such as the school stimulus package. Every community has stories like these ones – of mismatched spending that has not responded to community needs. Regional Australia Institute's Jack Archer, who consults with many different communities, says dissatisfaction with government template spending is a common theme that highlights the disconnection. 'Every time I mention this, people lean forward and tell me a story.' He tells me the story of how the federal government wanted to fund a night bus in a particular Indigenous community to stop inter-clan violence. The community came back and said, We don't need a night bus to stop violence. We need some resources for mediation, and if we do that the bus will still be good but it won't have much of a job to do. But the government did not have the flexibility or the 'agility' to direct the funding to a different action such as mediation. Government pretty much said, Sorry, what colour bus do you want?

It is these interactions that have contributed to the straining relationship between all levels of governments and citizens in smaller communities, because they are visible examples of why government processes feel broken. In a small community, where change is less obvious, decisions like infrastructure spending – on anything from footpaths to school halls – is immediately noticeable and remarked upon. Observation is truth.

People also notice when grants are rolled out, such as at election times or when winning margins get slimmer. When a local community group got a grant for some construction work, the office bearer told me, 'I'm sure that's because we are causing a little bit of a problem for them, and they are looking at this area very carefully and how can they appease us a little bit, so they looked at it and said, Here's one for the seat. Let's give them something.

'This is where politicians underestimate the general public. They are trying to pull the wool over our eyes and we are awake to it.'

Another policy example of the gulf between the Parliament and the main street was Malcolm Turnbull's 'Jobs and Growth' slogan in the 2016 election campaign. For all the discontent with government, on the main street the one issue over which there was no dispute was the need for jobs. Long-term jobs. Not scraps of jobs, skerricks of shifts, but solid jobs with futures. Jobs that you could point to for a housing loan. Jobs that you could build a life around. After this Coalition mantra in 2016, some 400,000 jobs were created over 2017, of which 300,000 were full-time and 100,000 were part-time. But small towns have not seen it happening. They have seen casual jobs that come and go. They have also heard about corporate tax cuts, which might translate into a job in a city but not in their small town. 'They talk about when industry closes, there is always going to be jobs there. Well, what jobs are going to be there?' said one older man at the Men's Shed.

When I think about the gulf between the main street and the Parliament, I think it comes back to the biggest change in my reporting life, which has been the pace of the media cycle and therefore the pace of political, and specifically policy, announce-ments. Voters are expected to digest policy quickly and decide on its merits as they sit watching political debate speed past like so many train stations on the XPT. A small town proceeds at a slower pace. If I have learned something from my involvement in the local newspapers and progress committees, it is that change needs careful and patient explanation. This is hard enough at a micro level, when you can run into your councillors in the local supermarket. It is no wonder voters are perplexed and disconnected with modern politics and politicians.

Active voters want responsive governments to explain the logic of spending decisions. They need time to chew over government policy – time that is no longer there, given the speed of the polit-ical cycle. (I don't discount the fact that sometimes, no matter how appropriate the policy prescription or how well explained, the decision won't wash with voters until its wisdom is proven.) Voters also want responsive governments with mechanisms to change those decisions to better fit local conditions after feedback from community. Although this is what a member of parliament is for, small-town residents who are not connected find accessing their MPs difficult. With the size of rural seats increasing as popu-lation changes, getting to an MP is not an easy task. I live in an inner regional town and our federal seat, held by Nationals leader Michael McCormack, is 49,000 square kilometres. The federal seat of Lingiari, held by Labor MP Warren Snowdon, covers most of the Northern Territory, at 1.3 million square kilometres. Durack in Western Australia, held by Liberal MP Melissa Price, is 1.6 million square kilometres. These are not the MPs you bump into at the supermarket. And yet without more responsive mechanisms, governments at all levels will not get credit for their spending or efforts.

When I started political reporting proper in the early 1990s, journalists were able to get hold of public servants and policy advisors to explain and discuss the details of government policy. Relationship-building over lunch or coffee with mid-level to senior bureaucrats and policy advisors – people who know stuff – was the ordinary fare of the political reporter's day. There were benefits for both sides. The journalist was able to understand the policy and make contacts who were helpful for their job, and the bureaucrat could educate the journalist in her area of expertise and persuade said journalist of the best policy option. A journalist who understands the logic of a policy is one who will share that insight with the public.

That relationship-building is much rarer now. Governments are too jumpy to trust public servants; public servants lack confidence in journalists, or are simply not allowed to speak to the media because of public service rules, which determine only certain employees can do so. Journalists rarely have spare time between filing the copy needed to fill the insatiable internet editions of their papers. So policy stories are much harder to write, and even when they are written, those articles rarely get as much traffic as the latest outrage story or gotcha moment. Readers have to take responsibility for their own part in this story.

Yet paradoxically, in my experience living away from the city, there is interest in policy discussions among voters. In the months after I left the press gallery, I had more conversations with ordinary people about policy than I'd ever had in my recent years in Parliament. There, I'd covered many policy stories, of course, but they were framed in terms of whether a bill would fracture a particular party or whether it could get through the Parliament. At home, all I had to do for a policy discussion was to drive to town.

On one such day I went to fill a script with the pharmacist, Mark 'Dougo' Douglass. Mark came to town with his wife, Lyn, and children in 2002 to buy the local chemist. Mark and Lyn hurled themselves into the community. He stood for council, got involved in the rugby club. She taught swimming and is currently secretary of the local Country Education Foundation.

Issues relating to heart and blood pressure are big health problems in the town, in line with the rest of the country. But racing up the charts is the use of pain medications, such as the opioids – a subject that has received a lot of publicity in the US under the Trump administration. In the pharmacy Dougo starts talking to me about Australia's impending ban on over-the-counter codeine products that also contain opioids. He says regional communities will suffer because lower-dose codeine products are used to treat short-term pain, like a football injury or falling off a horse, especially when you can't easily get in to see a doctor, as is often the case in small towns.

I have heard about the rising use of opioids and tracked the debate in the United States. I question his resistance to the ban. So he invites me behind the counter to see the physical manifestation of his biggest concern. In the pharmaceutical dispensing station, Dougo shows me his 'Drugs of Addiction', or DD, safe. It's large, 1.5 metres square, and it's full of boxes, neatly stacked according to brand.

'It will last a week,' he says.

Dougo describes the trajectory of opioid use in Australia. In 1979, when he was a young pharmacist fresh out of university, he carried a set of keys on his belt for the DD cupboard. It was tiny, about a foot by a foot, and it was rarely used.

'For pain, we had Panadol, a bit of Panadeine, and when you needed something stronger you had Panadeine Forte, which was Panadol with thirty milligrams of codeine,' he says. Endone, well that was a big deal. Any usage was faithfully recorded in a drug of addiction book and the book would last for years. If someone was really sick they might get an injection of pethidine or morphine.

'When we got DD – drugs of addiction – in, it was a big thing. You might get one script a day, or every couple of days. When a person got Endone, you would go, Wow. It was usually for a really bad back, or cancer pain. We would get those and we would not sell much. If we got twenty or forty tabs that would be big. Your antennae would be up and you would say, We have to be careful with this. We would check the doctor had written it correctly and we would ring the doctor up and ensure he really did write the script. Every time a DD came in we would ring the doctor to make sure.'

Then it began to change. Slowly at first. Then since the mid- to late 1990s, he says, it has been exponential. 'It's gone *whooshka*.'

Dougo tried to work through the possibilities. Maybe it's because there are more people with cancer. It might be the ageing population. When he started as a young chemist, there were lots of veterans from the Second World War, a lot of people who had injuries caused by war and labour. He had quite a few Rats of Tobruk coming into the pharmacy back then, who had lived and worked hard. He would have thought there was a lot of pain in those days, but why have we got so much pain now? He keeps asking why.

'Some people believe that once you start a person on an opioid, they get on to a thing called the pain cycle. And once they are on the pain cycle, without a proper pain intervention by a pain specialist – and there is not many of those and certainly none around here – if they don't get into a proper pain specialist then this cycle devolves to higher and higher doses because you tend to build up a tolerance to the opioids like alcohol.'

People return, month after month, to have prescriptions filled, but with no other health advice to treat the causes. They are not seeing pain management specialists or physiotherapists or psychologists or other allied health professionals. 'They just go to the doctor and go, "I'm in pain" and he goes, "I'll give you this."'

Dougo feels that governments are swayed by a whole lot of people who know the theory but not what it is like on the ground – professors, bureaucrats, people with lots of textbook knowledge but who are not dealing with the public on a daily basis and seeing how their policies work in practice. In a small community it is stressful to see people who you care about not looked after in the best possible way. He worried so much he took months off to try to stop worrying.

When he started in pharmacy, Dougo saw one script a day for drugs of addiction. Now he sees twenty, and he hates to think how many scripts a city pharmacy would fill. 'They must have huge walk-in safes like a bank vault.'

At the end of August 2017, Australia's Annual Overdose Report 2017 was released by the Pennington Institute.[9] That report explained that more than twice as many Australians were dying from accidental overdose than were dying from car accidents. It found that Fentanyl, which it described as one hundred times more potent than pure morphine, was at the forefront of the increasing number of deaths. The report warned that Australia was 'on track' to experience a US-style drug overdose crisis. It also showed a marked increase in overdose deaths across regional Australia, as accidental drug-related deaths in rural and regional areas started to outstrip metropolitan Australia. (In 2010, the per capita accidental death rate between metropolitan and regional Australia was similar, at 6.0 (metropolitan) and 5.9 (regional). By 2015, accidental drug-related deaths in regional Australia had reached 7.3 deaths per 100,000, in comparison with 5.8 deaths per 100,000 in metropolitan areas.)

Dougo reckons that Australia is about five years behind America in our opioid addiction. He worries that in the current medical system, the path of least resistance is unwittingly encouraging people to get hooked. GPs do not have time to talk to their patients properly about the drugs they are taking, and the pharmacy-warehouse model does not have the relationship with customers to keep an eye on them. At the same time, community pharmacies are being squeezed by cuts to remuneration, cuts that reward high turnover.

He tries to impress on his customers the 'really, really dangerous side effects of the opioids'. Apart from addiction, the more immediate physical side effects are loss of cognition and falls, not to mention shocking constipation which requires ongoing doses of laxatives. 'That's okay if a person is terminally ill, but it's no good if you are forty-five.'

What really angers Dougo is government. Politicians should be charged with fraud, he says. And he has seen the influence of big health-care groups and lobbyists on governments, state and federal. When he began his work as a pharmacist, the doctor owned his practice, as did the chemist. Increasingly, big corporations have taken over and it is not unusual for him to get offers to buy his pharmacy. He has seen the growth of the Pharmaceutical Benefits Scheme – from 900 medicines when he started to 4900.

He describes a decoupling of leadership from decisions that are good for people. 'Leadership is about making hard decisions. They put seatbelts in and at the time I couldn't believe these things, they were so clunky. Or, remember when they first penalised you for throwing shit out your window. I remember going to Canberra and there were papers up against the fence. That was normal. There was shit everywhere, but now we think it's terrible.

'I understand we require brave policy decisions because we are going through all these changes – innovation. But government is scared to make any decisions. On renewables, on education, that has become churn and burn as well. You can deliver education in thousands of ways but the only measure is are people becoming educated?

'These things are important, but people aren't important anymore, and that is the shift. And politicians are gutless. Everyone knows how to solve it, but as soon as the Libs say one thing, Labor will say the reverse. And then there is the lobby groups. Ramsay Health Care is one of the biggest donors to the Liberal party. It's terrible. The policy is [that] everyone knows what to do but they just refuse to make a decision. They can't have a bipartisan result. That's the problem.

'And yet people I see are fatter and sicker and getting older. More cancers is one of the reasons, but there is weight gain; we have a lot of mental health issues for different reasons. You are more likely to be fat; you are likely to be involved in dangerous behaviours; and you might be more likely to be on pain medications and psychotic medications. We have thirty-five per cent of people with mental health disorders. Maybe that is the reason for some of the pain medications, as well.

'So it's the poor old punter that needs the outcome, and it's the doctors and pharmacists and nurses and dentists supplying services that are the meat in the sandwich.'

Dougo would prescribe a medical system that rewarded preventative health with a focus on the patient. It is a concept known as a 'medical home', where the GP sits on top of an overarching structure, like the head of triage or a traffic cop. The doctor would direct the services for patients in order to keep them well, whether it be specialists, allied health services, exercise physiologists, massage, physiotherapists, mental health services. The pharmacist would have a more active role, in much the same way as a hospital pharmacist, who works out exactly how much medicine the patient needs, rather than the generic instructions on a pillbox made in Germany. The pharmacist would also monitor weight, cholesterol and blood pressure. So the doctor and pharmacist would work in cahoots to keep the patient healthy and out of the doctor's waiting room. The sticking point is that the remuneration structure would need to change, but by Dougo's reckoning, 'You remunerate the doctor to keep them well and you are going to remunerate the pharmacy to dispense less. The doctor should still be remunerated to be the overarching guidance, and the patient should always be the focus.'

My mother was prescribed opioids for decades to treat the pain of rheumatoid arthritis. They were her sleeping years, when she took her double masters in literature and education to bed. When her joy of teaching was replaced by a fog of obsessions over when to take what tablets. Meals were spent nodding off. Sentences were punctuated with long pauses. It made me angry and frustrated – at the doctor, the chemist and the system. It took the tragedy of the death of her partner, the friendship and generosity of a group of nuns, and a committed doctor to wean her off the opioids. In twenty years she was robbed of her vocation, her quality of life and relationships. She went from a working person to a disability pension. Productivity, zero. Now she is contributing through volunteering in a high-care nursing home and we love her return to our world. For us, it was a family issue. But for Australia, it is a policy issue.

=

Main-street voters and the political class cannot operate without each other – they are two halves of the same democracy – and yet the thread that holds them together is stretching thin. Voters are increasingly turning to minor parties and independents because they have no faith in today's political outcomes. While some minor parties and independents have a lot to offer, demagogues only increase the risk of voter self-harm. People in my town report being disengaged from a political system because they see politicians and media serving themselves. Yet there is no shortage of political discussion on the main street; indeed, people are not averse to discussing policy. It is just that the policy changes so quickly and politicians argue from both sides of an issue in a short space of time so often that people are loathe to commit energy anymore. Rural voters around me have a kind of political burn-out. That they share with the city, but what makes my fellow country voters interesting is whether they will change their long-held voting patterns. They know that the most potent, last-resort political act they can carry out is to change their vote.

LESSON 11

Rural politics is stuck in an old model

My son studied Latin for the HSC. He was trying to memorise a speech by Cicero, in which the young Roman lawyer defends Sextus Roscius, who has been charged with the murder of his father. My son is bored with study so I ask him to tell me the story to humour me.

'Well, Mum [rolls eyes], it's a legal case. They are trying to work out who killed Sextus's father. Cicero argued that Sextus's cousins, who lived in the city, were more street-smart and more likely to murder someone than Sextus. This is because Sextus lived in the country and lived a rustic lifestyle. Cicero argued that country people were less likely to commit murder than city people.'

And right there is a theme throughout human history, which you have to acknowledge underlies many discussions on rural politics. It is an agrarian ideology – that the country is good and true, and the city is wicked and sinful. In Australia, this country–city debate has been a running theme in political discussion since white settlers crossed the Great Dividing Range. Almost as soon as areas west of the divide opened up to Europeans, those who inhabited rural areas began to complain about being left behind. In 1866, the *Wagga Wagga Express* reported that the squatters saw their 'prosperity crippled' and resources 'retarded', and believed they were 'swamped in the Sydney legislature'.[1]

City–country conflict drove the poetic cage fight between Banjo Paterson and Henry Lawson in the *Bulletin* debate over whether the Bush beat the City or vice versa. Sporting events such as the City versus Country rugby league match played up the conflict between metropolitan and the country, much to the delight of audiences. The city–country football match was played in some form or another for a century until it was scrapped in the 2017 season. As city populations grew disproportionately, and country populations dwindled, city teams dominated and were accused of hollowing out country ranks by buying bush players. Not even a 1987 rule change, which allowed players who originally played in country senior teams to represent the bush, could save the competition. If the same team always comes out on top, where is the fun in that? No one wants to watch a predictable match, so that game fell away.

As it is with sport, so it is with politics. Rural Australia is a minority population, notwithstanding the historical cultural imagination that holds it close, so with only 30 per cent of the population, rural issues do not dominate either the political agenda or media debates. Given democracy is a numbers game and 70 per cent of the population lives in cities, that is no surprise. The surprise to me was that rural people do not use their 30 per cent to vote more strategically, as the people who have made seats marginal on the outer edges of our big cities have done.

When I lived in inner-city Sydney, I never gave a rural party much thought. However, if you move out of metropolitan Australia and have a shred of political interest, your attention soon turns to the best way to get a bit of country representation. So in the years when my children were small I spent a lot of time delving into the history of rural politics.

The Country Party started as a loose coalition of independent-minded rural MPs who were cranky about their treatment by legislators and wanted to leverage influence in city legislatures. The party's foundation can be traced from the mid-1800s, when Europeans were settling west of the Great Dividing Range. Squatters were taking up land and shearers were organising, in the first of Australia's unions, a movement that quickly spread through Victoria, New South Wales, Queensland and South Australia. Farmers were also forming their own unions in most states, and they began discussing the best way to represent their interests.

The organisation of those ideas coalesced in 1920 with the formation of the Country Party. The party held the ideology of agrarianism at its heart. Australian political scientist Don Aitkin has described the Australian version of this ideology as 'country-mindedness'. Anyone who has followed Australian politics in the bush will recognise the ideas in Aitkin's oft-quoted definition:

(i) Australia depends on its primary producers for its high standard of living, for only those who produce a physical good add to the country's wealth.

(ii) Therefore all Australians, from city and country alike, should in their own interest support policies aimed at improving the position of primary industries.

(iii) Farming and grazing, and rural pursuits generally, are virtuous, ennobling and co-operative; they bring out the best in people.

(iv) In contrast, city life is competitive and nasty, as well as parasitical.

(v) The characteristic Australian is a countryman, and the core elements of the national character come from the struggles of

country people to tame their environment and make it productive. City people are much the same over.

(vi) For all these reasons, and others like defence, people should
be encouraged to settle in the country, not in the city.

(vii) But power resides in the city, where politics is trapped
in a sterile debate about classes. There has to be a separate
political party for country people to articulate the true voice of
the nation.[2]

Although Aitkin declared the death of countrymindedness as an
ideology in 1986, I can hear echoes of these sentiments today. When
Australia was locked in yet another debate about drought funding,
agriculture minister Barnaby Joyce argued that drought relief for
'mums and dads' was more important than assistance for redundant
car workers (who presumably were not mums and dads). It was early
in 2014 and the Abbott government was trying to run an argument
that the age of entitlement was over, at the same time as bringing
forward a drought assistance package. Joyce argued that farming was
different to other businesses because it was subject to the vagaries
of the weather. On ABC's *7.30*, host Leigh Sales suggested weather
was a contingency farmers would surely factor into their business
plan. Why should farmers be a special case when other businesses
couldn't rely on government to mitigate their risks?

'Well, because precisely this: you and I, Leigh, can only sustain
ourselves if we eat, so they are dealing with a product that is morally
good and that is right and therefore in itself engenders a desire by
the nation, a good nation, to make sure that we maintain our own
capacity to feed ourselves and those people who do the great job of
feeding ourselves and others.

'There's also just the human dignity side of it that these are mums
and dads, these are mums and dads who I believe are fundamentally different to a person who can go to the marketplace and secure

funding by reason of a share float or being able to raise capital on the back of a huge corporate backing.'[3]

Sales countered that the car workers who were made redundant as the car industry pulled out of Australia were mums and dads, too. Joyce came back: '[General Motors'] power is vastly in excess of a mum and dad who is living out in the heat and the dust and the flies with cattle dying around them, who has no opportunity to try and keep the sustenance of those cattle up so they survive. I think that's an entirely different scenario.'

Barnaby was following the script handed down from his fore-bears, as well as reaching back into the old vinyl collection for a sad song. I would like a dollar for every time I have heard city residents complain about whingeing farmers, 'privatising the profits and socialising the losses'. And why wouldn't they complain? That is what they hear from some of our most visible political representatives, though there is a fair proportion of farmers who opposed former drought assistance schemes such as the Exceptional Circumstances (EC) package. As one farmer put it to me, 'Why back a three-legged horse?' During the period of the EC program, which ended in 2012, there was a fair portion who believed that no-strings-attached interest payments were backing the wrong businesses. This diversity of thinking is rarely heard by city audiences, who mostly conjure up an image of farmers with their hand out.

Countrymindedness really took off in the second stage of rural political development, from 1920 to 1949. This was when the Country Party in its infancy experimented with varying levels of independence from its conservative partner, the forerunner to the Liberal Party. In the process, the party also toyed with the idea of grabbing the balance of power. It was a politically volatile stage, due to the Depression and the Second World War. During this phase, rural policies were driven either by the Country Party or rural inde-pendents who could not conform to the Country Party's approach.

The third stage in rural political development, from 1949–96, could be characterised for the longevity of country-based power that was by then embedded in government via the persistence of the Coalition. The return of the Menzies government allowed the Country Party to maximise its power under the leadership of John 'Black Jack' McEwen, and, during the years of the Fraser government, under Doug Anthony. For nearly fifty years there were no rural federal independents. Countrymindedness was effectively woven into government policy, causing complaints from some city audiences; in 1975 the party changed its name to the National Party partly in an attempt to appeal more to wider constituencies.

Historian and academic Ken Buckley's piece in *Meanjin* in 1972 still stands out for its blunt force. 'In GODZONE, these are the people who are most convinced that they are the Chosen and that if God fails them temporarily by sending drought or glutted markets, then the rest of the population owes them not merely a living but maintenance of their capital assets,' he wrote. He puzzled over the Australian Labor Party's refusal to attack rural interests, while acknowledging the ALP's motive to win country seats. He predicted that the 'tyranny of the country over the city' was due to be overthrown: 'The day of the sheep and their owners is ending.' The decline of the rural sector, he argued, represented 'one of the best prospects for Australia's future'.[4]

When Hawke came to power in 1983, he heaped praise on country Australia. 'No Australian resource is more important than our land. No sector of Australian industry is more important than our great primary industries, which still provide fifty per cent of Australia's export income in normal circumstances.'

Later that year Hawke urged national reconciliation when he compared the conflict between city and country people to the conflict between business and unions. He told the 1983 National Farmers' Federation conference that in the same way the government had started the process of business and the unions working to better understand each other, it hoped to 'end the artificial conflict of interest between city and country'.

'There are, in my opinion, far too many misunderstandings by city people of the problems and needs of country people. As a party and now as a government, we reject completely the concept of conflict between city and country. We depend on each other and we need each other.'[5]

Hawke did not mention any idea of the country misunderstanding of city people, which is also a feature of rural debate. Country people, myself included, sometimes fall back on the old sport of stereotyping city populations. City people garner all the government services. City people don't appreciate rural people or their industries. Instead, we need to think more deeply about how to assist with each other's problems and drive better national cohesion. A Hawke-style consensus.

Of course, consensus achieved under the Hawke government was precisely to bring about the big economic reforms which deregulated the Australian economy. And in spite of those first Hawke overtures at the beginning of his term, Labor lost support in the bush. Politics is a numbers game and the party turned towards more populated areas to win support. As the economic reforms began to bite, it was challenging for rural Australia, watching banks and post offices close in small-town main streets, watching the tariff walls come tumbling down, watching interest rates climb, watching banks foreclose on neighbours. Country towns turned inward and generally hung on to the belief that things would change once the Coalition came back to office.

And so began the fourth stage in rural political development: the years from 1996, when Liberal leader John Howard – a self-described Lazarus with a triple bypass – rose to claim government. That year – the year I moved to the farm – represented a turning point in the rural political landscape, because while the Coalition won a swag of rural and regional seats, voters finally understood that the newly deregulated economy had bipartisan support.

At the same time, a young, simultaneously nervous and inflammatory operator called Pauline Hanson was evolving. In her early days as a politician she had been dumped by the Liberal Party, and her defiance stood out in the 1990s political monoculture. Her plain, simple language mirrored a section of rural Australian sentiment that white working people (rural and regional) had been missing out while other minorities were getting ahead. From 1996, the revolt against neo-liberal economics began to emerge, not just in One Nation.

In the tradition of the underdog, the rural voter has a soft spot for any politician who will stand up against a more powerful force. In more recent times, the more powerful baddie could be a bigger regional centre, a big city, a big union, a big corporation (especially a big bank), the forces of globalisation or even the United Nations. I have heard complaints about all of these on my main street. So that stance of Hanson was not new. (The irony was that while she targeted more powerful major parties, she also picked on minorities that don't wield a lot of power: Indigenous people, Asians, and, later, Muslims.)

The National Party has tended to hold the line against the outsider political agenda. For example, the party has supported a free trade agenda for their agricultural constituency and economically rationalist policies that resulted in the sale of government assets like Telstra, albeit while establishing a telecommunications fund for the bush. In more recent years some National MPs have stepped outside their party policy on more popular and/or populist policies. Where the National Party backs the Fair Work Commission for its decision to cut penalty rates, Queensland LNP MP George Christensen opposes it. Nationals senator John 'Whacka' Williams was largely on his own in his party as he worked assiduously to pressure the banks over dodgy practices, and was ahead of his own party when it finally backed a Royal Commission to scrutinise the financial services sector. Nationals MP Andrew Broad spoke against raising the pension age to seventy, on the grounds that people such as shearers who labour physically cannot stay in the workforce for so long.

Still, the National Party is a party that aims to be in government as a part of a coalition and expects some of its MPs will be ministers. It is overwhelmingly seen as the party of country Australia. For people who live outside metropolitan Australia, there is something very seductive about a political party that purports to be devoted to country people. Until recently the National Party has been the only party that has sought to represent a specific non-metropolitan base. (Nascent minor parties have tried but have yet to take hold.) The Nats, as they are universally known, are stereotypically country. They present a strange mix of agrarian socialism and social conservatism, intimately connected to farmers and a section of small business people in rural areas. In their rhetoric, the Nats hold at their heart the family farmer.

Barnaby Joyce excelled at conveying this message. As agriculture minister he released the agricultural white paper in 2015 at the National Press Club and spoke about his childhood on the family farm. He described a land where Mum did the books, cooked and cleaned; and Dad and the kids chased sheep, drenching, mustering and shearing. It was a world in which bank loans were not for new cars but for properties. There was a sheep killed every Friday to feed the family, and the big outing was in the back of a Toyota ute and a Ford to Sunday Mass. His was a direct appeal to agrarianism, the idea that farming is a noble pursuit and the whole country – metropolitan and rural communities – was better for it.

'I hear from some quarters the day of the family farm is over, possibly walking out the door with the family business and the family house,' Joyce said. 'Like journalism without grammar, the land without the family farm is meaningless, soulless, it goes to the core fabric of our nation.'[6]

If you are the kid of a migrant, living in a large city, you won't recognise this childhood. But having lived that life and this rural one, I can feel the buttons being pressed for people like us on the other side, in parts of rural Australia. The childhood Joyce described is still the childhood of many kids around me, including my own. There are some differences. We don't do church, and generally churchgoing is dwindling in the bush as it is in the rest of Australia. After a brief flirtation with accounting, I don't do the books because much to the farmer's chagrin his talent for accounting far exceeds mine. But more than once I have interrupted my writing to help cut up and bag a sheep. Joyce's evocations may seem an anachronism if you are sitting in a café in Bondi, but he is narrowcasting to my family, not that Bondi family.

The central question I keep coming back to is whether a party that markets itself as the party of the bush should be doing more to appeal to the whole of country Australia, rather than speaking more exclusively to farmers and businesses. There are two constituencies that the National Party rarely mentions. One is the rural working class, which has helped build those farm businesses and industries. They feel largely neglected by National (and rural Liberal) MPs as well as Labor. The other is the #countrylife dreamers and tree changers, who are transforming country towns and villages. They are more politically progressive in their views than their long-time neighbours. These two constituencies are less rusted on to National and rural Liberal MPs who traditionally dominate rural electorates. They are open to other voting options.

=

The former Nationals senator Ron Boswell was quite the character around the Parliament. He was an important figure in the National

Party room for the longest time. He was first elected in 1983 when I was doing my HSC and the Hawke government came to power. He was the leader of the National Party in the Senate and took on Pauline Hanson's One Nation party in its first incarnation. In his later years, after he stepped down as Senate leader, he became the elder statesman and something of a Jiminy Cricket in the National Party room.

Boswell's valedictory speech came one month after Tony Abbott and Joe Hockey's budget in 2014. It was the Coalition's first budget, the horror show of cuts that marked the start of Abbott's decline as prime minister.

'Recently,' said Boswell, 'I had to remind my Liberal colleagues in the joint party room of the statement of their founder, Sir Robert Menzies, in 1970. He said: "Australian Liberals are not the exponents of an open go, for if we are all to have an open go, each for himself, and the devil take the hindmost, anarchy will result and both security and progress disappear." Just keep remembering it. These are prophetic words. The Liberal Party founder was saying that deregulation is not the answer to all problems and the free market will not always produce the best outcomes.'

It was a timely reminder of the contradiction at the heart of the Coalition. In that 2014 budget, the Liberal Party had clearly set out its agenda for a small government. The Nationals were less clear about their goals. Their then leader Warren Truss and his agriculture minister Barnaby Joyce talked about trade and dams and roads, but it was difficult to divine how the National Party fitted with the Liberal Party's small government mantra. The federal Nationals' big strength to a rural audience is that with a very small percentage of the vote it can keep the country front of mind by leveraging its larger Coalition partner when it chooses to do so.

The Nationals have chosen to use that power on defined issues: dams, roads, agricultural policy and regional development policy.

But their big failing has been their cultivation of close connections to established landholders and the business class in rural Australia while leaving behind the issues of the rural working class and underclass. In the 2014 budget, the National Party and rural Liberals signed off on punitive welfare measures, which would have forced people to move from their home towns to get work, Medicare co-payments, and half a billion in cuts to Landcare, a flagship program to improve environmental land management.

Note to MPs. You don't have to look very far in rural and regional areas to find people who are marginalised. The country has its fair share of pension-card holders, unemployed people and the working poor, including a number of Indigenous communities with complex issues to address. These constituents are mentioned far less by the National Party, even though it has long been acknowledged that rural Australia experiences higher levels of poverty than metropolitan areas. The National Rural Health Alliance calculated on 2015–16 figures that there was an 18 per cent gap between disposable household income in the capital cities and rural and regional areas. The gap stretched to 29 per cent when calculating net household worth.[7]

Metropolitan audiences assume that the Labor Party has the electoral monopoly on the 'poor' vote and the Coalition has a monopoly on the 'rich' vote. While the Coalition does hold most of the richest federal seats by household income, it also holds some of the poorest. According to analysis by Adjunct Research Fellow at Swinburne University of Technology Peter Brent, from the 2013 election, the Coalition held nine of the ten seats with the highest median household income.[8] The Coalition also held every single one of the ten electorates with the lowest median household income. Nine of the ten poorest seats were classified rural and one was classified provincial. Barnaby Joyce's electorate of New England was in the poorest twenty seats at that time.

When I tracked Joyce down after the 2014 budget to press him on its effect on his poorest constituents, he agreed. 'They don't live on farms; they are some of the poorest people in Australia; they are Indigenous and poor – for want of a better word – white people, who are the truly forgotten Australians, with no special program or department. If I can be belligerent and push economic progress, that is the part that lives on – it is economic growth.'

That sounded like trickle-down economics, but then he quoted US President Roosevelt's New Deal programs after the Great Depression and told me about his visit to the Tennessee Valley authority, which was a publicly owned power provider. 'The Tennessee Valley augmentation scheme . . . was a scheme that generated hydroelectricity and provided cheap power; it attracted industry, nuclear power, coal mines and provided jobs which increased standards of living, which are vastly better than social security payments.'

While he did acknowledge the issues for poor rural voters, I rarely heard any major party – including the National Party – talk about the poverty suffered by rural people, apart from farmers. Largely, it's as if this whole other group of country people do not exist. Who was looking out for the people who didn't have a lobby group like the National Farmers' Federation – based a block away from Parliament House? Who was looking out for the kid who worked in the bakery, the abattoir worker, the cleaner putting together a string of casual half days, or the kid on the supermarket till?

People in my town complain bitterly about the old country maxim: NSW stands for Newcastle, Sydney, Wollongong. They believe no one else gets any attention. And there's no doubt that in every election campaign until 2016, political journalists followed party campaigns that centred on the edges of Melbourne, Sydney and Brisbane, where the margins are slim and the voters are volatile.

Despite this, country voters are loath to support Labor. Even among blue-collar workers who might identify strongly with the traditional Labor economic platform, many have voted Coalition since Bob Hawke left the scene. At the more influential dining rooms in rural Australia, supporting Labor is akin to farting at a dinner table. Not the done thing.

When I write about rural politics, readers' comments about Australian country voters are fairly consistent. This comment from the *Guardian* website under a story on rural poverty is indicative: 'Most are still living in the days of Black Jack McEwen. They're so rusted on they haven't woken up to the fact that they are being shafted.'[9]

I don't agree that country people are always being shafted, but predictable voting patterns do ensure that less attention is paid to country seats: Liberal–National and Labor politicians feel that either we will always support them or we will never support them. 'Make it marginal' should be the catch-cry of country electorates.

====

Since 2016, political disruption has swept the globe, from the UK to the US to Australia's election right down to our corner of the world in state by-elections that have thrown up unexpected results. Around home, in October 2017 the New South Wales Coalition state government nearly lost the National-held seat of Murray with a 14.8 per cent swing, and there was a 19.6 per cent swing against the Nationals in my own seat of Cootamundra.

Later that same month, as Barnaby's life privately unravelled and he faced a by-election over his dual New Zealand citizenship, there were more signs he had noticed the neglected constituency. He told Fairfax journalist Peter Hartcher that he was writing 'a comparative analysis' that looked at the 'social opprobrium attached to poor white people' in rural and regional Australia. It was written in a story headlined: 'The shrewd tactic Barnaby Joyce will use to win the by-election in New England'. It sounded more like a political strategy than a philosophical agenda. He started talking about the people in 'weatherboard and iron', a nod to the white working class.

Yet almost as soon as he signalled he understood this lost constituency, Joyce's behaviour became emblematic of the sense of entitlement that pervades sections of the National Party. In the lead-up to the election, he left his electorate to fly to Canberra, where he accepted an oversized $40,000 cheque from mining and cattle billionaire Gina Rinehart as an 'award' for National Agriculture Day. The cry went up at the inappropriate nature of the award, and Joyce was forced to decline it the next day.

He won the 2 December by-election with a 7.2 per cent swing towards him. It didn't surprise me as people around me were firm in their conversations: frustration with the constitutional requirements MPs such as him were facing. They just wanted Parliament to get on with its job. The problem was, that was not happening.

By February 2018, the *Daily Telegraph* had published photos of Joyce's former junior press secretary and pregnant lover, Vikki Campion, on its front page. Then came other allegations of inappropriate behaviour, which Joyce denied. He described the whole affair as a 'witch hunt'. As it was unfolding, people in the main street were split over whether the affair was a private matter. The Nationals defended Joyce. 'It ends up taking a toll when you are working so hard to achieve a certain outcome,' said federal Nationals deputy Bridget McKenzie. 'Barnaby himself admitted that he wasn't home a lot and there were issues that occurred as a result of his focus and drive for regional Australia'. Sure, marriages break down for all sorts of personal reasons. Please don't tell me that regional Australia was the catalyst for his marriage breakdown.

When Joyce finally resigned, he said that as someone who had gone to Woolbrook Public School, just outside of Walcha in northern New South Wales, he was humbled to have been deputy prime minister. I would love to see someone from that one-teacher primary school, which in 2018 has an enrolment of ten students, three of whom are Indigenous, become deputy prime minister of

Australia. Half the kids at Woolbrook are in the bottom quartile when it comes to socioeconomic advantage, according to the Index of Community Socio-Educational Advantage (ICSEA) index, with none in the top quartile. Equally, I would be rapt if a child from our town's high school of 124 students, 63 per cent of whom are in the lowest quartile on the ICSEA index, led the nation.

But, like my kids, Joyce subsequently went to a Sydney private boarding school. At St Ignatius, 78 per cent of students are in the top ICSEA quartile and 1 per cent are in the bottom quartile. Could his Woolbrook classmates who didn't follow him to a Sydney school have made it to deputy prime minister? Those are the kids the National Party really needs to look after because they are also part of the future of country towns.

We are all flawed, but Joyce's very public downfall symbolised the darker side of small-town culture. We know our neighbours, as they do us. We see our councillors and our local politicians. We know their weaknesses and their strengths, as they do ours. In that knowing, we cut them some slack, as we hope they would for us. At its most extreme, the sense is: he is a dickhead but he is our dickhead. I love the idea of a party that represents the whole of country Australia, but it does not mean we should settle for anyone who's less than professional. Country representatives must be led by a person who understands the divide and challenges, without tugging the forelock to either Liberal or Labor. They should not fall back into the old rural political model of jobs for the boys. It is hard enough to gain traction in an upturned political environment. A good bloke or a good woman is not enough.

==

Some of the most interesting insights into the place of the National Party have come from Liberal prime ministers who have worked with the junior Coalition partner. In Heather Ewart's documentary *A Country Road: The Nationals*, the late Liberal prime minister

Malcolm Fraser reflected on the period of economic deregulation of the 1980s, in combination with the effects of the drought. The Nationals failed to differentiate during that period and it weakened the party. 'They didn't realise the inherent strength they could have had.'

In the 1990s, during the Howard leadership, amalgamation was discussed and supported by former Nationals leader John Anderson. Though it was opposed by Ron Boswell, Anderson was sent to sound out John Howard. (Liberal–National amalgamation has always had some support within the Liberal Party and the Queensland division is a merged party.) Howard ruled it out immediately. He believed that the Nationals needed to hold the country vote parking spot so other independents or minor parties did not fill the void.

'My great fear was if you forced it at a parliamentary level, it would not be accepted at the grassroots and then you would get people running as "authentic real Nationals" or they would even revive the old name of the Country Party and run against Coalition members and we would just be recreating the very disunity we were trying to get rid of,' said Howard.

So is rural representation about holding a parking spot for the Liberal Party or should it have a different philosophy? I recently asked a state National aspirant running in a country seat why she'd chosen the National Party now, given the candidate had previous involvement in the Liberal party? 'Because it's a country seat,' I was told. She obviously saw the parties as interchangeable, philosophically and politically, and she is not alone.

The predictability of rural seats in times past has meant that politically ambitious country candidates stand for the party that can win in those seats, not the one that best represents their values, if there are separate values. However, if voters are rusting off from the major party choices, it might be time to reimagine the old rural political model to represent newer models of country political representation.

That does not necessarily mean slaying the National Party. I am one who absolutely believes there is a place for political parties that represent country voters. But it certainly means country voters demanding more of our main country party as well as encouraging greater competition from political start-ups. It means thinking hard about the philosophical foundations of country culture as it exists now as opposed to as it was a century ago. Ultimately, it means assessing candidates on their merits rather than supporting our MPs out of tradition.

LESSON 12

Country MPs are not all Country Party

The National Party's trump card in the rural voter's mind is that it can still claim to be a party specifically for country people. Don't underestimate how powerful this message is in rural and regional areas. Historically, rural politicians have capitalised on city–country conflict to harvest votes, and the conflict has served the National Party well. The National Party effectively tells us that the city will never understand us and therefore parties of the city will never understand us.

That is a strategy designed not only to see off the Labor Party but also the Liberal Party, who probably pose the biggest threat to the National Party. There are more Liberal MPs representing country seats than there are National MPs in 2018. Rural Liberal MPs have been active behind the scenes with the National Party in totemic policy brawls such as the Abbott government's decision to stop the takeover of Graincorp by the US company ADM, and the backpacker tax.

Due to the Coalition's three-cornered contest rule, which stops one partner challenging a sitting MP, in most cases country voters get the option of either National or Liberal, independent, Labor,

Green, and then minor parties such as One Nation or the Shooters, Fishers and Farmers Party. (I would like a dollar for every farmer who has said to me, 'The Shooters never asked me if they could use the Farmers in their name.')

While the Australian Labor Party was born in the bush out of the shearer's strikes of 1891, Labor has been at best inconsistent and at worst has turned its back on its heritage. The reality is that the odds give Labor and Liberal the best chance of winning the most seats in the city. There have been Labor politicians who defied the odds. In my local political landscape, Labor's Billy Sheahan won the state seat of Yass, as it was then known in 1941, and held it until he resigned in 1973 from the by-then-renamed seat of Burrinjuck. Sheahan claimed 2000 relations in our area, though he did not even live here while he represented the seat, due to the travel issues in those days. Billy's resignation cleared the way for his son, Terry Sheahan, to take up where his father had left off. Terry Sheahan became a New South Wales Labor minister and held the seat until 1988, when the state Labor government was tipped out after the retirement of its premier, Neville Wran. Labor has not held this seat at a state (or federal) level since.

When Billy Sheahan ran for Yass, he put a picture of himself in his barrister's wig and robes on the how-to-vote card. Now a judge on the Land and Environment Court, his son Terry tells me, 'You would never get away with it now. The idea was "favoured son of the soil makes good". Yass–Burrinjuck were traditional Country Party areas that were stolen by my old man.' Billy was old-style Labor and his son Terry is a chip off the old block. When I ask how Billy did it, Terry says, 'Force of personality, force of service.'

Certainly personality or personal standing had something to do with the Sheahans' grip over our state seat for nearly fifty years. Terry's second cousin, Charlie Sheahan, stood at the 2017 Cootamundra state by-election, which saw a 19 per cent primary swing against the National Party, but it was not enough for another Sheahan to win the seat. The swing represented a protest vote against unpopular Coalition government decisions, including council amalgamations and the greyhound racing ban.

In 2016 Vivien Thomson had won the number three spot on the New South Wales Labor Senate ticket until Malcolm Turnbull called that year's double dissolution election. Without ceremony she was bumped down the ticket to make way for New South Wales Labor party vice president and union leader Tara Moriarty. Vivien had spent her time visiting little towns across the state and had worked on Charlie Sheahan's campaign in the previous state election and the recent by-election. She told me she has copped a bit of flak in the local area for standing for Labor. Farmers do not consider Labor their party of choice and social pressure is exerted on those who do not support conservative candidates. More than anything, Vivien believes that Labor's biggest problem has been that the party walks away from country seats after they lose them. 'You can't win if you don't turn up. We didn't keep a presence and that was to our own detriment. If we kept a presence, we would have had a chance at winning the seats back.'

Vivien believes that the Coalition are simply better at marketing to country people. In the country, if the Coalition loses a seat, the party treats it as an aberration, while Labor are just quietly grateful if they get across the line. 'The LNP, they put across this big hoo-ha, thinking people will follow along, which they do. What Labor does when we are defeated, we almost take it too personally. It sort of knocks us back too much, and we slink away instead of getting back in there and fighting and keeping a positive attitude.

'When it comes to leadership, I don't care what the forum, when you are beaten down you've got to stand back up. I just don't think we stood back up, and when that happens you lose a lot of support in any work environment. I don't think politics is any different.'

She is referencing the last twenty years, since she has been following politics closely, which coincides with my time around here. I have watched Labor run university students in the state seat; candidates acting as place holders and pamphlet distributors. That's told me that Labor does not value rural seats and that has been reflected right back at the party in the voting patterns. If you can't be bothered to stand a serious candidate, why would I be bothered voting for you?

Vivian counters that after Labor's losses the party branches were decimated. They maintained a core group of members but the party organisation walked away. It is still a struggle to get members for all political parties, let alone Labor branches in country towns. She hopes that is changing with Sheahan's candidacy. She wants Labor to run good, credible candidates, even when it expects to lose. 'Otherwise you have no credibility, so we have been learning that the hard way. We have got some good people on councils now; we have a lot of good candidates running for seats even when they know they are going to lose. So it's changing, but it's been a hard lesson.'

Before former Labor senator Sam Dastyari quit the Parliament over his links to Chinese political donors, Vivien took him to Griffith to do a 'politics in the pub' event. It was around the same time as Dastyari was abused as a 'terrorist' and a 'monkey' in a Melbourne pub by members of a nationalist group Patriot Blue. In Griffith, six and a half hours from Sydney and a little less from Melbourne, those country drinkers are just pleased when politicians turn up to listen – and they get extra points if they know they will probably lose.

'We had people in the room asking questions and they walked away feeling happy that: (a) someone listened to them and made an effort; and (b) they were able to meet face to face and ask hard questions, and it wasn't staged.'

Compounding Labor's Missing In Action status in the bush is the culture and history that have viewed rural politics through the prism of agriculture. As a result, so much of the time governments and media frame our conversation as if everyone outside cities is involved in farming. The National Party benefit from this narrative because they are the party most connected to agriculture. Influence in rural towns often rests with landholders, who are most likely to be involved in local councils, state and federal politics, or at least have connections to those who are involved. That class – the people I see most in my social network – has strong links to the National and Liberal parties. But what about the neglected people in towns and regions, who are pursuing completely different lives?

A few lights have come on recently in the Labor Party. When federal Labor was sent into opposition in 2013, the party established its Country Labor caucus to signal that a sub-faction would look out for country interests. It was a flag-waving exercise, but it acknowledged a deep political truth: Labor cannot win government without winning a portion of regional seats.

Labor's agriculture shadow minister Joel Fitzgibbon is the putative leader of the caucus. He holds the New South Wales seat of Hunter, which is classified as a rural seat, and there have been times in the past when he was the only rural MP around the cabinet table for Labor. So he set up the country caucus to filter Labor policies through a rural lens.

In 2016, Bill Shorten spent the first week of the Australian election campaign in regional Queensland, using the seat of Herbert as his base, and Townsville in particular – a regional city that had been hit hard by job losses in mining. Shorten spent that first week campaigning in the surrounding traditional National Party territory, including George Christensen's seat of Dawson, Michelle Landry's seat of Capricornia and even the independent Bob Katter's very safe seat of Kennedy. In that election, Labor won Herbert from the Liberals on the narrowest of margins, but none of the surrounding seats. Since then Labor has devoted regular attention via Shorten's town hall meetings to Queensland regional seats.

So why was everyone suddenly interested in country seats? A number of events had turned political heads towards rural voters. Britain had voted to leave the European Union on 23 June 2016 off the back of regional voters. Pauline Hanson had won four Senate seats in the 2 July 2016 election. Her party's support was higher the further you travelled from capital-city centres. Donald Trump was elected on 8 November 2016 with a strong regional base. The New South Wales National Party suffered a by-election swing of 34 per cent in November in the rural state seat of Orange – which had been a safe National seat since the Second World War. From a small town, it felt like things were changing. The sheep would not go through the usual gate.

In 2017, as Shorten's regional town hall campaign accelerated, Bob Hawke was recruited in a video to remind a country caucus meeting in Rockhampton, Queensland, that the Labor Party had its origins in the bush. Rockhampton is close to a bellwether seat these days, swinging between Labor and the LNP as governments rise and fall.

'The shearers' strikes back in the 1890s and the formation of the Australian Labor Party was very much connected with the Australian bush,' Hawke said in the video. 'The Australian Labor Party should always remember, and the country should always remember, that, as distinct from any other political party, the Australian Labor Party is more rooted in rural Australia than any other.

'I'm very pleased that modern Labor is stressing the importance of rural Australia. This has two aspects. There is the electoral aspect. We don't hold many rural seats. We should hold more because we are better for rural Australia than the conservatives, so Australia will be better served by having a rural Australia more strongly represented within the Labor Party, which is very much a party of rural Australia.'

The irony is that Labor and the minor parties are looking to capture rural and regional seats on the back of economic and cultural dissatisfaction at a time when the agricultural sector is more optimistic than it has been for years, notwithstanding the 2018 drought in Queensland and New South Wales. The 2018 Australian Bureau of Agriculture and Resource Economics (ABARES) has projected steady growth in farm production and exports over the next five years. The price of agricultural land continues to grow, which has certainly put a smile on the faces of farmers in our district. According to the Bendigo and Adelaide Bank's analysis of 2016 figures, the Australian Farmland Values Report shows the national median farmland price increased by 9.3 per cent in that year compared with 5.3 per cent in the previous year. And why not? Interest rates are low and commodity prices relatively strong. But this is where it is – once again – important to separate agricultural industry from the rest of rural and regional Australia. Remember, country people are not all farmers.

In the same year, 2016 census figures for median income by federal electorate show that the Labor and National parties share the ten poorest seats in the country. It is a reminder that in recent times economically some city areas are as disadvantaged as regional and rural areas. As of 2018 the Nationals hold four New South Wales seats, three of which are rural and one provincial; Labor holds six, five metropolitan and one rural.[1] In the poorest twenty seats by income, Labor holds ten, the National Party holds seven and the Liberal Party holds three seats. But Labor and Liberal hold equal shares of the ten richest seats, all of which are classified as inner metropolitan, and spread across Sydney, Melbourne and Canberra, though Julie Bishop's seat of Curtin in Western Australia sneaks into tenth spot. The other states and territories – South Australia, Northern Territory, Tasmania and Queensland – have no electorates in the ten richest seats, which tells you something else about the way the states divide on income and culture.

These lists again highlight the competing demands not just in the Coalition but also for the Labor Party in terms of demographic.

The Coalition's advantage is that the Liberals and the Nationals can talk to very different constituencies and work both ends of the spectrum, but Ron Boswell's valedictory warning to the Coalition highlights the tensions at its heart.

=====

In spite of Labor's efforts, the biggest threat to the Liberal–National coalition in rural seats is independents. Rural voters have proven they will vote for independents more often than their city cousins when they feel the major parties have failed them. Think about the three of five independents who sat on the crossbenches during the Gillard government of 2010–13. All came from rural or regional seats: Tony Windsor in New England (New South Wales), Rob Oakeshott in Lyne (New South Wales), Bob Katter in Kennedy (Queensland). A fourth independent, Andrew Wilkie, holds Denison in Tasmania. (Though Denison is listed as an inner metropolitan seat, Tasmania has many of the characteristics of regional voters due to its splendid isolation.)

Rural voters love someone to take a stand. Good independents hang on. Independent Cathy McGowan narrowly won the seat of Indi in Victoria in the same election, and increased her margin in 2016. Queensland National MP George Christensen essentially runs an independent campaign by standing against his own party and his government as the maverick, though he rarely follows through on his threats.

Looking at the pattern of rural independents, the Parliament has gone full circle. In the early days of Federation, rural independents or independent-minded candidates flourished. During 1920 to 1949, they included William Watson in Fremantle (then a rural seat), Bill McWilliams in Franklin, Tasmania, Henry Groom in Darling Downs, Adair Blain in the Northern Territory and Alexander Wilson in Wimmera, Victoria. These members had diverse interests but their common call was the shortcomings of the major parties.

McWilliams was a former journalist who became the first leader of the nascent Country Party in 1920. When he supported the Labor Party in a censure motion against Billy Hughes's Nationalist government, he was replaced by Earle Page, who said McWilliams 'had shown an increasing tendency to vote against the majority'. Page represented the coalitionists, such as former leaders Tim Fischer and John Anderson. As the National Party still notes in its potted history on its website, 'Page recognised that the best opportunity for the party to get its policy objectives on to the statute books would be by being a partner in government.'[2] McWilliams represented that strong strain of oppositional defiance disorder present in rural Australia and in pockets of the National party. (Think Christensen, Joyce in his early years as a senator, and Bob Katter before he left the Nationals.)

Alex Wilson was a farmer and member of the Victorian United Country Party. After the 1940 federal election Wilson held the balance of power with fellow independent Arthur Coles, a former Melbourne lord mayor, and kept Robert Menzies in power. In 1941 he withdrew support for Menzies, effectively handing government to Labor leader John Curtin. Wilson argued that the government was not providing enough relief to primary producers and that he had some sympathy for the Labor Party's platform.[3] He also took issue with the way the Menzies government was raising money for the war effort. Wilson preferred money through 'the people's bank', the Commonwealth Bank. His speech at the time echoed the words of Tony Windsor and Rob Oakeshott when they provided their support to the Gillard government in 2010. 'I consider that a change must be made in order to ensure stable and safe government for the effective prosecution of the war,' Wilson said. In 2010, Windsor and Oakeshott also shocked the nation by choosing a Labor government over the Coalition as the stable option. Bob Katter started negotiations but ultimately could not bring himself to support the Labor government.

Windsor and Oakeshott were in a similar mould to Peter Andren, another popular, liberal-minded independent, who won his seat at the same time as Pauline Hanson in 1996. In his maiden speech Andren, a former school teacher and journalist, said, 'People expect government participation and support in their lives as much as they respect the value of private enterprise for fair return, provided it both rewards the entrepreneur and is beneficial to the Commonwealth.'[4] Born in Gulargambone, New South Wales, Andren understood that country people were not cookie-cutter free market conservatives, represented by the right wing of the Liberal party. He understood that Australian country people expected active government, government that understood when to intervene and when to step back.

In his generally conservative electorate of Calare (incorporating Orange in New South Wales), which was usually held by the National Party, Andren was sometimes at odds with his electorate, but I would argue that his voters understood and respected that his views were deeply held. Here, again, authenticity rather than political positioning puts independents in the box seat in rural areas compared to major party MPs who have to bind with a party position. Andren supported some traditional country views of the day, such as opposing the sale of Telstra, but he also supported issues traditionally associated with the Left, such as opposing both Australia's involvement in the Iraq war and Howard's tough stance on asylum seekers.

When Andren died of cancer in 2007, his death united politicians across the spectrum, stepping above the usual polite words for the bereaved. His obituary read like that of the fantasy member of Parliament. John Howard praised him because he never tempered strongly held views. Tony Windsor said he was the conscience of the Parliament. Former Greens leader Bob Brown said he gave politics a good name.

Tony Windsor crossed paths with Andren when Windsor entered federal Parliament in 2001 as a former New South Wales independent and ex-National member. At the same time, Bob Katter won his first election as an independent after he resigned from the National Party benches two terms into the Howard government. Both Windsor and Katter had their priorities, but there were similar themes, converging on economic alienation, globalisation and the neo-liberal policies pursued by the major parties to the detriment of country people.

Katter had long been a rebel and, like the former Nationals leader Barnaby Joyce, he was known for crossing the floor while in the National Party. He finally dumped his party membership in 2001, saying the Howard government was as popular in Queensland as a 'brown snake in a sleeping bag'. Katter's move was a protest against the economic reforms instituted by Hawke, Keating and Howard. His immediate wish list was for his government to cut petrol prices, build better roads, stop its competition reforms and freeze any further sale of Telstra.

Likewise, Windsor's comments in his first speech in 2002 on the unashamedly economic rationalist framework adopted by the major parties reflected the rural independent agenda. 'All the major parties have decided to back a framework which will have very little regard for distance, remoteness, smallness and social equity ... the very policies that are emanating from this place, whether they be fuel policy or aged care policy – even policies relating to country doctors or the lack thereof – are emanating from that basic policy framework, which has not delivered equity to country constituents in particular.

'The message that the policy sends to country communities is to proceed to your nearest major regional centre, go to the coast, go to Sydney or go to buggery.'[5]

The solution for Windsor had its origins in the approach of independent Bill McWilliams all those years before. Windsor argued for rural representatives to better use their balance of power. 'With 30 per cent of the vote, country Australia has the potential to have the balance of power – irrespective of who is in power in this chamber – and influence the political process far more than it has in the past.'

Rob Oakeshott – a former New South Wales National MP – represented a younger, more mobile generation of independents. He urged Australians to embrace 'global citizenry' rather than fear it. This message was in many ways antithetical to most rural agendas and the anger over globalisation. 'I am a long-term believer in global citizenry and see it as a challenge that this island nation needs to overcome in the way we play our "cringe politics" whenever we engage with the world. I think the United Nations, for example, is an important and valued institution and our involvement at the highest levels should be encouraged, as should our participation, understanding and commitment to various international treaties, agreements and obligations. These are good, positive exercises, not negative ones, and the benefits to us through global participation far outweigh the alternative of isolation of thought and isolation of actions.'[6]

Neither Windsor, Oakeshott nor Katter had gained much attention in the federal sphere until the hung parliament thrust them into the national headlights. Windsor and Oakeshott dared to back Labor in country electorates, representing a more centrist take on traditional rural representation. Their agreement with Gillard extracted a range of commitments in a deal that was available to the public – unlike the Coalition agreement between the Liberal and National party leaders. The Windsor–Oakeshott deal supported the National Broadband Network (NBN) to provide 'fair and equal access' to fast connectivity in country areas. They extracted increased funding commitments to regional health, regional education, and later they supported the first Gonski education package because it funded schools by need, which by definition loaded funding for rural schools and Indigenous disadvantage. (Federal Coalition rural MPs opposed Gonski reforms, though New South Wales Nationals education minister Adrian Piccoli was its biggest champion.) They urged policy work on climate change and carbon pricing, more transparent processes in Parliament and a better basis for regional policy making. They wanted a national food plan and commitment to review the research and development of agricultural innovation. Both Oakeshott and Windsor also received from Labor specific infrastructure-spending in their own electorates, including dam projects, hospital upgrades and water infrastructure. Their unique position as the holders of the balance of power essentially allowed these independents to goldplate their electorates. In substance they walked a line that brought policies from both sides of politics: the regional dam, road and rail priorities of the Coalition with the health, education and communications policies of Labor.

The majority of their voters could not see past their delivery of government to Labor, and to Julia Gillard specifically. Gillard was demonised by then opposition leader Tony Abbott, conservative commentators and shock jocks. After a bruising term both Windsor and Oakeshott retired, so we don't know whether they would have held their seats when Abbott's government came to office. It seems unlikely, and when Windsor came back to contest the following 2016 election against Barnaby Joyce, he lost.

But if you take away the politics and look at the substance of the policies they supported, Windsor and Oakeshott's priorities reflected a political centre that has the potential to garner widespread support in regional areas. Like Ron Boswell quoting Menzies, they did not want an 'open go' or unfettered market competition without regard to fellow citizens. They shook rural political representation out of its complacency and it shocked their country electorates. But if rural voters are cranky about politics, perhaps it's time to change the old model. It doesn't necessarily mean smashing the machine, but it does mean we need to demand more of our politicians and reward them when they try something new that delivers for country people.

One of the most innovative grassroots political models I have seen in recent years was Voice for Indi (V4I), the mob that got Victorian Indi independent Cathy McGowan elected – by attracting 31 per cent of the primary votes from a standing start.

To those outside the seat, she seemed to come out of nowhere. To those on the inside, her 2013 win by a few hundred votes on a two-party preferred basis to throw out the sitting Liberal MP, Sophie Mirabella, was the culmination of many years of community work. So blindsided was the rest of country Australia that they inundated V4I to ask them how they had done it. As a result, V4I held a political masterclass to share what they had learned. Even the National Party was going to attend, until someone must have decided it would be a bad look, taking lessons from a political novice. I thought that was a short-sighted tribal decision to its detriment.

The attendees in Oxley Hall just outside Wangaratta in country Victoria in 2014 were a mix of community groups, unions, activists and aspiring independents. A fair few wanted McGowan to extend her organisation into other seats, a request V4I flatly refused. A number of participants wanted to smash the two-party system. McGowan was not interested in that, either. The aim of V4I had been to concentrate on improving conditions in the seat of Indi, not empire-building. The group had not been happy with the existing representation of their local MP so they'd sought to change it. They did not want to change the whole world, they just wanted to change their part of it. And they had done it through a form of participatory democracy.

To starry-eyed rural political activists, there is something stirring about campaigns to change a major-party MP, but to do so is incredibly hard, especially in vast and diverse electorates. Small-town community issues tend to be very local and can be hard to translate from one end of an electorate to another. Lack of profile does you in. Peter Andren was a TV newsreader. Windsor was a state MP in a hung Parliament. Oakeshott was in state Parliament. Their recognition was already substantial. The task in Indi should not be underestimated. Malcolm Turnbull's electorate of Wentworth is 38 square kilometres. Indi measures 28,500 square kilometres, but is still nowhere near the largest electorate in Australia. Imagine getting across that with a few corflutes and T-shirts in a six-week campaign without a major party structure behind you. Paying for it alone would break most people.

It wasn't good intentions that got McGowan elected. According to V4I, there were certain preconditions that helped change the representation in that seat. The group first came together to discuss what they considered was poor local representation. McGowan was just one of its members. They started with a values statement, which everybody signed to agree on the priorities for better representation. By asking each member to sign it, disparate individuals were committed to a similar direction. A skills audit of the members was completed, so they all knew their strengths and what they lacked. The group hosted what they called 'kitchen table conversations' with locals, asking people for their views and policy preferences. V4I drew up the report and presented it to the local member in the hope of improving the way their issues were addressed. They did not get what they considered an adequate response. As a result, the group decided the local MP was not serious about addressing their issues, so they ran a competitive preselection process to find an independent candidate. McGowan won, volunteers were recruited and trained in political process, volunteering and door-knocking while the original kitchen table conversations were used to draw up an achievable policy agenda. In Indi's case, voters were concerned about the efficiency of the train line, mobile phone coverage, broad-band, mental health support and education.

V4I was particularly keen to get young people involved – to inject some policies to keep youth in town and add dynamism and technical savvy to future campaigning. Young people ran the social media campaign, organised 'flash mobs' on the streets to heighten the candidate's profile and get voters talking. Volunteers were under strict instructions to keep the debates positive, acknowledging that independents must be perceived as different from major party politicians.

For all of that organisation, V4I and McGowan still admitted to big mistakes in their first campaign, including mistakes and misun-derstandings around scrutineering votes, and faux pas. In her first media conference, McGowan was asked what her policies would be, to which she replied, 'I won't be having policies as such.' What she meant was that she was consulting with the electorate and would be taking their priorities to work with the government of the day. Instead it sounded like she didn't have a clue.

I am conflicted by elements of participatory democracy. We cane major parties for constant polling to check how voters will react before taking a leadership stand. At one time capital punishment had majority voter support. Isn't this also participatory democracy? After the first Abbott budget, I asked McGowan what she thought about it. She said she wanted to talk to her electorate first. V4I set up listening posts throughout the seat, collated the feedback from 700-plus respondents and handed it to the government. This cannot always be done. In reality, so many votes come before the Parlia-ment that McGowan has to vote on instinct and values.

After seeing off a challenge in 2016 by the former Indi MP, Sophie Mirabella, McGowan only consolidated her electoral margin with a swing of 5 per cent. These days her team is closer to a well-oiled machine. She has worked with V4I to extend their novel campaign approach to teaching the electorate more about how politics works. For example, community group representatives work in her parliamentary office, beside paid staffers, to expose locals to the political experience. It means that as those community groups try to achieve their goals, they know how to work within the political system, which remains a mystery to most people who work outside it. It gives the community power by using the local MP's office as a community resource.

The lesson from Indi is that country communities can organise if they are unhappy with representation. To be clear, this is not a call for revolution, but, as V4I proved, if communities are upset with being taken for granted by their sitting member, change is possible. There is no point in us whingeing about our representation, trotting out the old NSW acronym, Newcastle, Sydney, Wollongong, and singing sad songs. With social media, it has never been easier to organise political campaigns. If your MP is not working for you, organise someone who will.

LESSON 13

Farming dominates rural politics but stuff still gets ignored

I'm not a farmer, I just hang out with one. I don't really know my phalaris from my fescue so I don't pretend to be an oracle when it comes to all the issues facing agriculture. Like the rest of rural Australia, farmers vary by region, environment and commodity. A cropper is different to a grazier is different to a sheep farmer is different to an orchardist, and so on. All I can tell you is that the farmers around me are mostly diligent and innovative. They attend field days, learn new things and try to adapt to changes in both technology and climate. The modern farmer needs a range of diverse skills, from a knowledge of scientific process, biology, genetics, to that of futures trading, digital literacy, technological know-how and finance. The idea that farming is the easy way out as a career could not be further from the truth. But my interest has been in the historically dominant place of farmers in the Australian political landscape and the cultural imagination.

Historically, rural economies have relied on agriculture. And the combination of the historical importance of agriculture, not just to the town but to the Australian economy – farmers own and manage 61 per cent of the land mass – and the familial ties between city and bush populations in the past has placed farmers in a powerful position. Stories of farmer lobby groups prowling the parliamentary corridors striking fear into the hearts of politicians might be apocryphal, but if you listen carefully you can still hear a great deference given to those groups. Politicians are loath to criticise a farmer because in the past he (or she) carried pockets full of political capital. Generally, people with more influence on government policy have more assets – as happens in the cities. It was ever thus. That is not to say that all farmers have lots of assets. There is as much of a range in the industry as any other. There are farmers with a lot and farmers with little. There are farmers who are really good at what they do and others who suck. There are environmental stewards and there are slash and burn artists. Still, as a group their dominance in Australia led to the formation of the Country Party, and its rise on the eastern seaboard became a self-enforcing mechanism in towns. If you wanted something done, if you needed to influence policy, or at least have a say, historically the best vehicle was association with or membership of the Country Party. Country Party membership for my father-in-law's wartime generation was more common than it is now for my husband's generation, but the National Party still has a stronghold on a lot of rural organisations and councils, extending out to land management boards, particularly in New South Wales and Queensland.

Traditionally, the National Party and farmer lobby groups have concentrated on trade and tax policy, drought assistance, industrial relations, old models of decentralisation, water policy and primary industry bodies. In the past few decades, they have crossed into native title issues and environmental stewardship programs such as Landcare, while lobbying hard at a state level to wind back clearing restrictions on native vegetation laws. I don't have the space to go into all these so I want to stick with three political issues where interaction between agriculture as an industry and the political process is changing: climate change, land usage and regulation.

═══

Most mornings, I take a well-worn path through a paddock that was planted with canola in 2017. The crop had an inauspicious start and in many ways it represents the challenges of farming. We had good rains for the area in autumn so there was an optimism building about the season. But due to a machinery malfunction, the paddock wasn't sown down properly and when the green seedlings came up there were stripes right through the crop, a situation that vexed the farmer every time he drove past. He got over that, only to see the crop suffer frost damage from an unusually dry and cold winter. Spring rains promised but then held back, leaving us with what old timers call a bobtail spring. That is, a season, cut off in its prime. I knew the aphids must have moved into the area when my roses were covered in them, sucking the life out of the blooms. I complained but the farmer didn't want to hear it. Reckon they are bad here, go out and have a close look at the canola in number 2! Then, when they were spraying broadleaf weeds in the next paddock, the canola was hit in one corner by spray drift, killing that section. After that, a fierce hailstorm cut a swathe through the paddock, damaging the canola seed pods, leaving little bruised pock marks. There was still one corner of the paddock left which missed the hail and the spray drift, so the cockatoos went to work on that.

Comedy of error, or season, rates highly in our household. The farmer's preferred morning line to reflect his day comes from a Leonard Cohen song about stumbling out of bed and getting ready for the struggle. When your family's life and finances revolve primarily around agriculture and the increasingly unpredictable vagaries of climate, it breeds a certain equanimity of outlook, which I have tried to learn through yoga and meditation. That outlook teaches you to value what you have now because it could all turn to crap at any moment. It teaches you to always have a little slack in the system just in case that does happen. It teaches you to keep your expectations low and, hopefully, to come out of the year pleasantly surprised. The culture of low expectations partly explains the poem 'Said Hanrahan': 'We'll all be rooned.' It is a fine balance, though. Pessimism cannot be given its head completely because optimism must make an appearance in order to pay for putting the crop in. Every year has an order of hope and lament.

As it turned out, when that canola was harvested it wasn't great, but nor was it as bad as the farmer thought. These are the bits farmers can do. They can sow or plant or cut or muster or shear or milk or harvest, but it is a stony fact that so much of the business crosses into government policy. I am reminded of this as I shuffle past that paddock, now just an expanse of stubble left over after the crop was harvested. The paddock rises from a gully favoured by kangaroos to a hill on top of which sit two shiny silos on a concrete pad. Every time I look at those silos I think of the former Liberal treasurer Joe Hockey, because he introduced the tax discounts in 2015 which encouraged us to buy them. I wrote about that tax discount in the budget lock-up that year.[1] The giveaway was designed, according to the government, to encourage drought preparedness. (It also had a lot to do with repairing the damage done by the unpopular 2014 budget.) I often think I should put a plaque on our silos to Hockey, who has since left politics to become Australia's ambassador to the US. They serve as a constant reminder to me of the link between the Parliament and the people, and how policy can shepherd individual decisions.

If ever there was an issue that illustrated the effect of politics on grassroots cohesion it is climate change. Here is an issue directly challenging rural communities, and one of their key industries. It was tackled in a fairly bipartisan way until the turn of this century, when the policy rubber needed to hit the road.

This was evident in the old cabinet papers right back from Malcolm Fraser through to Bob Hawke's terms in office, when there was the first cabinet submission to reduce greenhouse gas emissions. The Keating government signed Australia up to the United Nations Framework Convention on Climate Change (UNFCCC). John Howard picked up the ball and ran with it when he came to office in 1997, establishing a world-first agency dedicated to reducing greenhouse gas emissions. Somewhere late in the life of the Howard government, things started to fracture. Perhaps Howard's political antennae was twitching. The Australian Greenhouse Office, formed in 1998, was in 2004 merged into the Department of Environment and Heritage. The Howard government negotiated on the Kyoto Protocol to the UNFCCC and signed the treaty shortly after, but then in 2002 refused to ratify it because it was not in 'Australia's interests' as a 'massive net exporter of energy' and it would 'cost us jobs and damage our industry'.

Kevin Rudd became prime minister in 2007, and set up the Department of Climate Change to deal with the 'greatest moral challenge of our time', but his carbon trading scheme was rejected by the Senate, failing without the support of the Greens. Then opposition leader Malcolm Turnbull was politically keelhauled for his support for carbon trading, and climate policy generally went to the pack from there, even though momentum had been building for years towards an emissions trading scheme (ETS). Pushed by the Greens and the independents Windsor and Oakeshott, the Gillard government overcame massive opposition to implement an ETS. New Liberal opposition leader Tony Abbott made its destruction his raison d'être and smashed the carbon-pricing architecture on coming to office in 2013. When the Abbott government announced its policy white paper on agricultural competitiveness, climate change was not mentioned in the terms of reference. The agricultural white paper was released two years later and in it the government reluctantly acknowledged that climate change was a thing and that farmers should build resilience 'in light of the challenges presented by such long-term trends'.

All of which is a short history of a long story on one of the major issues that hangs over farms like the death's head at the feast. If you ever needed evidence that lack of clear government leadership has the capacity to fracture the community, consider the changing position of the National Farmers' Federation, which appeared to be a direct response to conservative backtracking on climate. In 2006, the NFF was calling for action as we headed into the wheat harvest that December. Then its president, David Crombie, announced that the federation's policy council would be joining the Australian business roundtable calling for early action on climate change. The following year the lobby group backed an emissions trading scheme, saying it might be the 'greatest threat' confronting farmers and their ability to put food on Australian tables.[2] He said it also threatened the long-term sustainability of at least 60 per cent of Australia's landmass.

Then we had the 2009 leadership spill that saw Malcolm Turnbull dumped and climate sceptic Abbott take the helm. With dissenting voices in politics, the public mood changed and suddenly Crombie was welcoming the contribution of sceptic Ian Plimer as making a 'valid contribution' and lending support to other voices in the debate. Climate change became a partisan issue, in which climate policy was overwhelmingly considered a Labor issue. Tony Abbott's campaign against the carbon tax, which got rid of an emissions trading scheme, also successfully drove a wedge between conservative country voters and climate change.

'We've heard ad nauseam from those scientists convinced that climate change will ruin us all and, seemingly, hell-bent on making grim doomsday predictions. But we've heard precious little from those experts for whom the jury is still out, or, in the case of Professor Plimer, say their research shows extreme climate change predictions are overstated,' David Crombie said.

'Now, before I'm carted to a stake for public torching, I'm not saying Professor Plimer is right, nor that his colleagues with differing views are wrong. Just that it's about time we had a balanced, informed discussion and debate . . . free from vilification of those who dare to question conventional wisdom.'[3]

By 2017, under the new leadership of president Fiona Simson and chief executive officer Tony Mahar, the NFF had swung back to a more comprehensive policy to recognise 'that climate change poses a significant challenge for Australian farmers. As a nation, we must act to ensure that our economy is well placed to cost efficiently reduce our national greenhouse gas emissions profile.' The organisation again backed an emissions trading scheme as farmers, like everybody else, were hit with electricity bills that were 200 to 300 per cent higher than the previous year.[4]

It feels like a waste of time because it is. There could not have been a household in Australia that did not notice the rise in power prices, including ours – and we were supplemented by a solar power system. I watched that policy rollercoaster while gauging opinions in the farming community around me, and they are divided, just like the politicians. They range from acceptance of the science to entrenched opposition.

My near neighbour Peter Holding has been an outspoken advocate of action on climate change for as long as I can remember. He was involved in the Climate Kelpie website, which rounds up climate tools to help farmers make decisions about managing their land. He is also a member of the more recent Farmers for Climate Action, designed to push for mitigation policies that will help farmers adapt to a changing climate. It drives him nuts that governments and political parties have squandered good policy, and that an albeit decreasing number disregard climate science.

He and I meet in the same week as the local show, the first week of September when it should still be cold as charity. We remark, as everyone in the country does, about the weather. The wind is picking up. It is a horrid warm northwesterly.

'The more I see of it,' says Peter, 'climate change is going to become such an impacting thing by 2020. It's not the rain, it's the temperature, and the farmers can't get their head around the temperature business. They just don't seem to get it and that is the one bit of climate that is settled. It's the temperature bit that the [scientists] know all about. It's how the rainfall will be impacted, they don't know.'

A number of farmers remain sceptical about anthropogenic climate change, but generational change is happening. The take-home message from the climate policy debate, though, is that no matter what side you stand on, the political system is not working anymore. Gone are the days when governments would build a legacy and the opposition would move into government and move on to their own legacy. So much time has been wasted in this area by successive governments simply ripping up each other's policies. It underlines again in the voter mind that there is little downside in supporting minor parties because the cycle of political wrecking under major parties means nothing is getting done anyway.

Things started to change in the climate policy space in rural areas when farmers were affected by land encroachment issues, particularly from mining. Land usage is the second agricultural issue that is changing the rural political landscape, particularly after companies began activating petroleum exploration licences awarded by former New South Wales Labor minister Ian Macdonald, who has been since found guilty of misconduct in a public office over a mining licence and jailed for ten years.

Coal mining applications by the Chinese state-owned Shenhua coal company and BHP Billiton over prime agricultural land on the Liverpool Plains in northern New South Wales mobilised some very influential farmers and got them talking publicly about climate change. Mining was the thing that opened that door. The first female president of the National Farmers Federation, Fiona Simson, cut her political teeth in campaigning against Shenhua's mine.

In Queensland, the Lock the Gate community action group recognised the power of farmers' political capital early on in its fight against coal seam gas development. The National Party had been largely unresponsive to farmers' concerns about mining issues until Lock the Gate started organising and providing them support on a broader political scale. The movement fundamentally under-stood the potential of leveraging off political goodwill to farmers.

Farmers have resisted joining environmentalists to protest against mining ventures affecting their land because in the past the two have not been natural allies. Most farmers have been scathing of 'greenies', thinking of them as hippies and layabouts. Some still do think that way, but those whose livelihoods were threatened have changed their minds. And if you think about it, the prin-ciple of 'leave it as you found it' is really a conservative concept. Conservative thinker Edmund Burke wrote that we must act as trustees of the world – what he called 'temporary possessors and life renters' – rather than its 'entire masters', so that we don't leave future generations with 'a ruin instead of an habitation'.

So notwithstanding their traditional enmity, there is a natural overlap between environmentalists' and farmers' interests. Yet the two groups never really came together until Lock the Gate got busy with farmers in their battles against coal seam gas in Queensland. But it was the coal seam gas fight in the Pilliga State Forest in northern New South Wales that really caught my attention. When nightly news bulletins showed local farmers dressed in the preferred royal blue work shirt chained to property gates or earth-moving equipment, I knew things were changing.

I covered the land usage issue first in 2015 on the north coast of New South Wales when farmers began joining green groups to protest against a Metgasco coal seam gas licence in the little town of Bentley. I spoke to farmers in the region, a number of whom had transitioned from dairy to beef cattle after the deregulation of the dairy industry in the late 1990s. They stood with a growing horde of protestors as they became afraid their land and water could be affected by drilling.

In spite of the New South Wales Coalition government being the natural choice for conservative farmers, the state had initially disregarded the farmers' concerns, and the brush-off from government became the tipping point in getting the farming community in that region emotionally involved. It pushed people from passive but worried observers to active participants. It didn't help that the then state Liberal resources minister Chris Hartcher called the farmers 'anarchists trying to wreck the state's economy'. Government representatives were dispatched to check whether farmers were being fed misinformation from social media. An older farmer told me that he knew how to read Joseph Conrad but not a computer manual. 'I assured them I was not swayed by social media,' he said.[5]

After long battles, the state government bought back the Metgasco licence to stop the coal seam gas mine in the area, but that was also after the local New South Wales National MP had suffered a 25 per cent swing against him and nearly lost his seat. As the state government's political troubles increased, it also bought back BHP's Caroona coal licence on the Liverpool Plains in 2016, and half of Shenhua's licence over the Plains in 2017.

The fights that led up to this government capitulation signalled a shift on the ground. The issues had echoes of the debates over global political disruption. Outer city seats had learned to send clear messages to politicians. Don't count on my vote unless you work for it. It echoed calls from independents to use the vote more actively.

And speaking about the issues, those farmers opened up to me about the wider political process. The mining issue and the issue of licences became tangled with their worries over political nepotism and the power of money and lobby groups on government decision-making. In the past, there have been few options in country seats, but the rise of outsider candidates has meant other choices are available.

Frustrations over land issues fused together all the hot buttons for outsider politics. These farmers felt separated and distant from the hub of power in the city that was making the decisions. They considered their political representatives had let them down and they felt abandoned by establishment politics. As a result they began casting around for alternatives, and the further those political alternatives were from the major parties, the better.

The third issue – excessive regulation – also underlines the sentiment that city-based decision-making too often fails to grasp conditions on the ground in regional areas. Government regulation in the form of red tape, form-filling and box-ticking sends blood pressure skyrocketing. And politicians have pandered to it.

One of the more ridiculous past political contrivances in this area was Tony Abbott's metaphorical bonfire of red tape. It was a political response to an issue that caused ongoing angst in every sector, not least in farming: the Abbott government threw more than 9500 regulations and 1000 acts of Parliament into the figurative flames, with much fanfare, in a political show designed to send the message that politics was responding to voter needs – 'abolishing the unnecessary, counterproductive and redundant laws and regulations will save individuals and organisations more than $700 million every year, and "make people's lives easier, not harder"' – without actually achieving much in the way of meaningful policy reform.[6] The government published its plans in a brown-paper-covered booklet tied with red tape. It felt like a *Hollow Men* episode in which a bunch of people sit around with a whiteboard scrawled with REGULATION so they can workshop possible public relations strategies to build a political campaign while setting aside the original problem.

This sort of thing drives voters to distraction. One local man in his thirties describes it to me as snot. 'You know what really annoys me. The snot money that government spends on nothing. It's the shit that doesn't get anything done.'

Soon after that conversation, a contractor turns up at our farm to windrow that crappy canola paddock. He is carrying 180 pages of printed documentation to certify that he has permits to cross local roads with his large machinery. The contractor and his family have a farm but also run a business harvesting and carting grain. He lets fly on the state government requirements, which mean he has to identify the exact time and date that he will need to move his bloody great header or windrower during the harvest months.

It would be hilarious if it wasn't so time-consuming. Harvest is a tricky time. You watch a crop change colour, examine it, estimate, look at the grain's moisture content, annoy the hell out of the contractor if you use one, start up your own header if you don't. Do a round to check the paddock. Check the results. Consider the options. One paddock might look ready, but it might turn out that actually another one down the road is right to go. Predicting which paddock will be ready first is like predicting the day of the birth of a baby. Fine in principle but dodgy in practice. So for the contractor, predicting the date and time he will use certain roads while juggling his many different clients is damn near impossible.

It all starts with a good idea – safety – but it ends with a state government application process that begins three months in advance, with twenty-eight days for the Roads Department to consider the application to move one piece of machinery. If the date changes, the permit doesn't apply. The contractor has to start the process again. And that applies to one local government area. Pity the poor contractor who has to cross several local government areas or state boundaries. Then you are looking at the *War and Peace* of permits, which must be kept in paper form on the contractor at all times.

Some contractors say bugger the process and cop the fine because the application time taken is not worth the effort. They factor in the fine as a cost of doing business. And it's not like this problem is unknown. The Productivity Commission's report on transitioning regional economies late in 2017 was not clear why single permits were required when multi permits or local exemptions would do. The Commission recommended removing unnecessary stuff like this; that to do so would be a 'win–win'. It was both justifiable and would allow regional communities to adapt to change.

It is these sorts of daily frustrations caused by rules with no obvious logic that reflect badly on lawmakers. Voters like our header driver hear state and federal governments exhorting us to lift our productivity at the same time as requiring reams of useless permits to be carried on the dashboard – in an age when every contractor is carrying a smartphone or a tablet. While these voters distinguish between state and federal issues, when they hear Malcolm Turnbull's call for more agility and innovation, they feel governments are not lifting their own games. Direct experience with regulation reinforces the belief that government is a hindrance rather than a help, and makes the voter more inclined to whack the incumbent in the ballot box.

These three issues – climate change, land usage and redundant regulation – illustrate a clear mismatch between actual problems and the 'solutions' imposed by government. There is a sense that government is fiddling around the edges, and that even if one party comes up with a reasonable solution, the other party of the Parliament will act to destroy it for political advantage. Agriculture is an industry that's benefited historically from high-profile political representatives, and here are three central issues to its productivity that continue to fester. What hope for individuals and industries without identifiable representation? Can politics see those people, let alone address their problems?

LESSON 14

There is a neglected class and they are swinging

Australia is different from the US in the way we perceive government. Voters here who are fed up with politics-as-usual still expect government to be active, though they often can't articulate in what way; similarly minded American voters want government to get out of the way. In a small town, Australians have expected more from their governments because traditionally government has done more. What people around me want are jobs so they can stay in their place; they want infrastructure; and they want the access to the health, education and broadband services that city people enjoy, but they want it without the crap that city people have to put up with. The congestion, the pollution, the pressure. They expect the world to change but not too fast.

Conversations about discontent with, and the failings of, government in country areas are invariably followed by 'but I wouldn't live in the city if you paid me'. People tend to be slightly more socially conservative (though not always) and economically interventionist. Their big beef is with the lack of trust they have in government and the lack of consideration of them from city-based power centres. They know their MP can't fix every issue, but they want he or she to have a go. They don't mind immigration as long as it's done on the nation's terms not the immigrant's terms. They feel if migrants want to come to Australia, they should be grateful. These voters have many similarities with the swinging voters in the outer edges of the cities, but geography and culture differentiates them – those around me identify strongly as country people.

These are obviously broad brushstrokes. I think of these country-town people as the neglected class, sitting between those who rely more heavily on government payments and landholders and businesses who have enough assets to cushion them from economic shocks. The neglected class comprise the people who service the farms, look after the very young and the very old, keep the schools going, keep the hospitals running, do the council work (in the streets as opposed to sitting as councillors), stock the supermarket shelves. The neglected class are the very foundation of country towns, and you don't hear about them from most rural MPs.

The neglected class feel they have no sway over governments or politicians, and they feel inadequately represented by the media. They have no lobby group wholly representing them. They can see an educated elite on both the left and the right looking after themselves and shouting at each other in a conversation that is largely held above their heads, away from their main streets. Their issues are often taken in vain by both sides if their concerns suit the agenda of the day, but if you consider the agenda of the major parties, the neglected class are mostly disregarded.

The resentment creeping back within this class towards the land-owning class approximates the local version of the insider–outsider dichotomy we have seen play out globally. The neglected class are breaking away from the majors because they feel taken for granted by the conservatives and ignored by Labor. The neglected class are happy to shake up the parliamentary house in a bid to be heard because a vote is their only chance. The hopeful vote. They have voted Labor sporadically in the past, but as Labor has taken up socially progressive causes they have looked again towards the Coalition. There are resonances with Howard's battlers on the urban fringes, but the neglected class strongly identify with their rural places and their rural culture. They are aspirational. The angriest of them want to be recognised, to be acknowledged in a world that is changing and moving past them. In other words, the finest economic reform could put an extra $50 a week in their pockets but it would not change how they are feeling. The gentrification of some country towns has the capacity to make them angrier. Who can afford a $40 steak or a $25 brioche burger? Likewise, high commodity prices and inflating rural land prices will only stretch the gap between landholders and these voters. The neglected class feel as though they are losing ground and if you keep an eye on flat-lining wage growth figures you might understand why.

In contrast, the landowning class that influences country areas often have connections to politicians, business and public servants. Perhaps people within this stratum have gone to school with people in power or, like me, they may have worked with them. They can find solutions to individual problems, or at the very least they know who in the system they can bother to get these problems addressed. The landowning class might be cosseted with tea and sympathy, but the neglected class have no such solutions or comforts. Their people are disconnected from power.

Pauline Hanson has made a career of talking to the neglected class. Her standard response has been to blame outsiders. In 1996, it was Indigenous and Asian people. In 2016, it was Muslims.

'In my first speech in 1996 I said we were in danger of being swamped by Asians. This was not said out of disrespect for Asians but was meant as a slap in the face to both the Liberal and Labor governments who opened the floodgates to immigration, targeting cultures purely for the vote, as expressed by former Labor minister Barry Jones – to such an extent that society changed too rapidly due to migrants coming in the front door but also the back door, via New Zealand. Now we are in danger of being swamped by Muslims, who bear a culture and ideology that is incompatible with our own.'[1]

In Hanson's first speech to the Parliament – second time around – she blamed migrants for both being on welfare and taking jobs, creating city congestion and causing 'everyday Australians' to suffer by filling schools and hospitals, leaving the aged and sick to 'fend for themselves'. She blamed federal and state governments, who were telling people that high immigration stimulates the economy, but in reality, she said, it was only to create a bigger market for multi-nationals, big banks and big business. Her message in the Senate was 'Clean up your own backyard before flooding our country with more people who are going to be a drain on our society.' She called for an end to further immigration.

The response from commentators to her speech was horror. The entire Greens Party walked out of the Senate. Sitting in the chamber, I could not believe we were going over this old terrain again – Hanson 1.0, circa 1996.

Certainly, Hanson likes to use race and culture as a bludgeon, but we have to be careful to distinguish between One Nation's specific appeal and the general protest vote by the neglected class. From my conversations with voters, Hanson's support base splits between voters with concerns over immigration, race and cultural issues, and those who want to protest against the political system and the major parties. Sometimes it is both.

'I feel I'm more minority [parties], and the vast majority still vote Coalition and Labor,' says Adrian Stadtmiller, who voted for Hanson's party in the 2016 election. 'They are rusted on Coalition and Labor. It doesn't matter if they have the exact opposite view to me. I even say, "I don't want to get into a fight with you or insult you," but the Left is trying to shut down reasoned debate within Australia. [Those people] obviously see even the moderate Right as the enemy, and because they want to put their view forward, they want to make their views normality and people can't give other views.'

Adrian and Trish are concerned about immigration, but they also want to protest because they feel people west of the Dividing Range are pretty well forgotten when it comes to politics. Regional Australia has been left out of the equation. Get this side of the divide and they don't give a hoot. Lack of trust is the big thing, says Trish.

'People feel disenfranchised. They have their vote but so bloody what? Even the ones you vote for lied to you,' says Adrian. 'They feel betrayed, they are west of the divide. If you are at Cobar and you see all these politicians sitting up in either house, plush leather seats, $200 a day living allowance, $200,000 on top of that, Commonwealth cars, flights into all the electorates. You are busting a gut rounding up billy goats in 45 degree heat – I think people are just jack of it. They really are.'

It is important not to forget that Hanson is not the only anti-politician attracting protest votes, and the other parties have agendas other than immigration and race. Nick Xenophon does not push the same anti-immigrant agenda, nor does Justice Party leader and former journalist Derryn Hinch. They have all attracted enough votes to get into the Senate, in Xenophon's case repeatedly so until his political demise in 2018. Jacqui Lambie has spoken against Muslims in the past but much of her agenda also revolves around the trust deficit – in politicians, big banks and big corporations. If there is a common thread, the first order of business for those voting for the Parliament crossbench is that their elected representatives either smash the machine or hold up policies for review. These people want to wrong-foot the major parties because politics is not working for them. A protest vote is the only way they can do that.

Traditionally, when we vote for a politician we place our trust in our member to represent us based on their policy agenda. Given not all political dilemmas can be foreseen, we hope to understand an MP's views and values because that is our only guide as to how they will behave over their parliamentary term. What I see among main-street voters is a rewriting of that contract with politicians, and the main reason for this is that lack of trust. We can no longer trust that our representatives will act in our interests according to the political roadmap they have set down in the promises and statements made before an election. Therefore, if we cannot trust our representative, if our expectations are so low that we cannot rely on their behaviour in future, then we can only send a message in the present. Increasingly, that means turning to a minor party or an independent. In the white noise of politics, with its proliferation of viewpoints in the internet age, brand recognition is everything. With a recognised brand, a Hanson, a Xenophon, a Lambie or a Hinch does not have to provide a full policy suite. Upsetting the major-party apple cart may be all a voter needs.

As many commentators and major party advocates have recognised, a minor party can get very little done in a Parliament that relies on a majority vote, unless they are in a hung Parliament where government is forced to listen to a list of minor party demands. (Hence Tony Windsor and Rob Oakeshott getting so much for their electorates out of the forty-third Parliament.) More often, minor parties and independents have had more success opposing policies by combining with major opposition parties to stymy government plans. That phenomenon reflects the main street. Political satirist Simon Hunt hit the nail on the head when he sang, 'I don't like it' as the Hanson parody Pauline Pantsdown. Tony Abbott's most successful political period was in opposition, a period *Financial Review* cartoonist David Rowe captured perfectly by drawing Abbott in trademark red budgie smugglers with NO shaved into his chest hair.

This negative outlook is one of the most disturbing changes to witness in recent years, given it has infected not just crossbenches but government benches. True to his persona, Abbott spent more time in the forty-fourth Parliament unpicking policy than creating it. He promised to stop the carbon tax, stop the mining tax and stop the boats, and he delivered. The keyword is 'stop'. The theory is that if we can't see our way to start something positive, we will stop something we consider bad. In that action, we can say we have delivered. That becomes the value of the protest vote, and in the process, governments start to be measured on what they can stop rather than what they can create.

And that is because negativity sells. Here I want to say something positive about politicians. Politics is hard and getting harder. The life, in spite of the pay, is hard. One of the best political essays in recent times was by my colleague Katharine Murphy in the literary journal *Meanjin* on this subject.[2] Politicians deal with the physicality of upside-down life routines, separation from family, getting around large electorates, abuse and expectations, as well as being in the grip of ever-changing whims, which stymy even the best policies. In the late 1990s at the *Australian*, I interviewed as many parliamentarians as possible for a feature on the political life. Their private lives were marked by divorce, alcohol, disappointment and frustration. With even the best intentions, the politicians become jaded by the systemic blockages that have left their agenda constipated. I would not go into politics, though I give them plenty of advice.

One of the best-connected residents on my main street, who crosses all local social groups and works across many community organisations, is Darren Sargent, truck driver and quarryman. I ask him whether he would consider politics.

'Never. You can't achieve anything in politics anymore. You can do more at a local level if you want to do some good.'

==

Matthew Stadtmiller told his parents, Adrian and Trish, he had been preselected for the Shooters, Fishers and Farmers Party just before the 2017 Cootamundra state by-election. Both Matthew's parents took up their son's candidature with gusto.

Matt represents a certain strain of outsider politician: he became involved in politics because he was 'pissed off'. His parents have strong political opinions so he'd always heard political conversations around the dinner table. Though it was before his time, he liked the fact that Bob Hawke skolled a schooner and suggested that any boss who sacked a worker on the day Australia won the America's Cup was a bum. He interpreted it to mean that Bob understood the 'common man'.

The first election Matt actively noticed was in 1993 – Paul Keating's win, when opposition leader John Hewson tried to sell the Goods and Services Tax to the electorate. The fact that Hewson could not explain the GST on a birthday cake showed Matt that policy must not be too complicated for the 'real person' to understand and that journalists 'can trip interviewees up'. (Of course, Howard sold the policy five years later.)

Matt went to primary school talking about old movies he had seen at home – *The Scarlet Pimpernel*, *To Kill a Mockingbird*, *Picnic at Hanging Rock* and *Breaker Morant*. He came away from those early years thinking he might be unusual: 'The other kids would look at me a bit sideways. I've always been stuck between the sporties and the geeks.'

He rebelled at school, completing his HSC but refusing to apply for a university entrance score, much to his parents' horror. Later, when he changed his mind, he says the school didn't lodge the paperwork. 'I didn't want to be judged on a score anyway.' He headed to

Canberra to try out for a rugby union career, but he wasn't built to play the second row at a higher-representative level after playing ACT Brumbies 18s. Back injuries from years of scrums took their toll. So he needed to try for uni via a bridging course in Canberra. 'I worked out I wasn't silly.'

While studying an arts degree in Canberra, he decided he liked international studies, but he thought it might be too straitlaced and he wanted a creative outlet, so he pulled the pin. 'I started a cleaning business while continuing study, by correspondence.'

With a BA – in TV production at Wagga – he went to an advertising job at the same local newspaper in 2012 as I worked, five years after I was there. In his time, Fairfax shut our town's office and Matt had to move to Cootamundra and sell advertising there as well. He felt the paper was moving away from its local focus as the offices were rationalised to bigger regional centres, and that made him angry so he started to think about setting up his own paper. He worked with his brother erecting steel while learning the business from a regional independent operator. Focusing on local news, the *Twin Town Times* started in December 2013 with a computer, a desk and a $5000 loan. He took $500 a week for the first six months and worked eighty hours a week to get it off the ground.

Around the same time, Matt joined the local council. He was spurred on to protest against a streetscape upgrade (which I had worked on as a community member) because he did not like aspects of the landscaping or the parking arrangements. After he was elected to council, Matt worked as a newspaper editor, reporter and councillor. He rose to deputy mayor for a time.

The New South Wales government started talking about the possibility of amalgamation, and urged councils to get together. Self-determination, it was called. The process was going ahead regardless, so better to work out your dance partner from the beginning. Meetings were scheduled, negotiations ensued, town hall meetings were called. Two years passed and an accommodation was made. Harden decided to go with Cootamundra. But in the middle of harvest, the state government dropped the news that the town would go with Young and Boorowa.

All politics is local. Here, I really get into the weeds. It seems like a small thing, going with one council or another, but it was totemic: a government betrayal. People around me were furious because they considered the decision was yet another symptom of government failing to listen. Or, worse still, duplicitous. Though this was a state government decision, it was marked down as a failing of government with a capital G. They are all as bad as one another.

I was aghast at the stupidity of a political process that encouraged people to get emotionally engaged and educated in the options, but then forced them to live with a different result altogether. People were energised. No correspondence was to be entered into with Mike Baird's New South Wales Liberal–National government. Conservative people were threatening to vote against the conservatives at the next election.

Matt was furious, too, attacking the new amalgamated administration in his paper nearly every week. He had been talking to the Labor opposition and the Shooters Party about whether anything could be done to stave off the merger.

In the meantime, the government announced the greyhound ban. There is a dog track in Young, but there had not been a lot of greyhounds walking the main street. What upset people, most of whom had never watched a greyhound race in their lives, was the imposition of another arbitrary decision. They felt spurned, again, by state government. The state National Party MP Katrina Hodgkinson, who had been quiet on the merger, crossed the floor to vote against the greyhound ban. It was too little too late for a large section of her voters. Soon after, she resigned.

Matt considered his political options. He identifies with some of his mother's Labor tendencies. 'Trish taught me a lot about compassion for people in need.' He favours a republic if the constituents get to vote for the leader. 'The SFF were standing up for the little guys; the people who didn't have a voice or weren't being listened to.' He was thinking about where to channel his political energy and says he only joined the Shooters, Fishers and Farmers Party a week before he was announced as their candidate, though he had been studying their policies for some time. 'They appeared to be a good fit for me, and they have continued to prove that.' He liked what he considered as 'commonsense policies' and admired the party's campaign in Orange in 2016, which had tipped out the Nationals. Like the Orange by-election, the political strategy of the Shooters Party in the Cootamundra by-election was a protest vote. Local voters were exhorted to put the Nationals last. Much of Matt's language was around the National Party taking country people for granted. The amalgamation and greyhound decisions represented a 'betrayal' of country people. He said the most consistent theme in his conversations was the desire to punish the National Party.

'I've had eighty-year-old farmers and Light Horse members come up to me and say, "I voted National or Liberal my whole life and I'm not voting for them again." I think it's because they have been betrayed a little bit. I think it's the lack of democracy that occurred in the forced amalgamations. They are meant to be for regional New South Wales. National Party members have the opportunity to cross the floor and at least put up a fight for the people they claim to represent.'

While he did not win the seat, Matt won 23 per cent of the primary vote from a standing start, just pipped by Labor's Charlie Sheahan. The National candidate, Steph Cooke, won the seat on 60 per cent with a two-party swing against her of 10 per cent, which masked a much bigger swing of 19 per cent of primary votes. In nearby Murray, the Nationals suffered a primary swing of 14 per cent.

Regional seats are clearly getting more volatile, and Matt says he will run again because he is convinced that state government decisions continue to take the town in the wrong direction. He looks back with nostalgia – and he is only in his thirties – to a time when the abattoirs were still running and the railway was bigger. There were jobs in town and 'things were here that we no longer have anymore'.

'It seems to me the town I was born and grew up in and went to high school in was going backwards by the time I was in my late twenties.' Health, education and energy dominate the concerns, he says. He highlights the divide between education in the city and the country. 'When you look at NAPLAN results in this region, nearly all of them are below or substantially below where they should be. If you look at [New South Wales premier] Gladys Berejiklian's seat, between 3 and 6 per cent of the students are in the bottom 25 per cent, where we have 50 per cent of our students in primary and high school in the bottom 25 per cent.'

'People who had traditionally voted with the National Party strayed away from them because they thought they needed to be taught a lesson. I don't think the Nats realise. The National Party out here are just doing what the Liberal Party want, when they could stand up more for regional areas. They have got to change what they are doing. Don't be a rooster out here and say you are going to do this, and then be a feather duster. We are engaged through social media now.'

Taught a lesson. I have heard many variations of this classic protest-vote sentiment. Matt's motivation was to make our seat a marginal seat so that 'the government might spend more money'. Like Windsor and Oakeshott before them, minor parties and independents are beginning to understand that if they are lucky and neither the Coalition or Labor parties win majority government, the outsider politician has the opportunity to sit in the political sweet spot and win maximum gains for their electorate.

Even if an outsider candidate doesn't win, once a seat becomes more marginal, MPs must work harder with voters to win. Since Labor and the Shooters and Fishers cut the Nationals' margin in half in the 2017 by-election, a lot of attention and money has been lavished on the Cootamundra electorate: a $113,500 grant to the Young football club, which happens to use the same oval as the Young greyhound club; $680,000 announced for the Temora Memorial Town Hall; and $100,000 to upgrade Ariah Park community facilities. Rural challengers are beginning to push home the message: Make It Marginal.

———

What I hear most from Matt's story is, once more, that sense people around me have of being abandoned by governments, corporations and by political parties that formerly paid more attention to country areas. Again, there is the question of trust. Trust that government once would do the right thing, trust in the compact that government acted for the nation as a whole, trust in the system – that if you worked hard you could get ahead.

When I ask the main street if the individual can get ahead if they work hard enough, the answers are mixed. Shiralee's family spend their weeks and most weekends working, and she is not sure that her kids' lives will be easier than her own. 'The rate things are going, I really don't think so.' She believes there is work for young people if they look for it, but worries that larger companies in regional areas are not giving younger people a go – she sees a lot of older people at the checkouts.

Farmer Peter Holding's family has been in the region since the 1800s. He recently sold off some of his land to pay down debt, and decided to lease other country to achieve certain economies of scale. Peter is a terrier, unafraid of controversy and going against the tide. This is unusual in a small town. He has voted for most parties in the past, though he has 'drawn the line' at One Nation. He has very different views to Matt, but he reflects the rising sentiment that politicians must work harder for their votes. Peter worries about climate change; he worries about agriculture being taken over by global conglomerates; he worries about the divide between the haves and the have-nots.

'In the seventies we were always fed this idea that if you worked hard and educated yourself, you would get ahead,' he says. 'It doesn't matter what you do [now], the economy has stalled, the rich bastards are ripping everybody off and we see that every day, and politicians have forgotten about the deal they made with the public; and everyone is just totally annoyed. I mean, I find it disturbing.'

When he looks around the world, he is dismayed at the rise of large corporations to the detriment of communities. For him, he is thinking about big parties and big business, and its control of the system. He has watched with concern while global companies like Cargill and Hassad have bought up Australian farm land. Agriculture and food giant Cargill is America's largest private company, while Hassad is a wholly owned subsidiary of the Qatar Investment Authority, the country's sovereign wealth fund that also has a mandate to ensure Qatar's food security program.

Peter worries that an economic downturn will force multinationals – which often demand set returns – into a big sell-off. 'If they put all this country on the market, it will be like someone let a nuclear bomb off in Australia. I can see a situation like Oklahoma in the 1930s, where people are just walking off.'

About 88 per cent of agricultural businesses in Australia are wholly owned by Australians, while 12.4 per cent of agricultural land is held by businesses with some level of foreign ownership.[3] About the same level (12.5 per cent) of total Australian agricultural water entitlements are owned by companies with some level of foreign ownership. While foreign ownership of land is not as big as people perceive, the issue continues to press buttons in the bush, but not always for the reasons the media and politicians think. Foreign ownership is often reported as xenophobic, and sometimes it is. But Peter Holding thinks about the foreign ownership of Australian land in the context of it threatening national food security in the shadow of climate change.

'All I ever hear when I go over to Canberra is [that] we have to look after the consumers. That's great – and eventually you kill all the farmers off and then you have to import all the food from China, and how is that looking after the consumers? Imagine if food prices went up 50 per cent. There would be a scream come out of the western suburbs like you would not have heard of. It wouldn't come out of here, it would come out down there. There is twenty electorates gone.

'We saw the Arab Spring start because some bloke could not sell his oranges in Tunisia. It is serious business, and when people get hungry they do some pretty strange things. And I don't think they quite get that out here because we have always had plenty of food.'

Peter believes Australian voters are angry because economics have pushed people to the point where they feel powerless.

'I sold out because more or less if we didn't I would go broke to cut the debt. I mean, a large debt. Something had to be done. So we got rid of all that. Mum thinks that is because we got old. No, it happened because of debt and because that was an opportune moment. If you were young, you would have to face facts.

'I don't think a lot of farmers get this and the economics has moved to such an extent in agriculture that most everyone is starting to realise. They are like peasants. Go back a thousand years to the peasantry and the feudal system and you have a few rich people rapidly gaining all the land again. I lease land, more or less like a peasant, and there are people out there working the land, but they don't have a lot of control over it, and with climate change they have even less control, and they are fed so much rubbish.'

Peter thinks it is hard for kids from disadvantaged families anywhere to get ahead unless they have a good role model, let alone kids in small towns where the opportunities are fewer. They need a parent, a relative, a mentor or a teacher. He says that under most circumstances struggling kids do not have access to those people. 'The things that change people's lives are other relationships between people. The reason rich people get rich is because they hang around with rich people that know how to get the system to work.'

And that is where he believes governments need to intervene – with funding for school services to make up the difference, otherwise disadvantaged kids, or those with fewer options, fall through the cracks. 'They will probably leave school, go off and get pregnant, and the cycle goes all over again. It's just the way it is. The schools don't have enough counsellors to handle that. They do their best but they just don't have the money. That's what annoys me – $120 million to spend on this stupid bloody [same-sex marriage] vote that should be ticked anyway. $120 million could have gone into schools, hospitals, anything.' (Peter's view is probably not reflective of his sixty-something age group around me. From my conversations, generations were split on the issue, with the younger generations supporting same-sex marriage as unremarkable, while older males tended to be resistant to change.)

More than social change, though, the neglected class want something concrete. Notwithstanding the local confusion over building our second school hall, voters usually want physical infrastructure as well as substantive ideas that address what they see as service deficiencies. People have developed a keen smell for political contrivances and frippery. There must be a mathematical formula out there that reflects the inverse relationship between the increasing use of political war-gaming and political anger. As politics have become slicker, people have become angrier.

The past decade of intra-party turmoil has seen many internal wars break out. In Parliament, when someone wants to get at the prime minister's office, a favoured tactic is to leak the government's 'talking points': the cheat sheets that succinctly put to the public its messages regarding a range of topics. The unthinking MP can rattle off the 'talking points' without much thought and still stay on message. This is partly required because ministers expect, and are expected by journalists, to answer questions across all portfolios or issues of the day. That means they need to know what the hell is going on. In a strange way, I yearn to return to the day when ministers stuck to their portfolio, to issues they actually knew something about.

The odd thing about the 'gotcha' moment of leaked talking points is that close observers pretty much know what is on the daily sheet because we hear the messages ad infinitum. Yet there *is* something raw about actually seeing the written words, because they confirm to voters what they suspected all along: that some politicians don't think for themselves; that some politicians rely on spin.

Consider the leak last year to Fairfax after the 2016 election.[4] Under the heading 'Abbott–Turnbull war', MPs were instructed to state that the current and the former PMs were 'working in the same direction'. No one needed a talking point to confirm that the reverse was true. Likewise, in the dying days of the Gillard prime ministership, Kevin Rudd supporter Joel Fitzgibbon joked that he would consult the 'manual' on what to say about another dire poll for Gillard. 'It says I should say polls come and go but the only poll that matters is on election day.'[5] These moments simply confirm what voters think about the business of politics.

So often, people tell me they know what politicians are up to. Peter says it infuriates him that politicians won't answer the question. He knows they are just playing 'What do you call it? Small-target politics?' That's why he likes to vote for independents. 'People have got to say, "I have had enough." I just want to stick it up them for three years and then they might fight to get the seat back again.'

As a result, when minor-party politicians walk blinking on to the stage, unsure of their lines and mangling their words, the main street likes it. When Jacqui Lambie suggested that the Nationals 'grow a set [of balls]' and oppose university fee deregulation, many applauded because finally someone was speaking a language they understood. The policy issue is often less important in the voter's mind than 'standing up' against the major parties. That was part of Nationals' former leader Barnaby Joyce's appeal before his political self-destruction. When he arrived on the political scene in 2005, with what we journalists would call a 'colourful turn of phrase', the media laughed at him. In my town, his presence registered immediately because of his language. And as he rose through the ranks of the National Party, polls showed that country people thought Joyce was a future Nats leader, because he stood out.

So plain-speaking language registers with voters. Criticism from the media and other more polished politicians only serves to underline an 'outsider' status. It is toted up as further evidence that certain politicians don't belong to the elite class that runs the country, and that they deserve a place in politics for that reason alone.

Shiralee votes informal these days, partly because of the constant leadership changes. She just doesn't believe that whoever she supports will stay there for long. She's given up wasting the emotional energy on deciding who to back. 'I just got my name ticked off, folded the piece of paper and put it in the box. I have done that for a while. Matthew gets cranky with me and says, Your vote counts. I say, Don't tell me that my vote counts, for god's sake. He says that it does, You're one person. I said, My vote is not gonna make any difference, and he says, Yeah – that if you don't vote, you give it to someone else anyway. I say, So be it. I could vote for Tom,

Dick or Harry and then Eliza will probably get in, so it won't make any difference. So I do vote but I don't.'

Shiralee comes from a Labor family. Her grandfather was always talking Labor, but after she got married Matt's family was always talking Liberal. To Shiralee, they are all the same. She reels off the last five prime ministers. 'We had Kevin Rudd, then he was put out, then Julia Gillard got in. She was no better than Kevin Rudd, then they put her out, and put Tony Abbott in, and he was pathetic. Then they put him out and put Malcolm Turnbull in. It wouldn't matter who they voted in, they would be swapped out anyway. None of them are any good.'

Shiralee is doing well given that in 2015 paramedics stopped assessing a patient's level of consciousness by asking them to name the current prime minister.

=

The rise in voter support for minor parties and independents has created a political volatility that is heart-stopping for the average member of Parliament. Looking back at my stories in politics around the 1996 election of the Howard government, we counted marginal seats as those electorates with a margin of less than 5 per cent. That is, a 5 per cent swing would win the seat. In 2017, Liberal MP John Alexander declared he might be a dual British citizen so he needed to renounce and go to a by-election to win back his old seat of Bennelong. He was on a margin of 9.7 per cent and though he won, it was touch and go. When 10 per cent is marginal, life as an MP is a whole lot harder.

With this voter volatility comes lower expectations as to what governments can achieve. Major political parties have taught voters they cannot trust that governments will deliver on their promises or keep their prime minister in place, so voters are in the process of teaching political parties that they can't trust their traditional allegiances. Politicians acknowledge this fact but don't really know what to do about it. The unpredictability of voter behaviour has made it less likely that governments can achieve anything. Australian politics has become a self-fulfilling prophecy.

Most politicians know that voters are breaking from the mob to vote for outsiders. Most politicians know that people are unhappy with the volatility. When Malcolm Turnbull challenged Tony Abbott for the leadership, he said there must be an end to 'policy on the run' and 'captain's calls'. Australia, he continued, needed 'a style of leadership that respected the people's intelligence, that explained these complex issues and then set out a course of action and made a case for it. We needed advocacy, not slogans.' Turnbull diagnosed the disease but has yet to deliver the treatment.

The anger, meantime, continues with all levels of governments – federal, state, local – because Government with a capital G is seen as the problem. The neglected class feel like they are doing their job, but politicians, governments and media are not doing theirs. It might not be a fully formed coherent argument. Who has time or inclination for that? It is the vibe, as they say in *The Castle*.

When the New South Wales premier swanned into Young for the by-election, I asked fifty-something tradie Tim if he went to see her. Nah, he says, I only would have gone if I could have fifteen minutes with Gladys.

What would you say?

'What the fuck are you doing? You have got no idea. You don't have a clue, you are just fucking the place up. I just would have to say that.'

How are they fucking it up?

'They are just liars. I would cut their wage in half, get rid of half of them. Just don't be a liar.'

What do they lie about?

'Everything. You know that. You write about the bastards.'

255

Most of my fellow residents think I have an unhealthy and ulti-mately unfruitful job. 'How do you do it?' is their most common question. Whether this vein of discontent ends in tears for the major parties in Australia is the great unknown. But if I were to place a bet on the group that would be most likely to break away in a Brexit or Trump-style movement, it is this neglected constituency in the regions and outer metropolitan areas. People who are most aware of other people who are economically better off and worse off. They are largely white working class, the smaller end of business owners, or sole contractors and farmers who do not see their interests align with wealthier people who have connections into politics through the conservative parties. Rusted on electorates are rusted off.

LESSON 15

The economics of a small town are tricky

I started covering federal politics during the dying days of the Keating government, and the underlying message from economists since then has been that small towns do not work in an age of globalisation. This is an international argument. The most blunt statement of it in recent times was from Kevin D. Williamson in the *Nation Review*, talking about the near-dead tiny town of Garbutt, in New York state, prior to Trump's election. 'The truth about these dysfunctional, downscale communities is that they deserve to die. Economically, they are negative assets.'[1]

We know that towns change and at any one time in a nation some are thriving and some are in decline. It is an inconvenient truth to economists that people will always need to eat, but it is an equally inconvenient truth for towns like Harden-Murrumburrah that the agriculture industry is now able to produce more with fewer people. We are told that unless we have other industries, or a critical mass of people, our town is bound to fade like an old photo. I only need to look up in the shed out the back to see the scythes that were used for hand-harvesting wheat hanging in the rafters – a constant reminder that this farm and those around us needed many more people in the past. These days, dinner conversations are around driverless tractors and small-scale swarm robotic technology to solve paddock problems. A new tractor practically requires an IT degree to drive it. The metropolitan image of the farmer is old school, portrayed in shows like *The Farmer Wants a Wife*. But this farmer wanted a state-of-the-art drone. Using his drone, he checks water troughs, sheep mobs, pastures and crops.

The march of technology is not new, and as it has taken place much of the focus in small agricultural towns like ours, as we have seen, has been finding the Big Employer. In this fantasy, the Big Employer will ride in and build a bloody great factory/shed/complex producing widgets that will create masses of jobs. But there is a bracing fact in Labor MP and economist Andrew Leigh's book *Choosing Openness*. In Australia, manufacturing jobs peaked in 1948 – a lot earlier than some of the commentary would suggest. 'Even in the immediate post-war decades,' Leigh writes, 'as these countries kept their trade barriers high, the share of the population employed in manufacturing was declining.'[2] There goes the widget factory. Likewise in the main street. In our town, railway employment peaked in the 1920s, yet in our town's nostalgic memory the peak is closer to the 1950s post-war boom.

When I served on the local council committee in the 2000s drought, its goal was economic development, which meant finding creative ways to attract to the town jobs, industries and ultimately people. Kids for the schools. Implicit in the understanding in agricultural small towns is that while farming might be the traditional economic foundation, we need new businesses and industries to provide some stability to the rollercoaster that is food production reliant on weather patterns. That committee and subsequent local economic development officers spent a lot of time duchessing small and medium-sized businesses to move in. They had some success – a large duck producer moved to town – but it is hard yards.

Years later, after Brexit and Trump, I take the XPT train down the Sydney–Melbourne line to consult with John Daley and his colleague and program director Danielle Wood of the Grattan Institute. My school days were spent in largely white neighbourhoods in the east and the northern suburbs of Sydney. I have spent most of my time working at home, in Parliament or in Sydney's east. So when I step out at Southern Cross station in the heart of Melbourne, it's a culture shock even for me. I follow a country bloke up Bourke Street. He walks like Tony Abbott and is wearing the dogger boots which are common at rodeos, a big Akubra and an Ariat jacket, favoured by horsey types. I can see him looking around as if he has landed in another country. He looks left at the young Asian-Australian guys chatting next to him. He looks right at young Muslims wearing hijabs in the Bourke Street mall and then he turns and looks at me. His eyes skate over – presumably because as an Asian-looking woman I look like everyone else in that mall. I have waited for a long time to be the same as everyone else. But as I watch this guy, it does not require much empathy to work out that his head might be spinning from cultural discombobulation. Migrant kids – not to mention Indigenous kids – understand that more than anyone.

In the heart of multicultural Melbourne, Daley and Wood have no good news for my little town. In 2017, they completed a research paper called 'Regional patterns of Australia's economy and population'. The report highlighted Australia's ongoing march towards a service economy.[3] It showed that the share of jobs in agriculture, forestry and fishing has fallen from 6.1 per cent to 2.5 per cent since the mid-1980s; and the share of manufacturing jobs has dropped from 16.1 to 7.5 per cent. At the same time, the rise of service industries keeps going up and up, to 79 per cent in 2017. As *The Economist* wrote in 2013, services are things that you cannot drop on your foot, like accommodation, healthcare, transport, education and communications.[4] Services are not things like agriculture, manufacturing, forestry, fishery or mining. Daley is another in the long line of economists who tells me the Big Employer ain't going to happen.

'If you're an employer, there is usually no particularly good reason to set up your new whatever-it-is in the regions. We live in a world where the economy is dominated by services, and growth in the economy is even more dominated by services. There might be good reasons to put a manufacturing business out in the regions, but there is usually no reason to put a services business there. For most services businesses, what matters is being close to other services businesses.

'The only exceptions are businesses that provide localised services – your hospital, your school – that have to be located where people live. But most services businesses can supply people more remotely, and there is usually no reason for them to be in a regional area. Instead they want to be with as many other services businesses as possible – usually in a big city like Melbourne.'

And never mind my area of 3500 people, Daley is pessimistic about Adelaide. 'There are a lot of high-end services businesses that have left Adelaide and now service it out of Melbourne. [Adelaide is] not big enough in demand terms. And because clustering is particularly important to high-end services businesses, they are converging on Melbourne. Adelaide's economy is getting hollowed out because it's too easy for the big professional services firms to service Adelaide by putting someone on the plane. It's harder to do that for Perth because it's just too far, but they can do it for Adelaide, so they do.'

Of the big law and accounting firms, Daley says some would be lucky to have a shopfront in Adelaide with one person on the desk. 'The same is true of middle-order businesses. If you're a specialist law firm, why would you be in Adelaide, let alone Mildura? The only reason you would be in Mildura is if you were specifically servicing agriculture businesses and quasi-manufacturing business that hang off agriculture.'

This news is both comforting and not. Comforting because if Adelaide is up shitters' ditch, then our little town should not feel so bad. Not comforting because he paints a picture of a world where the only survivors live in big cities. Nick Xenophon should really place a travel ban on Daley going anywhere near South Australia.

So is he telling me that as the economy moves to more service-based industries, there is no answer for my country town, which has long been waiting for the Big Employer to provide jobs for 150 people?

'It ain't going to happen.'

Economic inequality has long existed between the cities and regions. Using the 2016 census and 2014–15 tax data, Daley and Wood found average incomes tend to be highest in city postcodes, though there are 'pockets of disadvantage' in Sydney and Melbourne and 'large swathes of low income suburbs' in Adelaide and Brisbane. Most regional areas in New South Wales, Victoria, Tasmania and southern Queensland have below-average incomes. At that time, regional areas in Western Australia, South Australia, the Northern Territory and northern Queensland typically had above-average incomes. Incomes were particularly high in mining areas in the Pilbara in Western Australia, the Bowen Basin in Queensland, and Olympic Dam in South Australia.

Daley and Wood found that inequality was actually worse within cities than in the regions, which makes sense given that super-high incomes are usually to be found in the cities, along with pockets of poverty.

But even though there is a clear perception that regional discontent stems from country people being left behind, the economic gap per person has not been getting wider. The income gap between cities and regions stayed steady over the past decade. Income growth per person was pretty similar across cities and regions in the past decade, with high blips in some remote areas, mostly for mining jobs. Unemployment is patchy, but it is not obviously worse in the regions when compared with outer suburbs, nor is it growing faster outside of the cities.

And yet, Grattan's research found life *is* changing for people in the country. One consequence of growing services industries is that more people are moving away from small regional towns, and more people are moving into the cities. Population growth is highest in and around the cities and the coast, with some good growth in mining regions. This growth is fuelled by migration, and most migrants, particularly people from non-English-speaking backgrounds, tend to go to the capitals. Daley and Wood found that around 12 per cent of Australia's total population was born in the UK, North America or Europe, compared to the 8 per cent from Asia and 2 per cent from Africa and the Middle East. It contrasts with my 'statistical area' of Young–Yass: 1 per cent of people in my region was born in Asia; 0.4 per cent in Africa or the Middle East; 6.3 per cent were born in Western countries.

Daley contends that in the post-war period more jobs were being created in regional areas, so more unskilled migrants moved there. These days, migrants are more skilled so they tend not to go to regional areas unless they find skilled work there as, say, doctors or nurses.

'For most migrants who go to regional areas, we are condemning them to a pretty ordinary outcome, because there aren't many new jobs there . . . unless they are a health worker. They are going to struggle, or wind up with a job that doesn't use the skills they have got. These bigger regional towns that are within cooee of Melbourne are doing rather better: Shepparton, Bendigo, Ballarat. They are growing populations.'

There is also the education divide, which, again, governments and media have long documented. Cities are generally home to higher numbers of people with tertiary educations, bearing in mind some pockets have lower rates of university-trained people. Certain coastal areas and university regions, such as Armidale, also have higher rates of tertiary education. But in the main, education rates in regions and rural areas are lower.

In Young and Yass, on the 2016 census rather than the Grattan maps, we have 16.3 per cent of people with a bachelor degree compared with 22 per cent for the whole of Australia. But if I drill down into Harden-Murrumburrah that number drops to 7 per cent. Compared with the rest of Australia, the town has fewer advanced diplomas, more certificate-three qualifications, fewer Year 12 leavers, double the number of Year 10 leavers, and twice the number of people whose highest school attainment was Year 9 or below. So the diversity and education divides are clear between city and country, as is the economic divide.

In 2018, Grattan built on their research to consider the reasons behind the accelerating support for minor parties in a final paper called 'A crisis of trust: the rise of protest politics in Australia'.[5] In the 2016 Australian federal election, the minor-party vote in the House of Representatives and the Senate reached its highest level since the Second World War. Wood and Daley note that in the 2016 election, votes for minor parties in the House of Representatives exceeded 23 per cent – the highest level since the 1950s and 8 percentage points higher than in 2004. In the Senate, the increase was more than 15 percentage points.

As self-confessed policy wonks, Daley and Wood were straying from economics into political science because they wanted to work out why reform was so hard. To do that, they needed to discover why the vote for minor parties has risen rapidly over the past decade, particularly in regional electorates. They started with the common explanation for the rise in the populist vote across Western countries: that many people believe Australia's regions are getting an economic raw deal compared to the big capital cities. But, they argued, 'Support for minor parties in Australia rose most when wages grew strongly and inequality was stable. Economic insecurity also doesn't seem to explain the widening city–regional voting divide: the regions are keeping pace on most indicators of individual economic well-being.'

Daley and Wood concluded there has always been an economic divide reflected in an income gap between city and the regions, but income growth has pretty much stayed the same. In other words, the anger must not be driven by the gap because the gap has always been there. Furthermore, they point out, 'international evidence is mixed on the link between populism and the economy' and Australian studies have 'failed to find any relationship between vote share of the incumbent and the health of the Australian economy'.

The Grattan Institute's findings suggest, then, that economically the divide between city and country has remained relatively static, or at least as unequal as it always has been. But there is another divide, which equates to the fact of more culturally and linguistically diverse populations in the cities and more culturally similar populations in the country. This cultural divide (unlike the economic divide) is getting bigger, Daley and Wood argue. The cultural divide is growing more because the cities are drifting away, rather than because the regions are changing. It's reflected in regional attitudes, which include concerns about the pace of change, the decline in traditional values, and the level of migration. This increasing cultural distance is playing out in politics.

Daley's key takeaway point is that there are no jobs out here, so the population slide will continue. Or, as Danielle Wood says, 'It's very hard to fight these forces – you can't push economic water uphill.' She argues that most regional jobs and population schemes have failed, though she believes there is a case for financial assistance to towns exposed to a sudden shock such as a closure of a large employer like the car industry.

But when you take the economic divide and add it to nearly thirty years of economic messages to small communities that they are not viable in a globalised economy, that some of your towns are dying and you have to move if you want to stay ahead, maybe it is as simple as reaching a tipping point. We did not desert the major parties ten years ago, but having been told we are the walking dead for the past decade, I for one have enough oppositional defiance disorder to say, 'Well, up yours.'

Or, put another way, there is a danger in assuming that if the economic divide remains consistent, it can't be a real cause of voter anger. That's a bit like concluding that because there's always been a gap between male and female wages that gap cannot be the cause of rising anger among women. Are women angrier now over the gender pay gap than they were? Too bloody right. Sometimes there is just a flash point, a #MeToo movement.

LESSON 16

You can't make assumptions about small towns and race

When I arrived in town, Yusuf Khalfan and his business partner, Mirza Datoo, had been the local family doctors for twenty years. They carved out a practice shortly after they arrived in the late 1970s and they must have treated just about everyone in Harden-Murrumburrah over the years. They worked from a little apricot-coloured terrace whose waiting room was the lounge room of the original house. It had a coffee table for magazines and a toy box. Many mothers, including me, had crouched on the little chair next to that toy box trying to keep our sick kids occupied. The ever-patient practice managers double-booked in patients. When you know everyone, it's hard to refuse a sick child or an older person struggling with the latest bug or a chest-rattling ailment. Never mind the emergencies.

Yusuf grew up in Kenya. His parents were Indian, one side from East Africa, one side from Zanzibar. He has Persian heritage, too: his Shia family migrated from country to country over generations. After an arranged marriage in Kenya, his parents settled down and had twelve children. Yusuf was number nine. His father was a law clerk, an expert in Islamic jurisprudence, assisting judges, particularly on the business of estates donated for religious purposes, known as waqf. He also worked for a British firm, but his main job was dealing with waqf.

As was common then in Kenya, his father pushed the boys towards education, but not the girls. His mother was also instrumental, insisting Yusuf go to a government school rather than the community schools run by each religion or religious branch. There were schools for Shia Muslims, Sunni Muslims, Ismailis, Hindus and Jains, as well as the African and English populations. His mother told him that if he went to a community school he would never progress, so he walked back and forth, four times a day, to the two sessions of government school. His family were fairly strict adherents to the faith, rising at 5 am to learn the Koran, visiting the mosque and saying prayers.

When Yusuf's father died, his older brothers had to leave school to support their mother and siblings. He had no intention of going to university and when he left school he taught at a local high school. Yusuf's brother, Hami, and his mother applied for a scholarship for him at the well-regarded Makerere University School of Medicine in Uganda. Yusuf had no idea the application had been submitted and was as surprised as anyone when he won a place.

Five years later, university dean and fledgling dictator Idi Amin handed Yusuf a medical degree, and after a three-year internship back in Kenya, in Mombasa, he travelled to Kericho, a tea-growing district in the Kenyan highlands. He was the only doctor covering around sixty health centres and one hospital with 120 beds. His saviours were the medical assistants, the equivalent of Australian bush nurses, who had learned their skills from experience. By the light of generators and a Land Rover, the assistants guided him through surgery in Swahili. 'They are the ones who taught me more surgery than the professors.' The assistants also acted as triage nurses, seeing hundreds of patients a day. Between twenty and thirty would reach twenty-five-year-old Yusuf.

He remembers a good life and friendships across divides. A government school taught him to mix with many different religions and races. His ambition was to return and teach at Makerere, but when Idi Amin's regime began throwing out all Uganda's Asian citizens, any hope of return to his old medical school vanished.

Fellow graduate Mirza Datoo came from a small village in Tanzania, the seventh of ten children. He trained as an anaesthetist. Political turmoil in East Africa in the 1970s pushed him and Yusuf, old university friends, to consider emigrating to the US, the UK or Canada. Then, at an opening night of the movie *Bonnie and Clyde*, they found themselves outside a cinema that was opposite the Australian High Commission. There was a long queue for the movie so while the pair was waiting they decided to ask about their chances in Australia. It was 1976, and an Australian staff member said, 'Sure thing, we will even pay for the ticket.' The rest of Yusuf's family eventually left as well but most of them chose Canada.

Malcolm Fraser's government paid the pair's airfares to Sydney and they were put up in the Endeavour Migrant Hostel in Coogee. They had very little money and were horrified at the price of a bus ticket – 80 cents – until the following week, when they received the first of their weekly cheques from the government to get established.

Chance struck again. A fellow medical graduate had a practice in the New South Wales town of Grenfell, and as Yusuf waited for his postgraduate course at the University of New South Wales to start, he and Mirza were told of a practice that might be for sale in Harden. The two doctors bought the practice with a bank loan but very little collateral and started treating in the town the year after.

Yusuf remembers being welcomed by most local people, though a few were hostile, and they happened to be from the more influential families in the district. Their reaction to the young doctors' presence caused a split on the Harden-Murrumburrah hospital board – some of whom supported a doctor who had arrived after them. The state government stepped in to broker a resolution, and it kept Mirza and Yusuf in town. And here they stayed for the next three decades. Yusuf married Jenny, a self-described working-class nurse, and Mirza married Sherryn, also a nurse. They sent their kids to local schools. They joined community groups, while tending the young, the sick and dying. Yusuf was Rotary president for years. He helped establish the Bendigo Bank branch as other banks pulled out of town, served on numerous health boards and played cricket in his younger days. Mirza helped set up the local bridge club. Together with the nurses and allied health workers, the doctors' presence and advocacy meant the hospital continued to function and the nursing home residents received attention. Mirza worked as an anaesthetist throughout the region.

New services came to town such as diabetes education, mental health services, and a Life Education van, which teaches children preventative health messages around eating, exercise and drugs. Immunisation rates increased. There is something fundamental in the trust that is forged with people who treat you when you are physically or emotionally low. That is how Yusuf and Mirza became sewn into the fabric of a little town.

Yusuf and Jenny have retired now, and spend their time between the town and the coast, connected to their professions through locum positions. Mirza and Sherryn have retired to Canberra. Both doctors have been awarded an Order of Australia medal for medical service to rural communities.

I caught up with Yusuf at the annual picnic race meeting and we sat down to talk about nebulous notions of race and the migrant experience in country towns. There were moments for Yusuf. There was the bloke who called him a black bastard, then became his patient. We agree that minorities have to jump a higher bar to prove themselves. That's how it is. Yusuf did not consider it consciously. Who would when they are making their way from the Kenyan highlands to Harden in their twenties? Like so much stuff in life, gut instinct ensured that he survived. That and a bloody-mindedness to make his new life work, and to prove to people 'I am here to stay, whether you like it or not.'

'I think that as a minority you have to really expose yourself,' Yusuf tells me. 'You have to go above that, and I still remember telling people when I came to this town, "I am the biggest wog," and that killed everything. The word "wog" has now gone off, but it was very prominent at that time.'

Like Yusuf, I was always proud of my heritage and put that cultural pride out there in our little town. I had as much fun as anyone, batting back racially loaded comments, intended or innocent. When I first arrived, I was picking up something in town when a man remarked on my arrival as the new bride. After I introduced myself, he said without malice, 'I often thought I'd get me a Chinese wife.' I stifled my laugh and guffawed with the farmer when I got home. I could laugh because racial divides are also about power. When you have power, as the town doctor, or, like me, when you are secure in your economic, cultural and professional place, it is possible to laugh those comments off because we are cushioned by a web of other supports. But it is crippling for those without power.

Yusuf remains grateful for the support of locals and other health professionals, whose own networks into community helped build a critical mass of support. He and Jenny stayed up late some nights, discussing their issues with other staff. Workplace camaraderie is made from little moments, and in a small community it spreads like a Facebook meme. Conversely, lack of support can break a person. In the end, after a lifetime of practice, Yusuf's issue was how to leave without hurting people rather than how to stay.

==

My instinct as the daughter of a migrant is always in favour of immigration. We are a migrant nation. I have covered immigration as a policy round in Canberra and as a larger part of the political story in recent years, as the asylum-seeker issue has become central to elections. When we think of migrants, we think of brown people, those who are visibly different. We do not think of white people because they do not stand out in most Australian communities. Then, as if to remind us that Australia is a migrant nation, in 2017 the dual citizenship issue arose. Barnaby Joyce's father was born elsewhere, as mine was. Yet I kept hearing, 'How could you be more Australian than Barnaby?' One woman said to me, 'It's not like he's Pakistani.' Would that work for me? Is Barnaby more Australian than me because of his Anglo appearance? Had they had to prove their 'Australian-ness', would Iranian-born former Labor senator Sam Dastyari or Singaporean-born Ian Goodenough have been cut the same slack as MPs of British and New Zealand heritage?

On the main street, acceptance of individual migrants or multicultural backgrounds sits side by side with a fear of the same migrants as a group. It is impossible to make assumptions. I grew up assuming country towns were filled with rednecks. This is not correct. Then I arrived in town and assumed that having two long-serving, loved and trusted Muslim doctors in Yusuf and Mirza would have softened hearts to Muslim migrants. This is not correct.

There are two contradictory impulses in country towns regarding migration. One is that remote and regional voters are more likely to believe that the immigration intake is too high. The second factor is the increasing trend for country towns to actively court immigrants to boost their populations or fill particular jobs such as health workers or abattoir workers. So people may be voting against more migration while at the same time trying to attract migrants into their towns to boost jobs, swell schools and staff health services.

This conundrum has also led to contradictory government policy and messaging.

Barnaby Joyce, for example, has argued strongly that country towns need temporary visa programs – previously known as 457 visas – to fill job shortages in the bush. At the end of 2016, he argued that the 457 visa program should be 'a demand-driven program'.

'If the demand is there and the visa holders go to regional areas, then they are growing Australia's regional economy. When a home-grown workforce is either unavailable or reluctant to move to regional Australia, we don't see 457 visa holders as a threat, we see them as a benefit.'

Joyce argued that the temporary skilled worker visa also helped to road-test new migrants, suggesting that a drop in the visa numbers in places like Rockhampton in Queensland was because '457 workers wanted to become Australians and constructive members of the community: buying houses, bringing up their kids. And that's exactly what happened.'[1]

But after Labor campaigned for a crackdown on temporary visa holders in the 2016 election, and Pauline Hanson won four seats in the Senate, the Coalition followed suit. The 457 visa was replaced by two classes of visas with greater restrictions on citizenship and permanent residency requirements as well as a reduction in the number of occupations eligible.

The language was squarely aimed at sending a message that Australian jobs would be quarantined for Australian workers. The political message to 'crack down' on temporary foreign workers was unmistakable, though it went hand in hand with a change that ensured employers could still get skilled workers in regions that needed them. One of the new visas also allowed the transition to permanent residency.

Politics does not happen in a vacuum. Not only have small-town residents been told for the past few decades they are not viable, but at the same time they have seen skilled migrants and asylum seekers attempting to get into Australia. So in some quarters it feels as if immigration could disrupt regional towns. There is a fear of being displaced or of being asked to change. All the while, people feel they have less control over the forces that have caused negative changes to their towns, such as government's withdrawal of jobs, globalisation and technological change, which has aggregated jobs and services in larger centres.

When the former prime minister John Howard said 'We will decide who comes to this country and the circumstances in which they come', his message was as much about having control as deciding the make-up of immigrants. After all, he subsequently presided over a substantial increase in skilled migrants. Most small towns and non-metropolitan regions do not have the diversity that makes other cultures commonplace. This may explain why individuals are accepted more willingly than larger cultural and religious groups, especially the newest migrant kid on the national block. Oddly, since Labor and the Coalition have moved closer together on policies such as boat turn-backs – forming a bipartisanship on tougher policy – the anti-immigration vote has bled to minor parties and to candidates on the right of the major parties in rural and regional areas.

If that isn't confusing enough, while the anti-immigration dynamic is at work, there are 150 local government areas out of a total of 537 across the nation that have lost Australian-born population but gained overseas-born population. Areas picking up population increased by 50 per cent to 2016 on the previous census period to 2011. These include western New South Wales, north-western Victoria and the wheat belt in Western Australia. Examples include the resettlement of 160 Karen refugees from Myanmar to the Wimmera's wheat-belt town of Nhill in Victoria to fill jobs at the town's largest employer, the duck producer Luv-a-Duck. When the Port Melbourne-based company planned an expansion in 2010, the low unemployment rate and the decline in the working-age population forced it to look further afield. A report from Deloitte Access Economics and the AMES settlement agency concluded that the initiative had added $41.5 million to the local economy and seventy jobs.[2] The crucial part, though, was strong communication and support from and between the local community leadership, the Karen community leadership, the local government, the employer, as well as the Nationals federal MP for Mallee Andrew Broad to ensure the transition went smoothly. You can't dump people in a small town, walk away and expect everyone to sing 'Kumbaya'.

Examples such as Nhill make it difficult to generalise about attitudes to immigration and difference in rural and regional areas, or indeed to predict any Brexit or Trump-style backlash. All I can do is go back to my main street, where the town is 86.5 per cent Australian-born.[3] As a whole, Australia has 28 per cent of its population born overseas, which is higher than other OECD countries like Canada (20 per cent), the US (13 per cent) and the UK (12 per cent). But our overseas-born gravitate to cities: 83 per cent of first-generation migrants were living in capital cities in 2016.[4]

Lorraine Brown's ancestor Robert Chamberlain was drawn to our area by the gold rush of the 1850s. He was one of the locals who signed the petition against the influx of Chinese during the Lambing Flat riots, which led to the White Australia policy. Many Chinese were injured and most likely killed in those riots, when they were set on by white miners upset at their lack of return and competition because of the Chinese.[5] Lorraine has worked hard to commemorate those events from the Chinese side through the Lambing Flat Chinese Festival. She and local historian Robyn Atherton have studied with others in the local historical society to research and restore the Chinese section of our local cemetery, which remains the last vestige of a larger Chinese presence left over from the goldfields. The graveyard is in a different section to the larger population, and in the past its headstones were tumbled and overgrown. Grant funding and working bees have restored it in memory of the Chinese who are buried there.

'I'm sure that Robert Chamberlain, when he signed that petition, was the percentage of people who feared the Chinese coming in who were different, who had different food, different clothing, everything was so different and totally alien.'

She believes it takes years for migrants to integrate comfortably and for the local population to benefit from the new culture coming in. Lorraine saw the discomfort of a visiting Chinese delegation who arrived in town to commemorate the Chinese contribution to the area for the local goldfields festival. She watched them getting out of the bus and by their body language she realised, 'To them, this is quite alien.' It was no different to my lived experience.

The Chinese were the old migrants and their genetic heritage carries on in some families. The newer group to arrive in the region are Lebanese Muslims in the nearby town of Young, though the first Muslims were attracted by the orchard farms in the 1970s.

I have long heard reactions against Muslim immigration in my conversations, in spite of the doctors' contributions to the area's people. I have also heard strong support from many voters of different shades for attempts to ban the burqa, the full face and body covering worn by a tiny minority of Australian Muslims. When Pauline Hanson wore a burqa into the Senate, it was a big topic of conversation on the main street.

'I think she was just trying to make a point in doing what she did,' says Lorraine. 'I admire her for that. She has taken the ridicule and so forth that goes with it. Most people are tolerant of the Muslims and that, but they are predominantly in a Christian country, and our rules and regulations here say you can't go into a bank with a helmet on, or a face covering, yet we give in to a very small proportion of the people and allow them to do the same thing. And I think that's wrong in our society.'

Lorraine contrasts the Muslims and the Chinese to a community of Anglo-Saxon people. She says that while people were frightened of the Chinese migrants during the gold rush, they 'never imposed their religion on us as does some of the Muslim community'.

'The radicals impose that religion on everyone else.'

She also feels the doctors were accepted because they married into 'our community'. Lorraine is worried that the newer migrants might take generations to marry into the larger community. 'That's the objection that people think about. If you know on a personal basis a Muslim person, it's probably no different to a Chinese person or as I knew the Jewish people, who are persecuted. I think it's always the threat of that community imposing their values on your community; that you have your own rules and regulations. The Muslims probably more so than the Chinese community. Probably early generations intermarried within their community. They never enforced their ideologies on the rest of the community, but that is different than some of the radical Muslims. I do believe that happens worldwide because that is where all the hotspots are. That frightens people, including me.

'For us out here, it's probably no threat at the moment, but I do see the threat of the radical Muslims and that's a bit scary if they get into politics, and that's where we think about dual citizenship.'

Lorraine thinks the resistance to other races and cultures might be a 'a hangover from the early British', but she fears the rules are being changed to suit minorities. She cites her son's city school which, she says, forty years ago banned some old hymns to suit Muslim families at the school. 'We were giving in a long time ago to this very small minority of people who were here, and assuming they have come here for a better life and yet trying to impose their things on us. They have come in accepting that that is the rules here. Within that society, you can still have your own religion and things you want, but there are certain standards that we have that you have to abide by, and one of them as far as I am concerned is the full burqa.'

I was live-blogging the Parliament for the *Guardian* when the One Nation leader walked into the chamber dressed in a burqa. It was one of those moments, the end of a long parliamentary day and week, when you can't quite believe your eyes. Hanson took off the burqa and asked whether Attorney-General George Brandis would work to ban it. Shaking with emotion, Brandis said no and outlined the security reasons why her actions were dangerous. He said it would marginalise a certain section of Islam. He reminded her there were half a million law-abiding adherents to Islam. Brandis got a standing ovation from Labor and the Greens, though not his own colleagues. His strength of feeling was palpable. Having reported through Tony Abbott's 'death cult' national security campaigns, which had all the nuance of a house brick, I was relieved that Brandis was not going to use the moment for a dog whistle. I wrote at the time 'GO GEORGE!' but I returned home to find most people on the main street had reservations about the burqa.

Farmer Peter Holding has voted for many different parties and is not socially conservative. He described Hanson's wearing the burqa in the Senate as a 'stupid stunt', but he is against the burqa because he sees it as a symbol of female persecution. He has no time for Hanson, describing her as a 'sad and bitter person', but he can understand why she wants to ban the mode of dress. 'I think women who wear burqas have no personal freedom and [opponents] want to do something for women's rights, but you can't go round saying you want to ban the burqa. That is simply an attack on Muslims. If she stood up and said, "We don't agree with the burqa in this country because it's a symbol of female persecution – it's like Saudis saying women can't drive. All of these rules have got to go", then I would say, Yeah, that's great. But to do that stupid stunt and pretend they are all terrorists . . .'

Shiralee agrees with Hanson's stance. She has seen women in burqas in Young and when she can't see a face she finds it 'confronting and uncomfortable'. I ask about a number of doctors in the region who are Muslims. Does that bother her?

'It does but it doesn't.'

Adrian and Trish Stadtmiller were family patients of Yusuf Khalfan for thirty-five years and great supporters of him. But, like Lorraine, the couple link mass immigration with the perception that unnecessary changes are made to accommodate minorities. At the same time, Adrian acknowledges that Indigenous people had white culture forced on them by British settlers. His feeling is that immigration has gone too far.

'Immigration is a big issue for me,' says Adrian. 'We had the post-war immigration boom and that was great for Australia. I don't mind if they don't integrate, that's up to them. It would be great if we could all integrate and get along fine. But when a few radical Muslim people arrive here and start demanding that sharia law replace democracy as the way of life in Australia, it's not on.

'It's not what we are used to and we don't want it, obviously,' says Trish. 'Also, what angers us is when they come and they suddenly say, No, their way is the right way. That's probably a very Aussie thing to say but we were here, it's our country and they are very welcome to share it but when they say we are going to do it their way, I don't think that is on. I really don't.'

Adrian cuts in: 'Whites can be accused of doing that to the Aboriginal people as well,' to which Trish suggests that is a 'whole other issue' that goes way back. She says, as someone who has worked in welfare for many years, 'I saw how much money the Aboriginals had thrown at them but was it used effectively?'

There is discussion about the development of what the couple consider 'elite Aboriginals', who make money out of the government bureaucracy but do not help anyone. We are speaking at a time when the Indigenous 'Voice to Parliament' has been proposed, following the Uluru Statement from the Heart. Malcolm Turnbull has immediately dismissed the idea of an Indigenous voice, characterising it as a 'third body' of Parliament, even though the Indigenous representatives deliberately did not define the concept.

Adrian counts storyteller and Yorta Yorta elder Francis Firebrace as a good friend to his family. 'I think we are very lucky that the Aboriginal people haven't gone to town – terror-wise – like some immigrants have, because of all the crap that they suffered from 1788 onwards. But I think even [the Aborigines] are pushing it a bit far when they want the third body of Parliament.'

=

Perhaps the conflicted main-street response to other cultures is a little easier to understand when you consider that our town's demographic is closer to Australia in the 1947 census, when one-tenth of the country was born overseas. In my region, which stretches from the thriving town of Young to the booming Canberra satellite town of Yass, our Australian-born population is 84.2 per cent, and the top five migrant source nations by birth are England, New Zealand, Netherlands, Germany and America – in that order.[6]

Compare my region to Australia's two largest cities and they are chalk and cheese. In Greater Sydney, at the 2016 census just over 57 per cent were Australian-born, and China is the top migrant birthplace, followed by England, India, New Zealand and Vietnam. In Greater Melbourne, Australian-born citizens make up close to 60 per cent of the population, and the top migrant source nations are, in order, India, China, England, Vietnam and New Zealand. The cultural divide between my little country town and the city in which I grew up is cemented into the numbers. As journalist and author George Megalogenis writes, the nation is quickly being separated into a series of 'distinct cultural identities'.[7] While the nation's south-east corner can be counted as 'majority new Australian', in the rest of the country 'old Australia dominates'. Megalogenis argues that the migrant intake, which remains at 190,000 a year, helped to create a 'top ten world economy' but that policy makers have a job ahead.

'Migration helps shape the character of each city. What will challenge policy makers and politicians is the economic and cultural separation of our two largest cities from the rest of the country.'

Two-thirds of the migrant intake are skilled migrants, who enter the country ready to prosper, with education levels higher than the average Australian. Of those recent migrants who arrived since 2006, around 65 per cent had a non-school qualification. Of that 65 per cent, 76 per cent had a bachelor degree or higher. A third of recent arrivals achieved a non-school qualification after they arrived and half of those qualifications were a bachelor degree or higher.[8] Compare this to my region, close to Canberra and its job supply, and still the proportion with bachelor degrees or above is 16 per cent compared to 22 per cent across Australia. Another 8 per cent had advanced diplomas or diplomas, and 18 per cent had certificate three or four.[8] Go to Mackay in Queensland, the heart of National MP George Christensen's electorate, and you will find the numbers with a bachelor degree drops to 12 per cent. Here, again, is these two countries expressed in numbers.

We have decided that as a nation we want skilled migrants because they are young when our population is ageing. They hit the ground running. They need less support and have a better chance of finding a job, or starting a business that will contribute to the Australian economy. But after more than twenty years on this main street, when I think about the cultural conundrum – the disassociation between individual and group; the disquiet in a section of the local-born population regarding unexplored and unexplained cultures – I turn my previous impulses upside down.

Governments, policy makers and community leaders have a responsibility to ensure they bring along the local-born population so that the gap between these two distinct sections of Australia does not widen. Identity politics, so criticised by the right, have been powerful for those of us who have needed to explore mixed versions of who we are. Who is not a cocktail? I am incredibly proud of my Chinese heritage and identify with it strongly. Likewise, my Anglo heritage. I am country and city. I grew up in a time when identity politics gave me the space to traverse these different identities at different stages. I can choose to be both or either at different times. When I consider the identity of country people, the increasing gap between the very look of urban and rural populations pushes our main street to identify more like the minority we have become. We are sometimes sneered at, sometimes lauded, and this makes us at once oppositional, defensive and proud in equal measure. Governments can't let this gap widen anymore because, as we have always taught our kids, no one should get left behind.

If that is not enough, consider this. If you are of a progressive bent like me, or a migrant kid who suffered racism like me, and are about to burst a valve at the very idea of thinking of a largely white rural population as a minority, think about an Australia that leaves behind an entire identifiable group. Then think about Brexit. Then think of Donald Trump. Then think again.

LESSON 17

Cultural tolerance is possible anywhere but it needs work

Young is one of the larger towns in our area, just over 10,000 people and growing. Its streets are busy, it can be hard to get a parking space, and it has a dynamism that is unmistakable. It is known for its stone-fruit orchards, so as you leave the town in summer you pass cherries, peaches, apricots and nectarines. The orchards have long been attracting a temporary workforce of backpackers, grey nomads and itinerant workers, who stay in caravans or camp in roadside parking areas. Once you pass the fruit trees, you hit more conventional broadacre farming, filled with crops of wheat, canola and mobs of sheep and cattle.

Young's population is creeping up, slowly but surely. One of the more unlikely sources of growth, causing an in-migration that has sparked a mini housing boom, is the Lebanese-Australian Muslim population. The community's pioneers came to Young forty years ago for the orchards. They were older migrants who had lived a semi-rural life tending citrus and olive orchards in Lebanon before coming to Australia in the 1970s. The old Young drive-in cinema site was purchased for a mosque in 1996 with very little opposition. In the past decade, the next generation has begun to arrive, sick and tired of the congested city, worried about the effect of urban crime and drug rates on their children. When these families talk about their reasons for leaving Sydney, they fit the quintessential tree-changer mould.

Ayoub* is married with four children. He was born in Sydney after his parents migrated from the Middle East in the seventies. His father had been a guest worker there, and they were trying to escape poverty and unrest. 'Something opened up, and at that time Australia was welcoming: Please come, please come. [My parents] thought there was a better chance for working.'

Ayoub is a tradesman who built a business and a life in Sydney. He moved from one suburb to another, hoping for respite from the pressures of dense living. 'We thought [each] would be better and it was just as bad. It's all the same. I don't think there is any suburb better than the other in Sydney at the moment.'

For relief, he would escape to the country to camp with his older boys, taking his four-wheel drive out around Bathurst, Sofala and Lithgow, along the Turon River. Exposure to the natural world started to change him. He remarked to his wife, Yaseera*, 'I think this camping is changing my relationship with the kids.' He felt more bonded. Living in Sydney, he never seemed to have time through the week for his family. He got home late from the business and once work was combined with his community duties at the mosque, the kids were often in bed when he pulled into the drive. He thought a weekender might be the answer. He didn't want to buy again in Sydney.

'I couldn't raise the kids in Sydney anymore. That's my number one reason. Sydney was getting too congested, too crowded. You couldn't even park a car in front of your own house. It got so ridiculous, the kids kick a ball, the neighbour yells. If that one doesn't, the other neighbour yells. The ball goes over and some neighbour won't give it back. It was tough on the kids.'

His brother was working in regional New South Wales, and suggested Young. Ayoub thought it was too far from Sydney but he drove his family up for the day. That same day they made an offer and bought a property a few weeks later.

'There was a community and that was one of the main reasons; obviously if there wasn't an established community, honestly we would not have moved here.'

Ayoub has established his business in Young while immersing himself in the community. We talk overlooking rolling countryside as he supervises a renovation at his mate's place. He talks about the money being spent in the area by the Sydney tree changers.

'There is $50,000 being spent behind you there, the plumbers are booked out with new people moving up and building on acreages; the sparky is out of Young and the earthmover is out of Coota. New people bring a lot of money to town. We need more jobs, we need more businesses, we want our kids to have jobs.'

Past the building site, the view is expansive. It is a green valley with a ridgeline of trees on the horizon. Ayoub points to his acreage nearby, a house shielded by mature trees. We discuss the effect of space and nature on humans. When he was looking for a weekender, he originally thought of the coast. The sea, the sea. Everyone wants to look at the sea. He and his mate were keen to move their families to the south coast. When Ayoub chose Young, his mate thought he was weird. Then he came up and saw the land. The space. 'He said, "Ayoub, I never thought looking at the landscape was the same as looking at the ocean. Looking at this gives you exactly the same feeling as looking at the ocean. It's even better." He ended up buying here.'

When Ayoub travels back to Sydney now, the kids pass on the opportunity to return, though the smallest one misses her cousins.

Most days, he finishes work and picks them up from school. He can't see the kids ever moving back and he is convinced their new life has changed them. They spend their time differently. They are more independent. They take more responsibilities. The older ones collect firewood and check fences.

'I think it's very important to be cautious, to know what things are. You need to feed your chickens and your sheep, check on life. It will teach them a lot of good lessons, and I really believe it changes the kids as people. They become more self-sufficient, more hands-on, more thinking outside the box. In Sydney it was play handball on the small courts or back on the Xbox. Outside. Xbox. Outside. You can't even ride your bike, you have to drive somewhere to ride your bike. Here, they have all the freedom. They are outside kicking, playing soccer. They can do it in Sydney, but it's harder to go to a park. My eldest son, I can rely on him to do a lot of stuff now.'

Ayoub's parents intend to move up from Sydney when his youngest brother moves out of home, because 'Dad is in love with this place.' It reminds him of his home country, the open space, the orchards.

The clincher for Ayoub's family, apart from the space, was the mosque, because it provided ready-made community. In recent years, the Muslim community has established an Islamic primary school. While Ayoub fully supports the Islamic school, he has decided the best thing for their children is to use the Islamic school for primary and the state school for their high school years because there are more subject choices.

==

Social cohesion requires people to have something in common. A common purpose and a sense of belonging, which adds to a sense of worth. Sometimes that belonging may be created in opposition to something else. We are what you are not. In the moment I describe at the beginning of this book when our town was criticised, my first response was emotional, my second response was to attack. My third response was to think about why I found one journalist's hot take of my town so offensive. By criticising our town as strange and isolated, the journalist seemed to be attacking our sense of self, which is strongly reinforced by our place and our community.

Cohesion comes easier in a small, homogenous community, but it may also explain why breaking from the mob is harder. In the past this has governed party voting patterns. Vivien Thomson says people have regularly told her that if they vote Labor in her community, they don't dare speak about it for fear of being pilloried or losing business. Likewise, new people coming into a community often have an easier time if they come via an existing inhabitant, as I did. Trust is built on relationships, and if you cannot find those friendships in the first instance, fitting into the group will be hard. Harder still if you blow in without a job or the means to support yourself.

Throughout human history, there have been good reasons for tribes to distrust outsiders. Anthropologist Robin Dunbar came up with the optimal size of a group. Dunbar suggests that 150 is about the right size for a community of humans. He began his research looking at why primates spend so much time grooming, and ended up with a measure of how many relationships we can handle. The number is a measure of a social group and, like concentric circles, it falls as you measure the people closest to you. Think of your invitation list for a big party, as opposed to a small barbecue, as opposed to the people you call in a crisis, down to your unit of five or so intimates. The point is that we humans have natural boundaries and if you are on the outside of my boundary, I am less likely to trust you.

Before Labor MP Andrew Leigh entered politics, he was a professor of economics. After sociologist Robert Putnam's book *Bowling Alone: The Collapse and Revival of American Community*, Leigh set out to understand the effect of diversity on trust, and found that in neighbourhoods where more languages are spoken people are less like to trust one another.[1] It was an uncomfortable finding for someone on the centre-left, though he says it is not surprising.

'I don't like the fact that people hunker down in the face of difference. I think difference and diversity and migration have been a great strength on net for Australia, but unless we understand the reality – that places in Australia with more linguistic diversity tend to exhibit lower levels of trust – then we can't set about dealing with that. And there are smart ways of dealing with it. Programs aimed to build trust in diverse communities. Why devote just the same number of resources to St Ives as Cabramatta, when you know the challenges of building trust in Cabramatta are greater?'

Country Australia has a strange interplay between three elements: the economic challenges in some areas, higher rates of self-reported well-being and the lower levels of support for immigration and cultural diversity. In some ways, all three elements have a relationship with social cohesion.

The annual Mapping Social Cohesion survey lands at the end of the parliamentary year. Professor Andrew Markus of Monash University spends time in the House briefing media on his survey, which began in 2007. Since that time he has polled more than 40,000 people. The report, put out by the Scanlon Foundation, provides five useful measures when thinking about social cohesion: belonging, social justice and equity, participation, acceptance/rejection and worth. Markus notes that while there is no agreed definition, social cohesion relates to a shared vision and is an ongoing process rather than a destination.

From a baseline in 2007, on those five measures Australia is trending downwards. Markus warned that social cohesion is like money in the bank – 'but we are running out of reserve funds'. What he has found over the years is strong support for immigration and multiculturalism, with little support for selecting migrants on race or religion. The qualification is the trends. There are two main trends: increasing levels of distrust of government and significant disquiet over Muslim migration.

About half of the population holds some concerns about Muslim migrants, with people raising a perceived failure to integrate and worries about terrorism. Within that group, a much smaller proportion holds it as a 'burning passion', says Markus. This is reflected on my main street.

The other part of the equation is the lack of faith in governments, our institution which normally provides leadership on these issues. Here, as we've seen, the main street also agrees.

If you drill down to look at differences between the capital cities and non-metropolitan Australia, you see the trend is exacerbated on these two elements. The 2017 report, for example, finds 'There is a consistent pattern of lower support outside capital cities for immigration and cultural diversity'. That is, 33 per cent in capital cities consider that the nation's immigration intake is too high, compared with 42 per cent in 'other regions'.[2] The gap also holds when measuring responses to statements on the value (or not) of multiculturalism, diversity of migrant intakes and attitudes towards Muslims. On measures of trust in government, the difference between country and city is less marked but still there. Country people have marginally less trust in government than city people, but slightly more pride in the Australian way of life and sense of belonging.

Considering Putnam and Leigh's research, I ask Markus if higher rates of reported belonging and pride in Australia in regional areas might be linked to our communities' lower levels of trust for 'outsiders' like immigrants.

He points to the 2017 report: in major cities he found the sense of belonging to 'a great extent' was 66 per cent and the proportion who 'strongly agree' that multiculturalism has been good for Australia was 47 per cent.[3] When you travel out to regional areas, the sense of belonging to 'a great extent' was 75 per cent (9 per cent higher), and the proportion who 'strongly agree' that multicultural-ism has been good for Australia was 28 per cent (19 per cent lower).

'It is true that there is an association of high levels of national identification with lower levels of support for immigration and cultural diversity,' he told me.

Then throw in discontent and pessimism. On this measure, One Nation supporters stand out. A majority (63 per cent) have 'no trust' in political parties. A substantial majority agree that Australia's system of government 'should be replaced' or 'needs major change' (80 per cent), and close to a third (35 per cent) are 'very pessimistic' about Australia's future, compared with 10 per cent or less for the three major political parties. A substantial minority (37 per cent) of One Nation supporters consider that 'having a strong leader who does not have to bother with Parliament' would be a 'very good' or 'fairly good' way of government.

The report concludes that 'between 11 per cent and 13 per cent of the population is strongly negative regarding immigration and cultural diversity, a larger proportion – between 15 per cent and 20 per cent – are strongly positive, while the majority, close to 65 per cent, are in the middle ground, open to persuasion.'

This is where political leadership must come in. The hard part for politicians, though, is that people have stopped listening to them. A number have privately voiced concerns about these issues but find it difficult to know what to do about them, other than keep calm and carry on. One expressed a concern that if a clever poli-tician with a Trump-style bank account were to ever arrive on the Australian political scene, things could get nasty.

One of the lightning rods for discontent with Muslim migra-tion has been attempts in some areas to build mosques and Islamic schools. In Bendigo, a thousand people protested in 2015 against plans to build a mosque in the city. A portion of the protestors were outsiders, a portion from within the city itself, though no one has established a ratio. Markus analysed that protest and found there were two fundamental dynamics at work and they can push against one another.

As previously discussed, towns and regional centres generally welcome population increases because more people revive local economies and have skills that might be missing. For towns lacking a critical mass to populate local businesses with skills shortages, cultural difference is generally less important if 'extra people bring life'.

In a larger place like Bendigo, which has a population of around 110,000, people are still needed to fill important roles such as doctors, but the population base is less of an issue, so there can be wider concern about cultural difference. Building a mosque becomes a focal point for that concern. Then wrap it with some economic figures such as falling jobs growth and flat-lining wages. Add timing to that: the mosque plans followed the construction of a large five-storey Buddhist stupa near the town. The conditions were ripe for discontent. Yet Markus found that in the case of the construction of the stupa and a more recently approved Karen temple, there had been no similar protests. For country communities, these lessons hold the key to ensuring both population growth and diversity while maintaining cohesion.

===

When the Muslim population started to increase in Young a couple of decades ago, there were murmurs of disquiet. Generally, though, there has been little division over the issue and that is backed by conversations with longstanding community members. Former teachers have told me that while the schools were not really prepared when the numbers increased ten years ago, there has been much more work done to improve cohesion and there have since been Muslim captains at the high schools.

Since Ayoub moved into Young four years ago, he has experienced very little religious or racial intolerance. His wife and daughters wear the hijab and they do not get abused in the street. Someone did make a critical comment to Ayoub about the Islamic school – that it could foment division. Ayoub sat down with the complainant and they discussed how it was no different from any other religious school. The resident had not realised that, like Catholic or Anglican schools, anyone can attend. Young's existing schools were also perturbed at first, because they lost some students, and therefore funding, given governments fund per student. Teachers at the local schools report that numbers have since settled again.

There have been media sorties into the town. The *Daily Telegraph* ran an 'exclusive', which yelled 'Young New South Wales Is the Unofficial Muslim Capital of the Outback'. Apart from the hilarity of the *Tele*'s subs labelling the inner regional town part of the outback, it was a potboiler. A breathless reporter quoted unnamed local police concerns about the potential radicalisation of young people. 'The *Daily Telegraph* found one former musician convert who says he would marry off his thirteen-year-old daughter if Australian law permitted it.'[4]

The local paper, the *Young Witness*, reported 'Young Civic Leaders Hit Back at *Daily Telegraph*'. It quoted criticism from the then mayor and council general manager Peter Vlatko: 'Muslims have been part of our community for a long time and we haven't had a problem with them whatsoever.' At the time, I cross-examined some locals, whose response was largely 'meh'.

Tolerance in the town was tested again in 2017 when a forty-two-year-old Australian-Muslim electrician was arrested for allegedly helping Islamic State develop laser missile detection equipment. Ayoub says the arrest shocked the community, Muslim and non-Muslim, but he maintains the division was limited to one or two critical responses. 'You don't think of this as Young. We ran away from all this,' he says. 'Since then it brought us closer with the churches and the schools because everyone knows this is not what we are preaching – it is not us.'

The Muslim community organised an open day at the mosque and invited everyone in town to visit and ask questions. Hundreds came, ate lunch and heard about the religion and its practices. There were priests and the police, ambulance workers, councillors and townspeople. As a result, communication between the local populations and new residents increased. Unknowingly, this approach reflected best advice from academic experts like Andrew Markus. That is, act early, don't dismiss concerns, work to understand them, because there is a large middle ground that can be mobilised to cause unrest. This is particularly true in the era of social media, he says, when like-minded people can connect across the world to raise money and participants for demonstrations across the nation.

The proactive approach of Young has paid off not only for the community but the economy. Ayoub says the town's real estate agents are actively targeting the Muslim community in Sydney, and he estimates local house prices have risen 8 to 10 per cent. 'I think the majority want to get out of Sydney. A lot of people had houses paid off in Sydney, but they tell me they are over it.'

With the new residents come a lot more income for local businesses and services, but the biggest challenge is always jobs for new and longstanding residents. The self-reported unemployment rate at the 2016 census was just over 6 per cent, but Ayoub advises new residents to think hard about how they will earn a living before dropping everything in Sydney. He says it can be difficult to break into new communities, even with a trade. Longer-standing residents are used to dealing with established businesses; many farmers have been dealing with services businesses for decades. The relationship is set in aspic. Ayoub says all of his jobs are from new people moving into Young. 'Locals go to the same people, I understand that.'

He is now facing all the same challenges as other country residents in getting his kids further education. He asks new residents to think about what their children will do after school, especially if it means moving away from family. Ayoub's eldest daughter wants to go into a medical field, which means leaving home to go to university. It is challenging for him as a father and hard financially because she will need to rent accommodation.

'Being the parents we are, we will say she is too young, she has never lived on her own, but I will cross that bridge when she gets her HSC marks. You do what you have to do, I tell her and we will work it out. Study hard. Concentrate.'

Like most other country parents, he wants his children to move back to town for a career. His wife has told him he must let go, but he is prepared to build for them on their land if necessary to keep them close by.

In some ways smaller towns could be well suited to taking on migrants and culturally diverse populations because we appreciate the extra families for our businesses and schools. Locals can more visibly support newcomers if the transition is welcomed. Ayoub brings small business skills and he is keen to keep his family close by and thereby stem the loss of young people. Cultural diversity helps the local-born population better comprehend Australian metropolitan society and – ironically – reduces the cultural gap between the metropolitan and rural.

How is it that the political rhetoric on Islam over the past few years has travelled so far from the realities of many communities?

'I think the get-out-of-jail card is "attack the Muslims",' says Ayoub.

Certainly I have never witnessed anything like the rhetoric of the Abbott government in the forty-fourth Parliament and the pressure it placed on one cultural group. But, following many local conversations, the disconnection between rhetoric and reality goes to broader questions of anxiety about place in the world, the casualisation of employment causing economic insecurity, changing cultural values and loss of trust in political, media, religious and scientific institutions. Specifically, I think of some of the conversations I have had. The people putting together a week's work from a few shifts, which provides no certainty for financial security, or even a regular pay slip to take to the bank for a mortgage. The falling away of community focal points such as church-going or the big sporting matches of Tom App's day. The loss in the number of reliable volunteers to make up an agricultural show society committee or a local footy team, which in turn shrinks secular community focal points. The death of the Big Employer, which provided jobs as well as social capital in the form of picnic days and town bands. The drift of individuals into more socially segregated worlds, where fake news is quickly passed on.

==

So will cultural diversity in country towns change the politics of rural seats? Ayoub and his fellow tree changers have come from Western Sydney, the great pendulum of Australian politics. As we've seen, Western Sydney politicians are made to work harder than most areas in the nation as their seats are more volatile. In my own community, it is the reverse. I have watched people move in and change their party vote as they get to know local members. It will be fascinating to see if rural communities become more marginal as they become more diverse, sparking tighter electoral contests.

While most in my little town were ropable about being swallowed up into a larger council in the amalgamations, as a resident of Young, Ayoub was delighted. He liked the fact that the larger council's 'men's club' was shaken up and that people from smaller towns like Harden would dilute Young and refresh its direction while checking the capacity of the longstanding councillors to play favourites.

For Ayoub, as for so many I spoke to, the marginal seat is the key to getting attention. He says the old-school migrant communities were rusted on to the Labor Party. Personally, he has voted for all the parties over the years. When Ayoub considers his vote in any election, he thinks about his local community rather than federal or state issues. That is, he asks himself, 'What is needed locally? Whatever is needed by community in general, who is benefiting the local community?'

It infuriates him that people vote informally, just show up so they don't cop a fine. 'We need Nationals to get their act together. They need to listen to the community more. We had ALP come to visit for Charlie [Sheahan]. At least they put their hand up and ask what people want. My objective is to get this a balanced seat, [whereas] country towns just blindly vote. Next election, trust me, that will change.'

Ayoub told me he would like to see the Shooters, Fishers and Farmers Party get up to bring more attention to the seat, to make it marginal. I noticed more state Labor MPs in the 2017 state Cootamundra by-election visiting the area than I have seen in the past two decades. Labor MP for Lakemba Jihad Dib – whose seat covers Ayoub's former home suburb – campaigned for Labor in Young, along with others. Whether Labor continues to throw such resources at country seats in a general election remains to be seen, because the volatility in metropolitan seats happens between the major parties on the fringes of capital cities. But the volatility in the rural areas tends to happen between the major and the minor parties, making it harder for Labor. Adding to the volatility, people are making up their minds later when it comes to their votes. From my local conversations, my sense is that this is not so much among the rural established landowners, who largely remained rusted-on conservative, but among small and micro-businesspeople and the neglected class. And it is borne out by the Australian Electoral Study, which shows the numbers of people deciding their vote during an election campaign (42 per cent) has crept above those voters who decided 'a long time ago' (35 per cent).[5] This may have something to do with the fact that due to increasing competition in rural areas, we are seeing late entries of minor party candidates emerging from communities to run as protest candidates.

Diversity is a double-edged sword which I think is worth it in the long term. Concern over social divisions only lasts as long as a community will let it last. In the 1950s, journalism used to be dominated by men; female journalists were oddities. Now my editor is a woman and my political editor is a woman. It's no big deal. In my small town, as sectarian divides have largely broken down, other new divides are being conquered. They include ethnicity and non-Christian religions. But in country communities we are often quietly integrating on our own terms, and we do not need lectures about whether we are doing it fast enough or far enough. Lectures will only increase anger, and divisions.

LESSON 18

Hey, rat racers, over here!

Here are two facts. Number one: Australia has a population of more than 24 million and of those, 8 million are living outside the capital cities. Number two: our two biggest cities, Sydney and Melbourne, are both projected to have populations of 8 million each by mid-century. In 2017, Sydney's population topped the five million mark and Melbourne was well on the way to the same figure, at 4.9 million. That means that over the next three decades those cities will each cram another three million people into their streets.[1]

The United Nations has tracked the trend towards the megacity, and better policy brains than me are thinking hard about finding solutions to the myriad problems that come with shoving millions of people into the same space. The megacities of the world, such as New York and Tokyo, are stand-alone economies to rival nations. New York's GDP, at $1.5 trillion, is far higher than Australia's ($1.2). The trend is projected to increase, with the UN predicting that the number of megacities will rise while rural population is projected to continue on a gentle downhill slide.[2]

While Sydney and Melbourne have still got a way to go to get to the likes of Tokyo (population 38 million in 2018), the thing you notice when you travel to major global cities is their increasingly homogenous nature. Big cities are all different in their own way, but a traveller can see familiar islands in culturally diverse places. Shopping districts feature global brands, and similar issues are discussed as globalisation and technology has brought the world closer together. We can understand each other's worries and learn from each other's solutions. This is both good and bad: good for broader conversations and common ground; bad if your kids want to eat McDonald's in Phnom Penh.

The idea of city homogeneity is a staple in the city–country debate. It echoes the concept identified in country-mindedness that 'city people are much the same the world over'. Or, as Paul Kelly sings, he can order sandwiches in seven different languages but every fucking city looks the same.

Cities, though, are starting to flex their muscles. Urban policy makers such as Robert Muggah of the Igarapé Institute in Brazil are urging cities to find their political voice.[3] Muggah argues that cities should be advocating their own interests, since their heft challenges most nation states. This is fair and reasonable given the interests, economic contribution and communities that live in big cities. But if our cities do move further away from rural areas in a cultural sense, and closer to other global cities, the political rift between metropolitan and non-metropolitan communities has the potential to further fracture. Policies that weave the two communities together are more important than ever.

Our cities need a release valve. Policy makers in Australia could be thinking about regional areas in terms of providing potential relief to the millions of people struggling to live in cities choked by congestion. It requires infrastructure and jobs. It means we have to talk about the D word.

===

On a Friday afternoon in 1971, then opposition leader Gough Whitlam visited the New Albury Travel Lodge to share his vision of decentralisation with the Albury and Wodonga ALP branch.

'Victor Hugo is said to have concluded his last diary with the words "greater than the tread of mighty armies is an idea whose hour has come". The new decentralisation is now such an idea. Australians are faced on every side with problems which will remain insoluble as long as the interests of the city and the farm are seen as separate and even incompatible. The farmer whose property provides neither full employment nor an adequate income is a victim of the concentration of our population in six swollen cities; so too is the suburban householder who pays more than he can afford for an unsewered block situated in an under-serviced community and separated by twenty miles of overcrowded roads and inadequate public transport from the desk or bench at which he works.'

For people on the edge of Sydney or Melbourne commuting to the central business district, 20 miles might seem a dream. But this was the beginning of Whitlam's push for inland cities. There had already been a 1964 Commonwealth state committee on decentralisation, which came to a wishy-washy conclusion – that it was hard to prove the economic benefits of centralisation or decentralisation. Ipso facto, a proper program of 'selective decentralisation could be undertaken without necessarily inhibiting economic growth'.

Whitlam, though, was hot to trot for big inland cities to take the pressure off existing cities and stimulate the regions. 'There is room for another Canberra between Canberra and Melbourne. There is room for another Newcastle between Newcastle and the Gold Coast. New cities processing Australian mineral resources will rise at Gladstone in Queensland and within the iron belt of the west, as they have risen already since the war at Mount Isa and Whyalla.'

Once Whitlam got into government, he established the Albury-Wodonga Growth Centre project for the twin towns on the Murray.

It was the Canberra in between Canberra and Melbourne. He signed up the New South Wales and Victorian governments for a pilot scheme that might be used as a model for other regions. He predicted Albury-Wodonga's population would grow to 300,000, and provided funding for infrastructure. The Australian Tax Office set up a regional office in Albury. But as governments change so do priorities, and the project declined. With a combined population of nearly 100,000, Albury-Wodonga is still a major regional centre with a university; nonetheless, the official nature of the program ended in 1995.

Before you write off Albury-Wodonga as a failure at 100,000, some of the most innovative communities have blossomed off the trunk of Whitlam's dream, and when the outlying areas are drawn in, the town may yet fulfil his target. The little dairy town of Yackandandah, which thirty years ago was suffering terminal population decline – sliding into the all-too-familiar territory of retiree destination – has been reinvigorated by a core group of residents with broader community buy-in. One of the keys to its success is the twenty-minute commute to Wodonga, with its universities, jobs and large industry. There again, I saw communities pushing ahead of governments in their policy ambitions. Totally Renewable Yak (TRY) is aiming for its self-proclaimed goal by 2022. Already the organisation has installed solar power on the privately run health service (after government pulled out); the community cooperative petrol station (established after big petrol pulled out); the museum; the Men's Shed; and a mini-grid on a greenfield housing site with even smarter Ubi solar meters via Mondo Power (a subsidiary of Ausnet power company) to allow customers to share power. TRY's aim is to extend their goals to their electorate of Indi, held by Independent Cathy McGowan. Indi already has more than 30 per cent of households with solar PV systems, double the Victorian average. The dynamism has attracted tree changers and after the ABC featured it on *Back Roads*, its tourist bureau answered 800 calls.

Whitlam's grand experiment is still spawning smaller economic success stories.

Notwithstanding the twin town experiment, decentralisation policy drifted away from top-down solutions in the 1990s as governments began to recognise that different regions had different characteristics that required a bit of self-determination. By the end of the Keating government and the beginning of the Howard government, policy moved away from the notion of active job creation – by dropping government offices or their satellites into the regions – towards more general funding for projects to stimulate local economies. At the same time, regional voters started to flex a bit of muscle. Pauline Hanson 1.0 was elected in 1996.

There was a summit in 1999, from which grew a Regional Partnerships Program to deliver buckets of money to communities to try to deal with 'economic stagnation or population decline'. Areas could also qualify if they had higher population growth combined with high unemployment levels. Then came the Sustainable Regions Program under Howard and the Regional Development Australia committees under Julia Gillard's government after her agreement with country independents Tony Windsor and Rob Oakeshott. The stated aims of the Howard program was an attempt to identify communities in need. The stated aims of the Gillard program was to get local people involved in designing their own solutions. So often, politics lays a cold hand on so many of the solutions. As the Gillard government headed towards the 2013 election, it reclassified Western Sydney as a separate region, essentially providing access to the Regional Development Fund. Likewise, in the life of the Abbott–Turnbull government, there have been intra-party skirmishes over the definition of a region in individual electorates because it holds the key to accessing the regional funding bucket for local members.

In the white heat of a double-dissolution election, as leader of the National Party, Barnaby Joyce changed the story back to the plonk-down-a-government-office model when he announced the Australian Pesticides and Veterinary Medicines Authority (APVMA) would move to Armidale.[4] At the time former New England MP Tony Windsor was challenging Joyce for Windsor's former seat and Joyce announced the APVMA move without cabinet sign-off. Pressure was building and Joyce – performing a dance of the seven army-surplus blankets – said it was part of a broader strategy for decentralisation. He pointed to the Grains Research and Development Corporation, which had moved four of its satellite offices away from Canberra, and the Rural Industries Research and Development Corporation, which had relocated its core operations to Wagga.

But Joyce's APVMA decision was bad news for the cause of a more thoughtful approach to decentralisation, reinforcing in the minds of voters that governments are reactive and politicians are out only to save their own skin. The government scrambled to wrap the decision in a more respectable garb and Queensland Liberal MP John McVeigh was appointed to chair a committee to look again at this hoary old chestnut. Even that committee's issues paper notes: 'Commonwealth decentralisation policies have been ad hoc. Many policies have either not received bipartisan support or survived a change of government.'[5]

Thus far decentralisation policy underlines to voters that governments cannot follow a train of policy thought long enough to get it to the destination. So decentralisation's long political history reflects the past decade of broader policy, which has been marked by implementation and reversal. Think about the carbon price, mining tax, the major rewrite of Labor's Gonski schools policy, the full-fibre National Broadband Network rollout and, probably, the Coalition's Gonski 2.0 school policy. It happens from federal government to federal government, and between federal and state governments. There was the fight between the Abbott government and the Victorian Labor government over tied federal funding of $1.5 billion for the East West Link road project.[6] It was money promised by

Abbott to the former Liberal state government but rejected by the incoming premier, Daniel Andrews, who wanted to concentrate on the Melbourne Metro Rail project. Ideologies were drawn at ten paces and in the current political climate if you are a government with a big idea that takes more than three years, you have Buckley's.

Yet there are areas where parties agree. In spite of the Coalition's hysterical campaigning in 2013 warning of a debt and deficit disaster, there has been a coalescing of sorts around borrowing for productivity boosting infrastructure. The Reserve Bank, the Business Council of Australia and many economists have joined the call. In his *Quarterly Essay* 'Balancing Act', George Megalogenis argued that government had to get more responsive if it wanted to restore public confidence. 'The economy won't stabilise without a more active government. The default setting of politics in the 21st century – to trust in the market – has proven to be bad economics, even for Australia, the only high-income nation to avoid the Great Recession. It has left us with gridlocked cities, growing inequality and a corporate sector that feels no obligation to pay tax.'[7]

So the newest version, of sorts, of decentralisation is the Coalition government's city deals, which require three tiers of government to agree on development priorities for spending on infrastructure. They have their roots in the UK's city deals and were announced on the eve of Australia's 2016 election. The idea was to use the Commonwealth as a coordinator and underwriter for funds and ensure state and local governments were on board.

It is no surprise that existing city deals are going to three of the most marginal political areas in the country: Townsville, Launceston and Western Sydney. They are regions that are economically squeezed, so they are priorities, but they are also areas where voters are prepared to whack governments.

The City Deals architect and the then Assistant Minister for Cities and Digital Transformation, Angus Taylor, made no apology for focusing on these regions after the last election. He told me in 2016: 'If you look at the UK, if you look at Australia, if you look at the US, there is political disruption going on. And the disruption is coming from the outer suburbs and regional cities. That's where Trump has focused, that's where Brexit was focused and we saw that in the recent federal election. And that is because people in those areas are crying out for solutions. They want governments to come up with solutions and so that's where we are focused.'

Taylor implemented a simple yet brilliant aggregation of data via the Smart Cities dashboard, which shows any individual, industry or organisation the potential of a region.[8] And, being a regionally based MP, he ensured the larger regional centres were included. You can quickly drill down to, say, Mackay in Queensland, and look at anything from education levels and housing ownership to industries and innovation expressed as patents per person. You can also compare centres on any of those measures.

In terms of bang for buck, it makes sense for decentralisation policy to focus on satellite areas that have higher populations. But this may be no consolation if you live in a small town too far from a larger regional or city centre to commute. As demographer Bernard Salt has written, capital cities have a certain gravitational pull which extends to about 120 kilometres – what he calls 'just beyond the comfortable commute line'. He identifies these larger centres that orbit around Sydney, Melbourne, Brisbane, Perth and Adelaide, sending commuters into these centres for jobs. He notes that for smaller capitals such as Canberra, Hobart and Darwin, the commuter line drops to 50 kilometres as there are no large satellite towns sending workers in.[9] Though I would say that while Yass is just outside that line at 60 kilometres, there are plenty of workers who commute on the Barton Highway every day, as evidenced by the traffic and a bus service. Unfortunately for me, I live exactly 120 kilometres from Parliament House. Too far away for a daily commute given the House hours.

Like many Australians who have watched politics over the years, I had come to the view that decentralisation was never going to work. I have grown up in journalism and politics under neo-liberalism, from the market solutions of the Hawke–Keating government onwards. As George Megalogenis notes, trusting the market was the default setting for our generation. Certainly when I outline my dream of a larger, more economically diverse, sustainable home town hanging off Canberra, Grattan Institute chief executive John Daley's economically rational argument against decentralisation is compelling. People love decentralisation because in the city it means those who have houses don't get squeezed, and in the country we can fantasise about economically sustainable populations. Except 'We have had 117 years of policy to do that and nothing has happened so far.'

Daley's argument is that centralisation is not being driven by government policy but by the decisions of individual companies, and they want to be where the other firms are. He uses the example of Canberra – oddly, the same place Joyce uses to justify the success of decentralisation. Canberra was purpose-built from a sheep paddock as the national capital. And, explains Daley, 'The theory is, if you get a world-class university and fantastic infrastructure, beautiful roads and really good connectivity to all the centres, and a big international airport, and a really highly educated workforce, and the best schooling outcomes in the country, and a critical mass of people together, say 400,000 people, then all the private sector will turn up. We have done all of those things in Canberra and how much of the private sector there is not parasitic on government?'

He suggests for big corporations with far-flung managers, Canberra is so far down the pecking order it barely rates. Unless you sell to government, there is not a critical mass of businesses to feed off. So for a little family in a country town, he paints me a picture to limit my expectations. 'My hope for a little family in a country town is you are doing something which hangs off the agricultural business of those towns, or you are servicing the local people in the town, and you'll be fine. If you are the local doctor, there are enough local farmers who are going to get sick that the local doctor is going to be there for a long time.'

Daley says the harder gig is in towns of a few hundred where commuting out is really the only option. And the incoming tree changer, looking for a quaint little village to escape the rat race? They are all on the coast or close to a major centre, he says. To which I said, 'One word: Jugiong.' He tells me the success of the little town is rare.

Yet when you consider the divide between city and regional, people are facing complementary problems. City dwellers complain of skyrocketing house prices and rents, congestion, long commutes, crowded schools and childcare. In the country, we complain about empty shops, low capital gains, dwindling school populations and ageing infrastructure. This does not mean that the problems marry up. But the rhetoric of government has changed since the 2016 election. In order to put some flesh on the bones of Barnaby Joyce's rash decision to move the APVMA, then deputy Nationals leader Fiona Nash started working on a government policy that asked departments to report back on which functions could be moved to regional areas. Those departments were supposed to report back by August 2017, by which time the concept had moved from taking departments holus-bolus to smaller offices or functions.

Nash flipped the argument.[10] Rather than think about decentral-isation as the bush begging for favours – as many National Party members had done – she argued that government should do the city and the budget a favour. Strategic investment, she said, would 'help fix overcrowding of capital cities'. Nash also pointed out that it was cheaper to house people in the country.

'Building new roads or rails in capital cities costs multiples more than it does in the country because the city projects require bull-dozing houses and digging tunnels.

'The more people move to the country, the less it costs our nation – and I suspect that's something that many people have never considered. Work by the Department of Planning and Regional Development in Victoria revealed that housing 50,000 new people in Sydney cost the government $4 billion in infrastructure; to house those people in regional New South Wales cost $1 billion. For every 50,000 people who choose to live in the country, governments save roughly $3 billion in infrastructure costs. Being good doesn't necessarily mean big, it means being a community of choice.'

It was all seeming a more nuanced conversation until the citizenship crisis took hold and forced Nash to walk away from Parliament. The High Court ruled she was not eligible to sit due to her British heritage. Barnaby Joyce, as flawed as his decentralisation model was, has also died a political death. The 2018 budget heralded the return of the plonk-down-a-government-office model, with six more small government agencies flagged to move, four of them to other state capitals. It looked like the full stop at the end of the Barnaby thought-bubble. The danger is the process will again fall over because government cannot follow through with a more complex approach.

==

While there is considerable opposition to decentralisation among government departments, there are also cautionary noises from regional bodies like the Regional Australia Institute.

'Well-intended programs have had many inadvertent consequences. The decentralisation of government agencies in the 1950s to 1970s, for example, is thought to have undermined local economic autonomy rather than build long-term interdependency. For this reason, many regional service towns are heavily dependent on the ebb and flow of political ideologies where those in power determine the size and location of public agencies and investment.'[11]

But for the ordinary person on my main street, there is an almost universal view that the strained urban areas must relieve some of their pressure by sending people outside the capital cities.

Consider the view of this eighteen-year-old school leaver, who combined the idea of decentralisation with potential for immigration: 'Instead of cramming people into major cities, what they did after World War II is sent people into the country and got those communities thriving. Sending the refugees and the asylum seekers out into smaller country towns, it would help reduce racism and it would help those communities boom again. They need labour force and people there. It would solve problems. We are losing people here, too many people in the cities, and that would help, giving them somewhere safe. People would not know how to react at first but then they would get used to it.'

It is a common sentiment. As a forty-something local office worker said, 'They are saying the cities are overcrowded. So send them out – we have amazing country. Why can't they move to us? With technology, everyone can commute. To me, why do they need to be in George Street [Sydney]? Office jobs can be set up anywhere.'

Indeed, governments and companies have promised for years that workers will be able to telecommute, and it is possible if bosses are flexible and the nature of your work allows it. We have residents in town who do work with major companies and government departments, but they still spend a lot of time in planes, trains and automobiles, which is bloody hard if your job involves face to face contact. My own employers over the years, from the *Australian* to the *Guardian*, have been very accommodating with my life choices, but so much of parliamentary politics requires eyeballs in various chambers at once.

The other element of telecommuting is connectivity. Even though the NBN promised to revolutionise working from home, it is still unclear where it will lead, given its implementation problems. In our inner regional area, when I plug my out-of-town address into the NBN website, I come up with the option of the Sky Muster satellite connection, a service that has been inundated with problems. The NBN prompt helpfully points to the guide to 'getting connected in remote locations'. Word travels fast and at the end of 2017, as we considered whether to sign up for satellite, neighbours, friends and a (non-local) government MP warned against it until the issues were ironed out. As frustration in the community grew, a small start-up business called Wi-Sky, run by a smart young local farmer and Nuffield scholar, Jock Graham, hooked off a main spur to fill the gaps for homes and farm businesses. So here, again, many country communities have given up waiting for government solutions and are ahead of policy. I should add that, as on so many issues, I also feel for my city friends on connectivity. When I helped my daughter connect to the NBN in the city, her Saturday night speeds were much worse than our inner regional home speeds. Attempting *The Handmaid's Tale* was like trying to watch it underwater.

Without doubt, the hunger for more infrastructure and development in rural and regional communities has been recognised by politicians, and that's also driven by fear of losing votes. But the economists remain unconvinced. In 2017, the Productivity Commission argued strongly against the plonk-down-a-government-office model, finding that moving government offices to regional areas comes with costs and risks.[12] Basically, they said government is not creating jobs, it is just shifting them around. 'As a regional development strategy, decentralisation is unlikely to make a long-term, systemic difference to regional growth and resilience.'[13]

In fact, on regional development more generally, the Commission argued that the whole Regional Development Australia agency should be abolished and Commonwealth should largely leave it to state and territory governments to carry on their traditional role. All levels of governments, the commissioner Paul Lindwell found, were already spending a lot of money in rural and regional areas, and better processes should be put in place to get rid of the constant ad hoc approach, so regions were properly defined and states targeted their spending.

'It is expensive and generally futile for governments to try to artificially create and maintain an advantage for a regional community where such an advantage does not inherently exist. Time and again, grand-scale interventions, or even less grand but persistent favouring of perennial candidates for support, have not delivered measurable benefits. In addition, government support always comes at a cost to people in Australia, as taxpayers must find the money.'[14]

As to the views of the voters on the ground and the politicians responding to their pressure, the Commission was scathing of the tendency to throw out money in order to get political brownie points from electorates 'as the varying governments express concern that their expenditures are not sufficiently recognised by the populace. This is a worrying trend that should be addressed now. Political recognition is not a valid objective for good public policy. The Australian population expect and deserve good government at all levels, working cooperatively in the interests of the people of Australia.'[15]

Lindwell's bottom line was that big regional centres and small towns will continue to rise and fall, and governments should not shield them from economic change but rather provide a safety net to individuals who lose a job or cannot support themselves. That would mean social security, education or retraining and job services. 'There will be instances where regions face continued decline in employment and economic activity that cannot be feasibly reversed. In such cases, governments' efforts should be directed at managing family and labour mobility, facilitating movement and ensuring that residents who remain in a region have access to a minimum level of services. Inevitably, this cannot mean that services will always be provided within all towns, or at the same level as might be expected in major urban or regional centres. Like all sound policies, regional adjustment should not promise what it cannot deliver sustainably.'

In other words, get real. You can't stay in a small town if you don't have a job.

Even though only 17 per cent of Commonwealth jobs are outside the big five cities and Canberra, I don't hold much hope for moving many government offices into non-metropolitan Australia. What is more likely is smaller cities and towns leveraging off existing and new infrastructure projects, such as the inland rail project, which has bipartisan support. The Coalition provided for equity funding for the 1700 kilometre rail route from Melbourne to Brisbane in the 2017 budget, off the back of previous Labor support. Senior Labor frontbencher Anthony Albanese argued that the project deserved support because it would provide economic development in regional centres such as Parkes, it would take pressure off the coastal routes, improve safety and environmental outcomes and economic benefits by replacing heavy vehicle movements. In 2018, the Committee For Sydney, an independent lobby group made up of local governments, business and cultural groups, released a report calling for better links between Sydney, Newcastle and Wollongong to connect those regions and unlock greater job potential and affordable real estate.[16]

If the last decade of politics has taught us anything, it is that the government is getting less predictable as it is buffeted by the big political disruptions. At the beginning of the life of the Coalition government in 2013, I would not have predicted a complete change of attitude by the Coalition on government debt, let alone a big bank tax or a banking royal commission. The political disruption that created Brexit and Trump have the capacity to push governments to polar opposite stances in a relatively short time.

Even after 117 years of discussion, to dismiss the decentralisation agenda would be brave.

There is no doubt that low interest rates and political forces might favour infrastructure building to help cities cope with their load and improve services for larger regional centres. But it can't be all one way. We can't expect governments to do everything. We need to have a vision for our towns. Our communities need to work out where we are going and what we want to do next with whatever funding or skills we have available. Political disruption means there will be buckets of money thrown towards regional communities in an ad hoc manner through the average election cycle, and in spite of the advice from the Productivity Commission report, that won't change any time soon. Politicians will always respond to voter pressure, and if country electorates get more volatile that push-me-pull-you will only increase. Country towns need to get together and order their own priorities for development. In order to get best bang for the taxpayer's buck, government needs to allow community leaders to decide where their funding dollars are best used, and communities need to take responsibility for those decisions. Sympathy for rural communities is already on the wane and useless spending will only exacerbate the divide.

LESSON 19

Let's celebrate the whole country

As a young copygirl starting out in news, I had regular overnight shifts in the radio room. It was the early 1980s and the room was covered in orange laminex, with a line of speakers that broadcast the police radio simultaneously. It had no window to the outside world but looked on to another room full of copytakers, who waited to type out stories from reporters on the road. Copygirls and boys had to monitor a dozen or more speakers for breaking news, write it down and relay it to the police reporter. Each speaker had a dial below it, so you could regulate its volume depending on what was happening. When there was action on one channel you dialled up and updated the reporter, who was usually cruising the midnight hotspots with a driver and photographer or, on a quiet night, drinking in a bar. If action was happening on a number of channels it was like playing the piano, turning the volume up and down, silently terrified of missing any big news. In some ways it was analogous to current public debate – a wall of fuzzy noise full of codes and verbal shorthand to portray potentially significant events. I look back with a certain fondness at those times, leaving out the boring parts, the mistakes made, the confusion of a new job in a different world. In my head it was all excitement and wonder.

Conventional wisdom tells us that looking back is unhealthy, but academic research now suggests that nostalgia can be useful for regulating emotions during periods of transition.[1] Country towns are always being accused of wallowing in nostalgia. No one calls it nostalgia when inner-city professionals protest against a freeway to get outer suburban commuters to and from the central business district. More powerful social classes – and I am a fully paid-up member – get to write the rules about who is allowed nostalgia and who is not. It is entirely reasonable for Lorraine and Tom to yearn for bustling footpaths again. It is entirely reasonable for Bernie to want jobs and industry more than a strong flat white for his grand-kids. It is entirely reasonable for a neglected class disconnected from the political process to demand more attention. After all, the connected class, business and industry have been demanding atten-tion for years. If people can protest a freeway, farmers can protest against a wind farm or a mine. I support renewable energy but do I want wind turbines on the hills that provide the best view on the farm? Not really. I'll cop it, but I would prefer not to have clearing of the bush on the range, or the turbines spoiling my view. These impulses are completely human reactions to a local context, a world that was one way and has now changed to another. We like to think we are rational, but as the poet Les Murray said, 'We're all human and, therefore, deeply inconsistent.'[2]

Humans inhabit communities. We naturally fall into like-minded groups, and no harm in that. We reference each other through our communities. Like sheep, we hang in mobs. But once the gates are opened, we are all one mob. Australia bought into a social compact that relies on interdependence: tolerance of other cultures, a progressive tax system that redistributes wealth, a welfare safety net, an Indigenous policy that is trying now to right the wrongs of the past. All this is underwritten by the idea that Australians have a responsibility to each other. We bought into the idea that we are a cohesive group and cohesion is valuable.

If we forget our political leanings and agree on that fundamental point, then the idea that this place is drifting into two very separate countries should trouble us. Two countries that look different, speak differently and have different priorities. It is there in the numbers, in the numbers of Australian-born out here in the country, the numbers of overseas-born in there in the cities. Out here, there's a whiter country, where incomes are lower and growth is constrained; in there, a culturally diverse country where the economic growth is better, house prices are going gangbusters and jobs are being created daily. If one country starts to race ahead and leave the other country behind, then we should expect an Australian fracturing. Groups cannot be disconnected and disregarded. It makes people angry.

There is a lot of truth to comedian Chris Lilley's mockumentary *Ja'mie: Private School Girl*. Apart from belling the cat on the two worlds we have created for our children, Lilley's best idea was the exchange between two schools of wildly different demographics within Australia. While kids from metropolitan schools are regularly being sent on cultural exchange to Paris, it may be a bigger cultural leap to go from Melbourne to Meekatharra in Western Australia. Many of those city kids, like me at that age, have never actually been to a country town for longer than a petrol stop. Does the city kid benefit more from seeing yet another oversized shopping mall filled with global brands she can get at home? Or would she be better served to get an understanding from her contemporaries of some of the delights and challenges of a small remote community of fellow citizens?

Progressives like me often wear their compassion like a badge. We can be so sensitive to racial difference but so insensitive to class

315

difference. Maggie-Kate's cultural shock moving from her home town to a racially diverse campus underlined the two Australias. In some senses her story warms the progressive heart because we think education and interaction will fix any fear of other cultures. Then we will all think the same way, right? What about the people, though, who don't cross the geographical and cultural divide? Are we free to think less of them?

Country communities are confused by government and city-based narratives that tell us we are representative of old Australia, that we need to pay our own way or move to more economically viable places. At the same time, our lifestyles are appropriated to represent Australia in everything from Olympic ceremonies to television commercials. In public debate, we are either rednecks or salt of the earth. This may be the result of bush mythologising, which in the past has unreasonably held up country people as the true Australian. Then, as population and growth tipped towards cities, we pulled apart the myth, overcorrected and tended to label everyone in rural and regional Australia rednecks. Still, in a professional crowd the only identities we can safely make fun of are rednecks and Pommies.

Cultural and economic division does not just exist between city and country. Country society itself is very stratified. Small towns are like goldfish bowls. You can see the state and the status of every occupant. Class is ever-present and can be about money and education, but most of all it is about choices. It is about opportunities. The higher up the class ladder you go, the better your range of choices in life.

In a small community, this hierarchy can drive communities to improve conditions for people with greater needs because we know the people on the bottom rungs. Our Country Education Foundation is an example of communities taking responsibility for their own. Charities like CEF reflect the best traditions of country families who recognise their relative wealth and give back because they know the kids who their money will help. A lot of these organisations are run by farmers and town professionals.

But the visibility of hierarchy can also cause discontent. There is a discontent about that same local community leadership, which might include councils as well as active volunteers who traditionally wield a lot of local power and decide on town priorities. A sense of hierarchy can also cause fear of new people and groups. The race conundrum is clear on the main street. There are the contradictory urges of seeking greater population to pull life into small towns, but pushing back against immigration as a threat. A number of people I speak to have real concerns about immigration levels, particularly Muslim migration, all the while knowing individual migrants who have contributed enormously to their communities. It is not comfortable to hear, but it has to be heard to be resolved peacefully.

At the same time, the Regional Australia Institute analysis shows more than 150 out of 500 council areas are seeing a decline in Australian-born population but an increase in overseas-born population. Those 150 councils have cracked the secret to increasing populations for their small towns. The increasing diversity from Muslim Australians in Young has occurred with few tensions because both the longstanding residents and the new tree changers understand the importance of reaching out. It was our well-loved doctor Yusuf who said that as a migrant you have to expose yourself. To which I would add, the community has to reciprocate. In Young there were no demonstrations over the mosque or the Islamic school, none of the protests seen in other centres. The town leadership – including politicians, councillors, school leaders, police – joined the Muslim community leaders to ensure cohesion. My small town has taught me that country communities are not stereotypes. It has also told me leadership counts for a lot.

So, across the country we cast around for political leadership to tell us how to think about these things. Government, though, is a behemoth that cannot respond. We are told to be agile, to adapt to economic and social change and get with the program, but we do not see agile governments. We see slow, unresponsive, irrational governments making weird decisions which do not make sense at a street level. We see politicians who cannot follow the most basic rules (am I a dual citizen?) while we have to jump through more government hoops than a circus pony to claim a payment or run a business. We see politicians who use their positions for personal gain, transition out of highly paid ministerial positions into even higher paid lobbyists; and if they transgress, are forgiven or allowed to make amends. We are not.

Politics have made an art of playing up divisions and differences, though politicians have it within their power to act differently. This is how country communities have stayed compliant. The worst of rural politicians have taught us to blame city people rather than working on ways to bridge the gap. Media broadcast misunder-standings between city and bush rather than find common ground. I have done this myself. So country voters are asked to concen-trate on strawmen. It's not the latte sipper or the migrant who will kill country Australia. That is a sop to appeal to rural identity to avoid the harder policy work that will build community rather than divide it. It is the easy way out – the political equivalent of 'look, over there' – requiring less nuanced thought about rural policy innovation. Instead, we are served the standard answer: roads + dams = happiness.

The old-school country political model – so often relied on by the National Party – amplifies the geographical divide because it perpetuates certain myths about the country. That the whole of country Australia is about agriculture. That we are all waiting for the pork barrel. That we are not interested in innovative ways to solve the issues of distance and the gap between rural and metropolitan cultures. Or that we lack the capacity to find our own solutions.

And in doing so, it does a disservice not only to a whole sector of country towns, but the very farmers they claim to represent, who do not need pity.

In short, government has come to be regarded on the main street as part of the problem rather than part of the solution. So those of us who are financially inoculated from economic shocks just move about our daily business. The problem is, a whole other constituency is left out of most debates on country Australia. This constituency is sandwiched between larger asset holders and the poor, who are too busy struggling to survive to worry about politics. They feel neglected by major parties. They do not trust government; they are concerned about withdrawal of government support for industry. They accept individual migrants, but they are worried about the level of immigration, though their communities are less diverse than those in the city. Place is important to them and they resent being told they must move in order to get a job: they want jobs in their own towns. They are worried about the level of government services in their areas. They want to hang on to the local hospital. They want good teachers to stay in their schools but they also want to have the control to get rid of the bad ones. They want decent broadband services. They want politicians who listen to their concerns and they want governments who respond to their priorities.

A substantial portion of the neglected class is sick of the regional debate being framed through the prism of agriculture. The National Party – the old Country Party – talks constantly about farmers without talking about the townspeople who service those farmers or live completely separate lives. The people who staff the hospitals, look after the very young and the very old, fix the cars, serve the coffee, clean the houses and grade the roads. They are often the ones who keep their kids in country schools all the way to leaving, effectively ensuring the schools stay open. A section of the neglected class considers established farmers – with their properties, their 'fancy cars' and their expensive schools – to be part of the problem. The small-town establishment like me wield influence in small communities and our connections make us insiders but the neglected class feel shut out from power. They are outsiders.

The neglected class is acutely aware of the geographical divide, and up until now the old city–country tropes have been enough. They have loyally supported mostly conservative country political representatives for years, though historically Labor has also been represented in rural areas. But the neglected class are losing patience with the status quo. They are looking to other politicians, people who stand out because they don't talk or act like the politicians. People who speak the language of the main street. The neglected class are sick of being lectured to by city politicians, economists, professional classes and in some case their own community leaders who are tied to the governing class. They are attracted to minor party, high-profile politicians such as Pauline Hanson, Nick Xenophon, Derryn Hinch, Jacqui Lambie – if not for their policies then for their outsider value. My enemy's enemy is my friend. The separation from voting tradition reflects the fracturing in politics. It is clear from the main street.

The whole of rural society, top to bottom, is pretty much disappointed or angry at politics. They feel let down, they don't trust government and associated institutions like the media. This they share with city communities. If you prod people further, they fall into two groups. Those who shrug their shoulders and feel they cannot do much about it. And those who are more actively angry. They are the neglected class, and they represent a constituency up for grabs.

==

It is a very human instinct to lash out at those below if you can't reach those above. Unless we integrate the two Australias, discontent rules, okay? So major parties and country community leaders need to start thinking about the neglected class.

Here I look to technology for inspiration. Electronic cars provide traffic assistance to drivers. But each day, each car confronts individual situations through which it learns. Or, as Tesla founder Elon Musk said in 2015, 'The whole Tesla fleet operates as a network. When one car learns something, they all learn it.'[3] This is different to humans. When my kids learn to play the piano, I don't learn. But this is my hope for rural Australia.

Across Australia, individual rural communities are leading the way with innovative policy solutions seemingly beyond the scope of a log-jammed government. An organised bush telegraph could share those examples so that we are not each reinventing the wheel. Or, to mix metaphors, small-town swarm learning could lift all boats. And I would wager that country women's connections, particularly through social media, could give Telsa's learning algorithms a run for their money.

We need to come together as communities because we are a minority, though historically we have played an oversized role in the Australian imagination. We can't afford to be picked off and divided for politicians' major and minor to fill their own agendas. We need to better connect and learn from each other's experiences on what works and what doesn't. We need to pick up the passion for the country from the best Country Party traditions, the understanding of economic strictures of class from the best Labor traditions, and notions of individual responsibility from the best Liberal traditions.

Why? Firstly, because cohesion is good for the country and that is our social pact. Secondly, because country voters are becoming more volatile. Elections since 2016 prove this, including the Coalition's close-run 2016 election, one-term state governments in Victoria and Queensland, and the WA state election, in which not even the protest vote for Pauline Hanson was locked in. In the 2018 South Australian election, SA Best's Nick Xenophon's much-heralded attempt to break into the two-party system fizzed out like a wet firecracker. Country New South Wales by-elections since 2016 have delivered consistent anti-government swings. In my time in the press gallery I kept waiting for a 'normal' government term after the hung Parliament, but it was like waiting for a normal weather pattern on the farm. The farmer tells me that normal rainfall will happen any minute now, but it has yet to arrive in the twenty-one years I have lived here.

So when I think about what might happen in rural politics in the future, I look to the metropolitan electorates that hold the city version of the neglected class. No MP can get too complacent in the outer edges of our big cities. Those voters make their politicians work. Rural and regional main streets are starting to understand that. Like a bull led by a nose ring, rural electorates have more power than they think. That ring is an illusion. The bull still holds the power if he chooses to exercise it. Country electorates are in a time of political transition and no one knows which way the bull will jump. Country voters are one fright away from determining governments.

Town, nation and government needs to engage in public debate on uncomfortable topics like building community cohesion between the two Australias. Rural and regional politicians need to speak up for all their constituents' concerns, not just the influential ones. Governments need to have simpler ways for communities to have a say as to how money is spent in regions to better target local priorities. Country community leaders need to be aware of consulting with a wider range of residents to involve more people in decision-making processes to plan their own priorities. That way, we can tell governments we don't need another nation-building footpath. What we need is a community learning centre and hot-desking hub with high-speed internet.

We also need to acknowledge that we do in some areas receive generous government funding already. The range per capita for 'extra small' rural remote councils in 2014–15 was $3350, compared with

$21 per head for urban developed councils.[4] Of course, that doesn't mean services are better; it's because it costs more to provide services to smaller, more remote communities. So equally we must stop measuring our worth by the number of grants we get. We are more than the sum of our government funding. We already contribute a lot to the national economy through exports and other products. Don't forget, our farmers manage 61 per cent of the landmass.

Meanwhile, politicians and policy makers who tell us to move to big cities to find a job should also be thinking about what happens when our two major cities double their populations midway through this century. If governments don't want to think about the city infrastructure bottlenecks, then they should think about the political implications of squeezing that many humans with heaving mortgages and long commutes into one spot.[5] And then look at the way outer city seats are swinging.

Governments also need to think about the cultural divide for kids like Maggie-Kate. I felt her discombobulation when I moved the other way. As a child, my city suburbs were mostly white and my face represented a future Australia. Now, when the nation is becoming Eurasian like me, I live in a whiter part of the country. And governments could think about Maggie-Kate's classmates, the kids who don't strive to be doctors or lawyers or the head of Treasury, but just want to get a decent job they love, or at least can live with, close to their home supports and social groups.

A country town is not all good and true. I am not here to argue that country people are angels. A town like mine is simply a microcosm of larger places, but you get to see it all on the one page. It has the small-minded, pecking at people like so many galahs. It has expansive thinkers who are not limited by conventional wisdom because they don't see enough people to know the convention. I am not obtuse enough to know that if you had no choices about where you lived, a small town could be hell on earth. I have met people who feel trapped like dingos in the expectations of this place. They would rather chew their arm off than stay.

Still, there are many things I love about my home town. I love its rhythm, its seasons and most of its people. I like the fact that it's not polished, like the city suburbs I visit. I would not have met the people in this book without moving to this place, which appeared so alien at first. I don't claim objectivity. My approach has been as a convert and an advocate. It is hard to untie the subject from the person I moved for and the family we've created. It is a soup of cultural lessons, personal discovery and hard truths that I would not have seen without my displacement. Though I was born and grew up in a big city, my adult journey is as a metropolitan migrant to rural Australia. My alternative life would have been very different. It possibly would have been less whole. It would have been lived in a more diverse homogeneity – a contradiction, I know, but nonetheless true. My new home represents the other half of Australia that completes the whole nation; instead of thinking of two Australias, we can think of them as two halves. Two halves of the one place. I celebrate it whole.

Endnotes

Introduction
1 'From the land of fear, loss and dark secrets', *Sydney Morning Herald*, 6 December 2009
2 D. I. McDonald, *The Shire of Harden: A history of local government 1890–1990*, Harden Shire Council, 1990

Lesson 1: WTF? There are people west of the divide
1 'Tony Abbott's visit to Indigenous NT community follows a basic rule: keep the show moving', *Guardian*, 20 September 2014

Lesson 2: Place is everything
1 Transcript of the Prime Minister, the Hon P. J. Keating, MP, Interview with John Laws, Radio 2UE, Sydney, 17 June 1993; http://pmtranscripts.pmc.gov.au/release/transcript-8895
2 'Judgement Day', *Four Corners*, ABC TV, 3 May 2012
3 Ibid.
4 Ibid.
5 *Queensland Times*, 6 January 1996
6 Some names have been changed.

Lesson 3: Diversity is waiting to be found
1 Pat Dodson, 'Racial Discrimination Law Amendment, Second Reading, Free Speech Bill, *Hansard*, 2016

2 Ibid.

3 For more on frontier wars in the area, see George Main's book *Heartland: The Regeneration of Rural Place,* University of New South Wales Press, Sydney, 2005

4 'Bringing Them Home: Report of the National Inquiry into the Separation of Aboriginal and Torres Strait Islander Children from Their Families', Australian Human Rights Commission, April 1997

5 'Uluru Statement from the Heart', Referendum Convention at Uluru, 26 May 2017; www.referendumcouncil.org.au/sites/default/files/2017-05/Uluru_Statement_From_The_Heart_0.PDF

Lesson 4: Social divisions are highly visible in small towns

1 Joan C. Williams, 'What So Many Don't Get About the U.S. Working Class', *Harvard Business Review*, 10 November 2016

2 Joan C. Williams, *White Working Class: Overcoming Class Cluelessness in America*, Harvard Business Review Press, Boston, 2017

3 Nicholas Carnes and Noam Lupu, 'It's time to bust the myth: Most Trump voters were not working class', *Washington Post*, 5 June 2017

4 'Why Australia still ranks among world's best for income mobility', *Australian Financial Review*, 24 August 2017

5 'Australia far from a classless society', Australian National University, 30 October 2015; www.anu.edu.au/news/all-news/australia-far-from-a-classless-society

6 'Taxation statistics 2014–15', Australian Tax Office, Australian Government; www.ato.gov.au/About-ATO/Research-and-statistics/In-detail/Taxation-statistics/Taxation-statistics-2014-15/

Lesson 5: There is an education divide

1 'Seven decades of farming: Australian agricultural policy, passion and protest since 1940', ABC News, 10 August 2015; www.abc.net.au/news/rural/2015-08-10/seven-decades-that-shaped-australian-agriculture/6616308

2 'Glass floors and slow growth: a recipe for deepening inequality and hampering social mobility', London School of Economics and Political Science, 25 July 2017; http://blogs.lse.ac.uk/politicsandpolicy/glass-floors-and-slow-growth/

Lesson 7: Not all kids want to go to uni

1 Fran Kelly, 'Are universities failing students in the chase for research dollars', *RN Breakfast*, ABC radio, 25 October 2017; www.abc.net.au/radionational/programs/breakfast/are-universities-failing-students/9083208

2 For a history of federal and NSW TAFE policy, see John Wilkinson's parliamentary research service brief, 'TAFE organisation and funding in NSW: past and present', 2014; www.parliament.nsw.gov.au/researchpapers/Documents/tafe-organisation-and-funding-in-nsw-past-and-pr/Training%20in%20NSW.pdf

3 'TAFE New South Wales: Fee freeze not enough to save institution', Eryk Bagshaw, *Sydney Morning Herald*, 12 January 2016

4 John Ross, 'TAFE focused on industry needs under Jon Black', *Australian*, 18 January, 2017; www.theaustralian.com.au/higher-education/tafe-nsw-focused-on-industry-needs-under-jon-black/news-story/11ddc1d92204958de8aa45c2a0d7b14b

5 'Apprenticeship reform vital for national economy', New South Wales Business Chamber, November 2016

Lesson 8: You can lead a small town (or country) up or down

1 'Warren Buffett changes his mind about newspapers: "Newspapers are going to go downhill", Talking New Media, 11 August 2016; www.talkingnewmedia.com/2016/08/11/warren-buffett-changes-his-mind-about-newspapers-newspapers-are-going-to-go-downhill/

2 'Paragon Cafe's Peter Flaskas Passes On', *Twin Town Times*, 10 March 2016; http://twintowntimes.com.au/_/2016/03/paragon-cafes-peter-flaskas-passes-on/

3 Laura Tingle, 'Great Expectations: Government, Entitlement and an Angry Nation', *Quarterly Review*, June 2012

4 *The Age*, 30 January 2007

5 'John Howard's vision for the Murray-Darling hangs in the balance', ABC News, 17 February 2017; www.abc.net.au/news/2017-02-17/john-howards-vision-for-the-murray-darling-basin-betrayed/8277524

Lesson 9: Small town life is not all sad songs

1 '3218.0 - Regional Population Growth, Australia, 2016-17', Australian Bureau of Statistics, 24 April 2018; www.abs.gov.au/ausstats/abs@.nsf/mf/3218.0

2 '4159.0 - General Social Survey: Summary Results, Australia, 2014', Australian Bureau of Statistics, 29 June 2015; www.abs.gov.au/ausstats/abs@.nsf/mf/4159.0#Anchor2

3 'Wellbeing, Resilience and Liveability in Regional Australia', 2015 Regional Wellbeing Survey, June 2016; www.canberra.edu.au/research/faculty-research-centres/ceraph/regional-wellbeing/survey-results/2015/RWS2015_Web-Part-1.pdf

4 Agricultural Competitiveness White Paper, Australian Government, 4 July 2015; http://agwhitepaper.agriculture.gov.au/

Lesson 10: The gulf between the main street and Parliament

1 Iain McGilchrist, *The Master and his Emissary: The Divided Brain and the Making of the Western World*, Yale University Press, Connecticut, 2009

2 'Broadcasting legend John Laws reveals what will happen to his golden microphone when he dies', *Daily Telegraph*, 28 June 2017

3 'What do you have to lose?' *Guardian*, 20 August, 2016

4 'Donald Trump criticises United Nations during first address, urges accountability and reform', ABC News, 19 September 2017

5 'Trends in Political Opinion: Results from the Australian Electoral Study 1987–2016', School of Politics and International Relations, ANU College of Arts and Social Sciences, Sarah M. Cameron and Ian MacAllister, 2016; https://www.australianelectionstudy.org/

6 Dr Stephen Kennedy, 'Australia's response to the global national crisis', Australian Government, Treasury, 24 June 2009

7 George Megalogenis, *The Australian Moment*, Penguin Books, Melbourne, 2016, p. 343

8 David Uren and Lenore Taylor, *Shitstorm*, Melbourne University Press, Melbourne, 2010

9 'Australia's Annual Overdose Report 2017', Penington Institute, Melbourne; http://www.penington.org.au/australias-annual-overdose-report-2017/

Lesson 11: Rural politics is stuck in an old model

1 *Wagga Wagga Express*, 10 March 1866

2 Don Aitkin, '"Countrymindednes"': the spread of an idea', *Australian Cultural History* 4, 1985, pp. 34–41

3 *7.30*, ABC TV, 6 February 2014

4 Ken Buckley, 'The Great Rural Bludge', *Meanjin*, vol. 31, no. 1, March 1972, pp. 71–7; republished in *Australian Politics: A Third*

Reader, Henry Mayer, Helen Nelson (eds), Griffin Press, South Australia, 1973, p. 427

5   Bob Hawke, address by the prime minister to the 1983 annual National Farmers' Federation conference, 17 May 1983; http://pmtranscripts.pmc.gov.au/sites/default/files/original/00006115.pdf

6   Barnaby Joyce, National Press Club, 6 July 2015: http://www.barnabyjoyce.com.au/News/Releases/THE-HON-BARNABY-JOYCE-PRESS-CLUB-SPEECH/

7   'Poverty in Rural and Remote Australia', National Rural Health Allowance, November 2017; http://ruralhealth.org.au/sites/default/files/publications/nrha-factsheet-povertynov2017.pdf

8   Mumble election tables, median household income; http://mumble.com.au/fedelect13/wall/others/medinc/OZ2.HTM

9   'Coalition has budget blind spot when it comes to the rural poor', *Guardian*, 8 May 2014

Lesson 12: Country MPs are not all country party

1   2016 census figures provided by the Australian Bureau of Statistics for poorest ten seats on median personal weekly income.
    *Fowler (ALP outer metropolitan Sydney**)
    Blaxland (ALP inner metropolitan Sydney)
    Hinkler (NAT provincial Queensland)
    Calwell (ALP outer metropolitan Melbourne)
    Watson (ALP inner metropolitan Sydney)
    Lyne (NAT rural New South Wales)
    Wide Bay (NAT rural Queensland)
    Page (NAT rural New South Wales)
    Lyons (ALP rural Tasmania)
    Bruce (ALP outer metropolitan Melbourne)
    *Starts with lowest income first.
    **Australian Electoral Commission rated geographical region

2   http://nationals.org.au/about/our-history/
3   *Hansard*, 3 October 1941; http://parlinfo.aph.gov.au/parlInfo/
    search/display/display.w3p;db=HANSARD80;id=hansard80%2
    Fhansardr80%2F1941-10-03%2F0011;query=Id%3A%22hansar
    d80%2Fhansardr80%2F1941-10-03%2F0006%22
4   Peter Andren, address in reply, 9 May 1996, *Hansard*; http://
    parlinfo.aph.gov.au/parlInfo/search/display/display.w3p;query=
    Id%3A%22chamber%2Fhansardr%2F1996-05-09%2F0038%22
5   Tony Windsor, address in reply, 14 February 2002, *Hansard*;
    http://parlinfo.aph.gov.au/parlInfo/search/display/display.
    w3p;db=CHAMBER;id=chamber%2Fhansardr%2F2002-
    02-14%2F0092;query=Id%3A%22chamber%2Fhansardr
    %2F2002-02-14%2F0000%22
6   Rob Oakeshott, first speech, 22 October 1998, *Hansard*; http://
    parlinfo.aph.gov.au/parlInfo/search/display/display.w3p;query=
    Id%3A%22chamber%2Fhansardr%2F2008-10-22%2F0091%22

Lesson 13: Farming dominates politics but stuff still gets ignored

1   'Federal budget: tax cuts for small business as part of $5bn
    package', *Guardian*, 12 May 2015
2   National Farmers' Federation, 'NFF throws support behind a
    national emissions trading scheme', 4 April 2007; www.nff.org.au/
    read/1244/nff-throws-support-behind-national-emissions.html
3   National Farmers' Association, 'Climate change dissenter
    makes a valid contribution: NFF', 21 April 2009; www.nff.
    org.au/read/1589/climate-change-dissenter-makes-valid-
    contribution.html?hilite=%252522ian+plimer%252522
4   'Broken electricity system is devastating and the market should
    sort it out: farmers', *AM*, ABC, 7 March 2017
5   'Farmers joining environmental movement in their fight
    against mining', *Guardian*, 10 April 2014

6 'Abbott Piles Red Tape on Bonfire', *Sydney Morning Herald*, 23 March 2014

Lesson 14: There is a neglected class and they are swinging

1 Pauline Hanson, first speech to the Senate, *Hansard*, p. 937, 14 September 2016; http://parlinfo.aph.gov. au/parlInfo/genpdf/chamber/hansards/16daad94-5c74-4641-a730-7f6d74312148/0140/hansard_frag. pdf;fileType=application%2Fpdf
2 Katharine Murphy, 'The Political Life Is No Life At All', *Meanjin*, Winter 2017
3 '7127.0 - Agricultural Land and Water Ownership, 2015-16', ABS, 13 September 2017; www.abs.gov.au/ausstats/ abs@.nsf/Latestproducts/7127.0Main%20Features32015-16?opendocument&tabname=Summary&prodno=7127. 0&issue=2015-16&num=&view=
4 '"Abbott-Turnbull war": Leaked government talking points suggest ongoing leadership tensions', *Sydney Morning Herald*, 27 October 2016
5 'Joel Fitzgibbon reads from the manual', *Sunrise*, 3 June 2013; https://www.youtube.com/watch?v=Qr0O8pQTtlo

Lesson 15: The economics of a small town are tricky

1 Kevin D. Williamson, 'The Father-Führer', *National Review*, 28 March 2016
2 Andrew Leigh, *Choosing Openness*, Penguin Books, Melbourne, p. 97
3 John Daley, Danielle Wood and Carmela Chivers, 'Regional patterns of Australia's economy and population', Grattan Institute, 2August 2017; https://grattan.edu.au/report/ regional-patterns-of-australias-economy-and-population/
4 'The Post-Industrial Future is Nigh', *The Economist*, February 2013

5   Danielle Wood and John Daley, 'A crisis of trust: The rise of
    protest politics in Australia'; Grattan Institute, 12 March 2018;
    https://grattan.edu.au/report/a-crisis-of-trust/

Lesson 16: You can't make assumptions about small towns and race

1   'In the country we don't see 457 visa holders as a threat, we see
    them as a benefit', Barnaby Joyce, *Guardian*, 28 November 2016
2   'Karen refugees make $40m contribution to Nhill economy
    in Victoria's Wimmera study finds', ABC News, 24 April 2015;
    'Small Towns, Big Returns: Economic and Social Impact of
    the Karen resettlement in Nihill', Deloitte Access Economics
    and AMES, 2015; https://www2.deloitte.com/content/dam/
    Deloitte/au/Documents/Economics/deloitte-au-economics-
    small-towns-big-returns-nhill-resettlement-270415.pdf
3   Census QuickStats, Harden, Australian Bureau of Statistics,
    2016; www.censusdata.abs.gov.au/census_services/getproduct/
    census/2016/quickstat/SSC11851
4   'Mapping Social Cohesion', the Scanlon Foundation; http://
    scanlonfoundation.org.au/socialcohesion2017/
5   There are no deaths recorded but newspaper accounts tell of
    terrible injuries.
6   Young-Yass, Statistical Area 3, Census data 2016
7   *Australian Foreign Affairs*, Issue 1, 2017
8   'Characteristics of Recent Migrants, Australia', Australian
    Bureau of Statistics, November 2016; www.abs.gov.au/ausstats/
    abs@.nsf/mf/6250.0
9   Census, Australian Bureau of Statistics, 2016, http://www.abs.
    gov.au/websitedbs/censushome.nsf/home/2016

Lesson 17: Cultural tolerance is possible anywhere but it needs work

1 Andrew Leigh, *Choosing Openness*, Penguin Books, Melbourne, 2017, p. 88
2 'Mapping Social Cohesion', the Scanlon Foundation, p. 73; http://scanlonfoundation.org.au/socialcohesion2017/.
3 Ibid.
4 'Young New South Wales is the unofficial Muslim capital of the world', *Daily Telegraph*, 2 October 2014
5 Australian Electoral Study 2016 report, ANU, p. 18

Lesson 18: Hey rat racers, over here!

1 '3222.0 - Population Projections, Australia, 2012 (base) to 2101', Australian Bureau of Statistics, 26 November 2013; http://www.abs.gov.au/ausstats/abs@.nsf/Lookup/3222.0main+features32012%20(base)%20to%202101
2 'The World's Cities in 2016', United Nations; http://www.un.org/en/development/desa/population/publications/pdf/urbanization/the_worlds_cities_in_2016_data_booklet.pdf
3 Robert Muggah, 'The biggest risks facing cities – and some solutions', TED, September 2017
4 'Public servants told it's Armidale or find new jobs', *Canberra Times*, 10 June 2016
5 Inquiry into Regional Development and Decentralisation, Issues paper, August 24, 2017; https://www.aph.gov.au/Parliamentary_Business/Committees/House/Regional_Development_and_Decentralisation/RDD/Issues_Paper/section?id=committees%2Freportrep%2F024094%2F24935
6 'East West Link: the case for and against Melbourne's $6.8bn road', *Guardian*, 10 October 2014
7 George Megalogenis, 'Balancing Act', *Quarterly Essay* 61, p. 52

8 'National Cities Performance Framework Dashboard', Digital Transformation Agency, Australian Government; https://smart-cities.dashboard.gov.au/all-cities/overview

9 'Australia's tale of two nations needs a united front', *Australian*, 27 April 2017

10 'Investing in the future of regions', Fiona Nash, National Press Club speech, 19 April 2017; http://minister.infrastructure.gov.au/nash/speeches/2017/fns001_2017.aspx

11 Regional Australia Institute, 'The future of regional Australia: change on our terms', November 2015; http://www.regionalaustralia.org.au/wp-content/uploads/Change-on-our-terms-FINAL-20151126.pdf

12 Australian Government Productivity Commission, 'Transitioning Regional Economies', December 2017; https://www.pc.gov.au/inquiries/completed/transitioning-regions/report/transitioning-regions-overview.pdf

13 Ibid., p. 37

14 Ibid., p. 22

15 Ibid., p. 26

16 'Fast rail could turn Sydney, Wollongong, Newcastle into "mega region"', ABC News, 5 June 2018

Lesson 19: Let's celebrate the whole country

1 'A new view of an old emotion, or how science is saving nostalgia', *The Conversation*, 20 August 2013

2 Trent Dalton, 'The absolutely ordinary extraordinary Les Murray', *Australian*, 29 November 2014

3 'How Tesla is ushering in the age of the learned car', *Fortune*, 20 October 2015

4 Australian Government Productivity Commission report, 'Transitioning Regional Economies', December 2017

5 'NAB chair Ken Henry sees 'extraordinary' opportunity in the regions', *Canberra Times*, 7 June 2017

Acknowledgements

I always knew I wanted to write about the country, but it was still a daunting task. I wanted to tell the stories of people on my main street, and it was the encouragement and help of the subjects themselves that pushed me on. *Rusted Off* would be nothing without this generosity. If you see your words or echoes in these pages, I hope you understand my deep gratitude. The Levett family's message from the heart of Wiradjuri country showed me a way forward for Australia. The Minogue family story was integral to this project. Ayoub, thanks for your courage. Adrian Stadtmiller, as a fellow writer, was a particularly handy sounding board. Thanks also to Martin Parkinson and Jack Archer, who, as public figures, shared their personal stories in a challenging environment. The Harden Historical Society provided invaluable resources; John Daley and Dani Wood at the Grattan Institute kept my sentiment in check; Andrew Markus's work on social cohesion has been fundamental for me to understand the broader national story.

It was one thing to absorb the stories, but another altogether to craft them into a book that makes sense. So thanks to Nikki

Christer for acknowledging the germ of an idea. Meredith Curnow and Catherine Hill implicitly understood and respected my voice from the start while helping me to get the most out of the material for the reader. *Guardian Australia* editor and friend Lenore Taylor gave me airspace to land this plane. George Megalogenis, Lucy Clark and Katharine Murphy are the holy trinity of writing therapy. Their feedback at important stages and their enduring friendship were crucial. Mike Bowers put a bit of steel in my spine during a crisis of confidence and reminded me that the only thing worse than writing this story would be not writing it.

Thanks also to Tony Willsallen, Gabriel Mellick, Robert Hanan and Gail Shaw, who opened the gate to the house paddock. To my parents, Bill and Jenny, thank you for teaching me the value of observation, context and compassion. To our children, Genevra, Ali and Harry, thanks for your love and patience through a time of deep distraction. And here's to the farmer, who blew my mind from the very start and set my life on the wholly different path that led to this book.